Max Frisch
Three Plays

The Fire Raisers, Andorra, Triptych

'*The Fire Raisers* is successful on every level; the story is as gripping as an adventure story; each line is fraught with several meanings; as an allegory it is unique, and behind the whole organic structure of the play is a European brain that is as witty as it is adult.'   Edna O'Brien, *Encore*

Andorra: 'Max Frisch has written a supremely important play, one of the most important to be written in the German language since 1945.'   *Encounter*

Triptych: 'Frisch's last major work for the stage transcends the battlefield of secular politics to fathom the ultimate power, the power of death.'
      Peter Loeffler

The flexible and eminently speakable translations by Michael Bullock (*The Fire Raisers, Andorra*) and Geoffrey Skelton (*Triptych*) are here complemented by Peter Loeffler's lucid and informative introduction.

Max Frisch was born in Zurich on 15 May 1911, the son of an architect. After two years at the University of Zurich, he abandoned his studies in philosophy to become a freelance journalist, travelling in the Balkans and Greece. At the age of 25 he resumed his studies, this time in architecture and for ten years combined architecture with writing. Now equally established as a playwright and a novelist, his novels include *Homo Faber* (1957; published in England in 1959), *I'm not Stiller* (1958/1961), *A Wilderness of Mirrors* (1964/1965); reissued as *Gantenbein* (1983), *Montauk* (1975/1976); *Man in the Holocene* (1979/1980) and *Bluebeard* (1982/1983). His best-known plays are *The Fire Raisers* (1958; first staged in English at the Royal Court Theatre, 1961) and *Andorra* (1961; National Theatre, 1964), while *The Great Wall of China* (1947, revised 1955), *Count Oederland* (1951, revised 1961), *Don Juan, or The Love of Geometry* (1962) and *Biography, A Game* (1967) have also been published and performed in English. *Triptych* (1981) still awaits its English premiere. Max Frisch died on 4 April 1991.

METHUEN WORLD CLASSICS

This collection first published in Great Britain in 1992
by Methuen Drama
Random House, 20 Vauxhall Bridge Road, London SW1V 2SA
and Australia, New Zealand and South Africa

Reissued with a new cover 1993

6 8 10 9 7

The Fire Raisers first published in this translation by Methuen & Co Ltd in 1962,
original title *Biedermann und die Brandstifter* copyright © 1958 by
Suhrkamp Verlag, Frankfurt am Main. All rights reserved. This translation
copyright © 1962 by Michael Bullock.
Andorra first published in this translation by Methuen & Co Ltd in 1964,
original title *Andorra* copyright © 1961 by Suhrkamp Verlag, Frankfurt am Main.
All rights reserved. This translation copyright © 1962, 1964 by Michael Bullock.
Triptych first published in this translation by Eyre Methuen Ltd, in association with
Helen and Kurt Wolff Books, Harcourt Brace Jovanovich, Inc., New York
in 1981, original title *Triptychon* copyright © 1978, 1980 by Suhrkamp Verlag,
Frankfurt am Main. All rights reserved. This translation copyright © 1981 by Max
Frisch and Geoffrey Skelton.

The front cover shows *Ohne Titel (Leteres Stilleben)*, 1940 by Paul Klee
100 × 80.5 cm, Private Collection, Switzerland. The author photograph on the
back cover is reproduced by courtesy of Suhrkamp Verlag, Frankfurt am Main.

A CIP catalogue record for this book is available from the British Library

ISBN 0–413–66560–7

Printed and bound in Great Britain by Cox & Wyman Ltd, Reading, Berkshire

CAUTION

MAX FRISCH

THREE PLAYS

The Fire Raisers
Andorra
translated by Michael Bullock

Triptych
translated by Geoffrey Skelton

introduced by Peter Loeffler

Methuen Drama

Contents

Max Frisch: A Chronology

1911	Born 15 May in Zurich (Switzerland), the youngest of three children. His father was an architect, his grandfather a director of the Zurich School of Applied Arts.
1924	Enters the *Realgymnasium*, Zurich.
1927	Sends his first play (*Stahl*) to Max Reinhardt in Berlin. The play is rejected.
1930	*Abitur* (high school diploma).
1931	Enrolls at the University of Zurich, studying German literature and philosophy. Attends lectures by the art historian Heinrich Wölfflin.
1933	Interrupts his studies. Works as a freelance journalist. Travels to Prague, Budapest, Istanbul, Athens, Rome.
1934	Publishes his first novel, *Jürg Reinhart*.
1936	Begins to study architecture at the Federal Institute of Technology in Zurich. Destroys his manuscripts and stops writing for two years.
1939–45	Several periods of military service (artillery).
1941	Concludes his architectural studies with a diploma; wins first prize in a competition, and opens office of his own.
1942	Marries Constanze von Meyenburg. (Three children.)
1944	Completes his first full-length play, *Santa Cruz*. Begins life-long association with the *Schauspielhaus* (Municipal Theatre) in Zurich.
1946	Travels in Germany, Italy, France.
1947	Meets Bertolt Brecht; engages him in 'daily dialectics'. Participates in 'World Congress of Intellectuals for Peace' in Warsaw.
1950	Publishes *Tagebuch 1946–1949* (diary).
1951	Spends several months in the United States as the recipient of a Rockefeller Grant for Drama.
1954	Publication of his novel *Stiller*. Separates from his wife, and gives up architectural practice.
1956	Travels to the United States, Mexico, Cuba.
1957	Publication of his novel *Homo Faber*. Travels to Greece and the Middle East.
1958	*Biedermann und die Brandstifter* (*The Fire Raisers*) first performed at the *Schauspielhaus* (Zurich) on 29 March. Zurich Prize for Literature.
1959	Divorce from his wife.
1960–65	Lives in Rome. Meets the poet Ingeborg Bachmann.

1961   Completes *Andorra*. First performed at the *Schauspielhaus* (Zurich) on 2 November.

1964   Publication of his novel *Mein Name sei Gantenbein* (*A Wilderness of Mirrors*). Awarded Ford Foundation Grant for Drama.

1965   Returns to Switzerland; settles in Berzona (canton of Ticino). Prize of the City of Jerusalem.

1966   First visit to the Soviet Union. Visits Israel and Poland.

1968   Marries Marianne Oellers. Visits Japan. *Biografie. Ein Spiel.* (*Biography. A Play*). Engages in the political debate of the late sixties.

1971   Lectures at Columbia University, New York.

1972   *Tagebuch 1966–1971* (diary). Travels through the United States. Elected Honorary Member of the American Academy of Arts and Letters. Spends the winter in Berlin.

1974   Grand Prize of the Schiller Foundation.

1975   Visit to China.

1976   Publication of his *Collected Works*. Peace Prize of the German Book Trade.

1978   Completes *Triptychon* (*Triptych*). First performed at the *Akademietheater* in Vienna on 1 February 1981.

1979   Divorces Marianne Oellers. Foundation of the *Max Frisch Archives* in Zurich.

1981   Moves to New York. Honorary doctorate of the City University of New York.

1983   Returns to Switzerland, settles in Zurich.

1986   Begins work on a filmscript of his novel *Homo Faber*.

1989   Engages in Swiss politics with *Schweiz ohne Armee* (*Switzerland without an army*).

1991   Dies in Zurich on 4 April.

Introduction

Max Frisch, whose plays have been translated into many languages and are performed on all five continents, was the citizen of a small, a very small country. This singular experience of being born and growing up within the narrow confines of Switzerland, the 'shoebox of Europe', as Frisch once called it, was to have a decisive effect on both his life and his work.

Born in Zurich in 1911 as the son of upper middle-class parents, Frisch completed high school and enrolled at the university, studying German literature and philosophy. After only four semesters he swiftly changed course, gave up his studies, travelled, then went back to the university, now settling for something more pragmatic, the study of architecture. But soon after he had graduated and had completed a number of housing projects, his career took yet another swift turn. Writing now asserted itself as the all consuming passion.

Frisch had begun writing at an early age. At twelve he had edited a newsletter for his high school, and at sixteen he was bold enough to send a copy of his one-act play *Stahl* to Max Reinhardt, the undisputed master of the German stage; the play, not surprisingly, was turned down. Frisch was disappointed, not discouraged. He tried his hand at writing for radio, began contributing to papers and periodicals, kept a diary, sketched a variety of shorter prose pieces, and composed his first full-length play, *Santa Cruz*, in the spring of 1944.

Flawed in many ways, *Santa Cruz*, nevertheless, is an important work, because it contains, at least in seed form, the major themes of Frisch's later writing. There is the great longing for a real, authentic life; there is the search for one's identity amidst the continuously shifting images of self; there is the elusive quality of all human interaction; and finally, subsuming all the other themes, there is the potent fantasy about freedom.

Although set in a distant and exotic location, as are so many of Frisch's plays, *Santa Cruz* reflects the painful experience of enclosure and constraint that the author felt living in Switzerland. To Frisch Switzerland seemed small in more than just the obvious, geographic sense. It seemed small to him in courage, small in adventure, small in tolerance. He saw how the civic ideal of moderation had over centuries fostered a frightening degree of complacency, and how the national obsession with order, propriety and balance had ultimately stifled the creative unrest necessary for all artistic work.

Quite naturally, therefore, the act of travelling, both in a physical and a metaphorical sense, became essential to Frisch's experience. He left his narrow country, travelled widely, settled in Rome, then in New York, and in his novels and plays fictionalized journeys to Mexico, the Amazon, China, and Spain. Through travelling and writing the strictures of his native land had finally been broken, and the world had become his.

Max Frisch never regarded these journeys into foreign territory as an escape, but rather as a self-imposed exile. For him it was an act that was firmly and consciously undertaken, and that had a very precise purpose: to see and understand the country he came from through the prism of distance and time.

And so Frisch returned to Switzerland after having lived abroad; he returned wiser, but still in fighting spirit. Right to the end he fought for a country that would be less dogmatic and more tolerant; not encrusted in tradition, but open to the new; not small in heart and mind, but honest and strong. When he died on the 4th of April, 1991, both friends and foes in Switzerland agreed that the country had lost its most eminent moral voice.

* * *

Both in Switzerland and abroad Max Frisch is primarily known as a novelist and playwright. Yet some critics have claimed that his true mastery lies in the writing of journals and diaries. The *Tagebücher*, composed in irregular sequence between 1946 and 1971, are an extraordinary document indeed, placing Frisch in a kinship with such eminent diarists of the post-war era as Thomas Mann and André Gide. With them he shares the microscopic eye, a disdain for all matters trivial, a relentless, often brutal honesty, and above all the courage to wrestle with some of the most complex issues of the turbulent years after 1945.

The *Journals* are a literary and political document of the first order. Anyone studying Frisch's dramatic work will discover a further, immediate significance, for all the major plays, including *The Fire Raisers*, *Andorra*, and *Triptych* are already contained in some form within the context of the *Journals*. Often, as in the case of *Andorra*, this seedling could lie dormant for years, until the time had finally come and the appropriate form had been found to tell the story once again.

A very similar metamorphic process propels the characters and the narrative in all of Max Frisch's novels. From the early, delicate *Bin, or the Voyage to Peking* (1945), to the massive *I'm not Stiller* (1954), and still further on to *Homo Faber* (1957), the quest for change, for a new authentic self, forms the centre of all narrative energies. Characters continuously invent and re-invent themselves;

plot lines spin off into multiple configurations, until the reader is as perplexed as the central figure of Gantenbein, who is caught in *A Wilderness of Mirrors* (1964).

Max Frisch wrote adventure novels of the most private kind. His heroes set out on a journey, hoping to find the source, a source, however, that eventually will always elude them. And so the journey continues, with new hope, with new despair. There is a clear echo of Albert Camus' Sisyphus here, pursuing his task against all odds; and there is the echo of Samuel Beckett's tramps, waiting for relief, waiting for the pain to go.

* * *

By the mid-fifties Frisch had securely established himself as a leading writer of prose; yet it was to be the stage that eventually gave him the most visible presence both in Europe and beyond. His career as a dramatist has always been intricately linked to the *Schauspielhaus* in Zurich, the Municipal Theatre of Switzerland's largest city. It was here that his lifelong passion for theatre-going had begun, and it was here that his first attempts at playwriting were encouraged, and where his first play, *Santa Cruz*, was performed. The man who was decisive in helping to shape Frisch's vision of the dramatic was Kurt Hirschfeld, the theatre's leading dramaturge. Hirschfeld was convinced that all great plays were not written *for* the stage, but *with* the stage. The true playwright, therefore, had to grow out of the soil of a living theatre. Frisch, young and curious as any novice would be, was asked to attend rehearsals, to discuss scenic matters with designers, to engage actors in a dialogue, to debate concepts with the dramaturge and the director. Convinced by his mentor, Frisch took this lesson to heart: the daily operations of the *Schauspielhaus* were to become an apprenticeship that no other school could have offered. The results of this hard and complete training are evident in every one of Frisch's plays. Few authors of the modern stage have developed such a natural and precise understanding of theatre as theatre. Beyond the lessons in philosophy and philology, Frisch always fondly remembered Hirschfeld as the man who taught him the alphabet of the stage.

The second man who, in those same years right after the war, profoundly shaped Max Frisch's vision of the theatre was Bertolt Brecht. After leaving the United States and before settling, once again, in Berlin, Brecht spent a few months in Zurich, where he met Frisch. The two quickly engaged in an intense dialogue. Conversations centred on political matters: on why the ugly seeds of fascism had survived after the collapse of the German Reich; on how the growing nuclear threat could be averted; and on what had to be done to secure social justice. But above all their dialogue focused on the role of the artist in the modern age, and, more specifically, on the role of theatre in a rapidly changing world. It was in this clearly defined field of dramaturgy that the young Max Frisch learned from the older master.

At the centre of Brecht's system was the firm, impassioned belief that the theatre could indeed be a powerful tool of enlightenment. This, it seemed to Brecht, was its true merit. Far beyond being a mere pastime, or worse, a mere form of escape, the theatre had to fulfill its newly defined mandate as a forum for challenging, subversive ideas. It had to question and undermine commonly held beliefs, it had to set the process of critical thought in motion, and, above all, it had to take seriously an audience that was willing to think. This notion of the theatre as a laboratory of ideas struck the young dramatist Max Frisch with 'the clarity of lightning', as he later described it. It was a revelation that all through his long career would serve as a guiding light.

Frisch has always been an eclectic writer, ready to learn from others. An avid reader himself, he would appropriate stylistic features from other authors, whenever he felt that this would strengthen his cause. Yet, despite these consciously and critically undertaken borrowings from figures as diverse as Denis Diderot, Georg Büchner, Paul Claudel, and Thornton Wilder, the result in Frisch's work is always a style of a very personal stringency and cohesion, which, ironically, has influenced in turn the writing of other, younger dramatists. 'All art', it seems indeed, 'is collaboration', as J. M. Synge put it.

*   *   *

The Fire Raisers, (1958), the first play in this volume, brilliantly incorporates stylistic features from Brecht's and Wilder's canon. There is the direct address to the audience; there is the chorus with its mock-heroic stanzas, interrupting the action with its futile advice; there is the use of strongly drawn types rather than subtly drawn characters; and there is, finally, the presentation of the plot in clearly defined beats, in episodic units.

Frisch, like Brecht and Wilder, never conceived these devices as mere tricks of the theatre. His aim, like theirs, was precisely focused, namely to establish a set of dramatic rules that would allow for critical distance between the action and the audience. Only this critical distance would permit every single audience member to reflect upon the important issues raised on stage.

And the issues presented so clearly and debated so vigorously in *The Fire Raisers* are important issues indeed, although the story itself is straightforward and simple enough. Max Frisch tells the cautionary tale of a respectable bourgeois whose house one day is visited by three strangers. They politely but firmly demand to be taken in as house-guests, and, to the host's own amazement, they succeed. Biedermann, the host, soon suspects his guests of being fire raisers; yet, even when they begin to hoard barrels of gasoline in his attic, he refuses to believe that they would torch his house. Soon it is too late. When the strangers finally ask him for a set of matches, he hands them one, thus sealing his fate: Biedermann, his wife, his house, and the whole town go up in flames.

The thematic implications of this story are clear; they are indeed as clear as in a morality play, a form which *The Fire Raisers* echoes in a number of ways. The central character in Frisch's play is a modern Everyman, open to temptation, willing to compromise, and an easy victim of self-deceit. Biedermann sees the dilemma, but cannot muster the moral courage to confront it. He fails as a human because he is blind to the reality of evil. He cooperates with the devil only to be burnt in the end, and he learns his lesson only when it is too late.

Frisch manages to tell this chilling fable without ever raising the schoolmaster's admonishing finger. Like the authors of the medieval morality play, Frisch understood that to teach *and* to entertain simultaneously was a difficult but not impossible task. *The Fire Raisers* succeeds with elegance and wit in a delicate balancing act: the impassioned lesson on man's boundless gullibility combines with a dazzling use of theatrical strategies to create the modern masterpiece, the classic of the repertory, that this play has deservedly become.

When *The Fire Raisers* received its first performance in the spring of 1958 at the *Schauspielhaus* in Zurich, the play instantly won full approval both from critics and audience. While Frisch had so far gained recognition primarily as a prose writer, *The Fire Raisers* now propelled him in a sudden burst to the forefront of modern drama. The play was soon optioned by all major stages in the German speaking countries, was subsequently translated into a wide variety of languages, travelled to the centres of theatrical activity, to London, Paris, New York, Rome, and Tokyo, and conquered the minor theatres in the provinces as well. It was the play that more than any other work before made Max Frisch's name internationally recognizable.

Kurt Hirschfeld, his friend, mentor, and critical voice, suggested yet another play, not only because he wanted to capitalize on *The Fire Raisers'* success, but because he firmly believed that there still was a multitude of stories in Frisch that had yet remained untold. Frisch, who trusted his mentor's insight and experience more than probably anyone else's, took this advice to heart. Still riding on the high wave of *The Fire Raisers*' phenomenal success, he conceived a new play. Three years later, in early November 1961, *Andorra* was first performed, once again at the *Schauspielhaus*, the stage that had taught him so much about the craft of playwriting. Hirschfeld, in close cooperation with the author, directed a stellar cast. The difficult efforts with a difficult play paid off: *Andorra* was to become Max Frisch's major achievement as a dramatist.

Andorra differs from *The Fire Raisers* in a number of ways, the most obvious structural difference being its scope. While *The Fire Raisers* is in essence a chamber play, set in the narrow confines of a bourgeois residence, *Andorra* is vast in design, with its central scenes evolving, and finally exploding, in the town's public square. Yet thematically there are some distinct echoes, as if Frisch tried to give another, sharper look at the same dangerous and intractable issues. And so we encounter once again, although in a different key, the theme of human gullibility and cowardice; we hear of those small daily treasons that man commits for the sake of convenience; we see man's boundless capacity for compromise, and finally, in shock, we witness the catastrophe that comes, at the very end of both plays, hard and fast.

Andorra is the study of a catastrophe: its birth, its growth, its deadly conclusion. At the core of the play is Andri, a young man who has barely outgrown adolescence. He is believed to be a Jew, and although he is not, suspicion alone is strong enough to fuel the prejudice amongst the villagers. Slowly at first, then in an ever tightening grip, the community closes in on Andri. Some villagers brazenly flaunt their anti-semitic rage; others, quite helplessly, try to resist the lure of prejudice. In the end, though, prejudice does prevail in a victory that is both bitter and complete. Andri, the scapegoat, is slaughtered; the ugly sacrifice has been made. But his death has no redemptive power: spring does not return to the village. The bleak winter of prejudice has won.

There can be no doubt that *Andorra* had grown out of a very specific experience of Frisch with his native country. He had all through his growing years observed in horror how dangerous, even deadly forms of chauvinism could fester under the thin veneer of bourgeois respectability, how a small country could be in danger of betraying its ideals in a grand manner. Yet, *Andorra* is not about Switzerland. Rather, Frisch conceived the play as a 'model' in the Brechtian sense of the term. Far beyond any national or ethnic boundaries, the play serves as a strong parable for modes of human, or rather sub-human, behaviour. This open form of *Andorra* is precisely the reason why the play gained such international acceptance, both in its printed version and on stage. It served as a mirror, in which every country, every group, could discover its face, if it had the courage to do so.

The Fire Raisers and *Andorra* deal with the dynamics of power: how it corrodes individual morality, how it poisons and eventually destroys an entire town. In this sense both plays are political in the very precise meaning of the word. Beyond the single case study of Mr Biedermann and the young Andri, Frisch observes the operation of power as an immanent force within all social interaction. Much of Frisch's earlier writing as a Swiss journalist and pamphleteer had already focused on this phenomenon, on its often visible dangers, and on its open threats. Frisch was disquieted by the power of Swiss banks; he feared the power of a firmly entrenched middle-class, insensitive to the needs of the weaker; and he mistrusted the power of a supposedly defensive army. As a citizen and moralist Frisch felt an urgent need to reflect upon these issues, whether he was living in Switzerland, or living abroad. To him, morality and political thought were an inextricable pair: the Athenians would have called him a 'writer of the Polis'.

Triptych, the third play in this volume, and Frisch's last major work for the stage, differs considerably from its predecessors in theme, tone, and structure. Written twenty years after *The Fire Raisers* and seventeen years after *Andorra*, this late play of 1978 is a testament, a farewell, which explores the unexplored, the realm of death. *Triptych* is the work of an ageing writer who finds himself confronted with mortality. And so the play transcends the battlefield of secular politics to fathom the ultimate power, the power of death: Frisch has moved from the physical to the metaphysical.

Gone is the holy rage of the moralist that had fuelled the two earlier plays. Frisch presents his fable in a quiet, wise, and gentle tone of resignation. Here, amongst the dead who can speak, and the living who remain mute, the laws of gravity seem to have been overcome. When the director of *Triptych*'s first production, obviously perplexed, asked Frisch for help, the author offered only two words of advice: 'Helligkeit, Heiterkeit' (brightness, lightness). The dark tales of power, deceit, and corruption had given way to a vision where the pain of living is but a memory, and where the state of death offers comfort and peace.

And yet, despite its very distinct topic and tone, *Triptych* shares common ground with the two other plays, and indeed with all the other works. Through all the permutations of his writing, Max Frisch has aimed for enlightenment. In the act of writing he hoped to come closer, and ever closer, to it, and in constructing complex parables for the stage, he invites us, the audience, to follow him on this journey to clarity and light. In his plays, Frisch invites us to think, yet he never gives orders. He was, in the end, one of the least dogmatic of writers, and one of the most human of men.

* * *

Max Frisch has been praised as the perfect craftsman who builds his plays with the same delicate care that an architect expends on houses, and he has been admired for his mastery in creating characters so rich and complex that they are both a blessing and a curse for the actors. One strength that critics have too often failed to highlight is Frisch's superb work as a stylist. Like few dramatists writing in modern German, he has managed to develop a language that is supple and expressive, sensuous and precise. It is a language that is both seismographically accurate and rich in ironic ambiguity.

This central paradox has made Max Frisch one of the most difficult authors to translate into any language. But he has been lucky in the process, and nowhere more so than in English. Both Michael Bullock's and Geoffrey Skelton's translations are flexible, to the point, idiomatically secure and eminently speakable; they are convincing proof that good, even very good translations from the German are possible, and that translators do not have to be traitors.

Peter Loeffler
Zurich 1991

The Fire Raisers

A Morality without a Moral

with an Afterpiece

translated by

Michael Bullock

This play was first produced on 29 March 1958 at the Schauspielhaus, Zürich, and was directed by Oskar Wälterlin.

It was first produced in England at the Royal Court Theatre on 21 December 1961, with the following cast:

GOTTLIEB BIEDERMANN	Alfred Marks
ANNA	Ann Beach
SCHMITZ	Colin Blakely
BABETTE BIEDERMANN	Doris Hare
EISENRING	James Booth
POLICEMAN	Roger Kemp
WIDOW KNECHTLING	Catherine Wilmer
DOCTOR OF PHILOSOPHY	John Thaw
CHIEF FIREMAN	Norman Henry
FIREMEN	Trevor Danby
	David Jackson
	Roger Kemp
	Dickie Owen
	Gordon Rollings
	John Thaw
	Henry Woolf

The Place: Europe
The Time: Today

Directed by LINDSAY ANDERSON
Designed by ALAN TAGG

The stage is dark, then a match flares, revealing the face of Herr Biedermann, who is lighting a cigar. As it grows lighter he looks around him. He is surrounded by firemen in helmets.

BIEDERMANN One can't even light a cigar nowadays without thinking of fire! . . . It's revolting –
Biedermann hides the smoking cigar and withdraws, whereupon the Fire Brigade steps forward in the manner of a classical Greek chorus. A tower-clock strikes the quarter.

CHORUS Good people of our city, see
Us, its guardians,
Looking,
Listening,
Full of good will towards the well-intentioned citizen –

CHORUS LEADER Who, after all, pays our wages.

CHORUS Splendidly equipped
We prowl around your house,
At once alert and free from suspicion.

CHORUS LEADER Sometimes, too, we sit down,
But without sleeping, tirelessly

CHORUS Looking,
Listening,
For that which is concealed
To be revealed,
Before it is too late
To put out
The first few flickers
Threatening fire.
A tower-clock strikes the half.

CHORUS LEADER Many things may start a fire,
But not every fire that starts
Is the work of inexorable
Fate.

CHORUS Other things, called Fate to prevent you
From asking how they happened,
Monstrous events,
Even the total destruction of a city,
Are mischief.

CHORUS LEADER Human,

CHORUS All too human

CHORUS LEADER Mischief that wipes out
Our mortal fellow citizens.
A tower-clock strikes the three-quarters.

CHORUS Much can be avoided
By common sense.

CHORUS LEADER In very truth:

CHORUS It is unworthy of God,
Unworthy of man,
To call a stupidity Fate
Simply because it has happened.
The man who acts so
No longer deserves the name,
No longer deserves God's earth,
Inexhaustible, fruitful and kind,
Nor the air that he breathes,
Nor the sun.
Bestow not the name of Fate
Upon man's mistakes,
Even the worst,
Beyond our power to put out!
The tower-clock strikes the hour.

CHORUS LEADER Our watch has begun.
The chorus sits down while the clock strikes nine.

I

ROOM

*Gottlieb Biedermann is sitting in his room reading
the newspaper and smoking a cigar. Anna, the maid,
in a white apron, brings a bottle of wine.*

ANNA Herr Biedermann?
No answer.
Herr Biedermann –
He folds up the newspaper.

BIEDERMANN They ought to be strung up. Haven't I always said so? Another fire. And the same old story as I live and breathe: another hawker who settles down in the loft, a harmless hawker . . .
He takes the bottle.
They ought to be strung up!
He takes the corkscrew.

ANNA Herr Biedermann –

BIEDERMANN What is it?

ANNA He's still there.

BIEDERMANN Who?

ANNA The hawker who wants to speak to you.

BIEDERMANN I'm not at home!

ANNA That's what I told him, Herr Biedermann, an hour ago. He says he knows you. I can't throw that man out, Herr Biedermann, I simply can't.

BIEDERMANN Why not?

ANNA He's far too big and strong . . .
Biedermann draws the cork.

BIEDERMANN Tell him to come and see me in my office tomorrow.

ANNA I have told him, Herr Biedermann, three times, but he isn't interested.

BIEDERMANN Why not?

ANNA He doesn't want any hair tonic.

BIEDERMANN Then what does he want?

ANNA Humanity . . .
Biedermann sniffs at the cork.

BIEDERMANN Tell him I shall come and throw him out with my own hands if he doesn't beat it immediately.
He carefully fills his Burgundy glass.
Humanity! . . .
He tastes the wine.
Tell him to wait out in the hall. I'll be there in a

minute. If he's selling something, tracts or razor blades, I'm not hard-hearted, but – I'm not hard-hearted, Anna, you know that! – but I'm not going to have anyone coming into the house. I've told you that a hundred times! Even if we had three beds free I wouldn't consider it. We know what that can lead to – nowadays . . .

Anna turns to go and sees that the stranger has just entered: an athlete, his clothes are reminiscent both of a jail and of a circus, his arms are tattooed, and he wears leather straps round his wrists. Anna creeps out. The stranger waits till Biedermann has sipped his wine and looks round.

SCHMITZ Good evening.

Biedermann drops his cigar with astonishment.

Your cigar, Herr Biedermann –

He picks up the cigar and gives it to Biedermann.

BIEDERMANN I say –

SCHMITZ Good evening!

BIEDERMANN What's the meaning of this? I expressly told the maid you were to wait out in the hall. What possessed you . . . I mean . . . without knocking . . .

SCHMITZ My name is Schmitz.

BIEDERMANN Without knocking.

SCHMITZ Joseph Schmitz.

Silence.

Good evening!

BIEDERMANN What do you want?

SCHMITZ There's nothing to worry about, Herr Biedermann: I'm not a hawker!

BIEDERMANN Then what are you?

SCHMITZ A wrestler by trade.

BIEDERMANN A wrestler?

SCHMITZ A heavy-weight.

BIEDERMANN I see.

SCHMITZ That's to say, I was.

BIEDERMANN And now?

SCHMITZ I'm out of work.

Pause.

Don't worry, Herr Biedermann, I'm not looking for work. On the contrary. I'm fed up with wrestling . . . I only came in because it's raining so hard outside.

Pause.

It's warmer in here.

Pause.

I hope I'm not disturbing you –

Pause.

BIEDERMANN Do you smoke?

He offers cigars.

SCHMITZ It's terrible to be as big as I am, Herr Biedermann. Everyone's afraid of me . . .

Biedermann gives him a light.

Thanks.

They stand smoking.

BIEDERMANN To come to the point, what do you want?

SCHMITZ My name is Schmitz.

BIEDERMANN So you said, well, how do you do?

SCHMITZ I'm homeless.

He holds the cigar under his nose and savours the aroma.

I'm homeless.

BIEDERMANN Would you like – a slice of bread?

SCHMITZ If that's all you've got . . .

BIEDERMANN Or a glass of wine?

SCHMITZ Bread and wine . . . But only if I'm not disturbing you, Herr Biedermann, only if I'm not disturbing you!

Biedermann goes to the door.

BIEDERMANN Anna!

Biedermann comes back.

SCHMITZ The maid told me Herr Biedermann was going to throw me out personally, but I couldn't believe you really meant it, Herr Biedermann . . .

Anna has entered.

BIEDERMANN Anna, bring a second glass.

ANNA Very good.

BIEDERMANN And some bread – yes.

SCHMITZ And if you don't mind, Fräulein, some butter. And some cheese or cold meat or something. Only don't put yourself out. A few pickled cucumbers, a tomato or something, a little mustard – whatever you happen to have, Fräulein.

ANNA Very good.

SCHMITZ Only don't put yourself out!

Anna goes out.

BIEDERMANN You know me, the maid said.

SCHMITZ Of course, Herr Biedermann, of course.

BIEDERMANN Where from?

SCHMITZ Only from your best side, Herr Biedermann, only from your best side. Yesterday evening in the local – I know you didn't notice me in the corner – everyone in there was delighted every time you banged the table with your fist, Herr Biedermann.

BIEDERMANN What was I saying?

SCHMITZ Absolutely the right thing.

He smokes his cigar, then:

They ought to be strung up. All of them. The quicker, the better. Strung up. All these fire raisers. . .

Biedermann offers Schmitz a chair.

BIEDERMANN Take a seat.

Schmitz sits down.

SCHMITZ Men like you, Herr Biedermann, that's what we need!

BIEDERMANN Yes, no doubt, but –

SCHMITZ No buts, Herr Biedermann, no buts! You're one of the Old Brigade, you still have a positive outlook. That explains it.

BIEDERMANN No doubt –

SCHMITZ You still have civil courage.

BIEDERMANN No doubt –

SCHMITZ That explains it.

BIEDERMANN Explains what?

SCHMITZ You still have a conscience, everyone in the local could feel that, a real conscience.

BIEDERMANN Yes, yes, of course –

SCHMITZ Herr Biedermann, it's not of course at all. Not nowadays. In the circus where I wrestled, for example – and that's why the whole circus was burnt to the ground afterwards – our manager said to me: Take a running jump at yourself, Joe! – my name is Joseph, you know – take a running jump, he said, why should I have a conscience? Those were his very words. What I need to keep my beasts in order is a whip. Those were his very words. That's the kind of fellow he was. Conscience, he laughed. If anyone has a conscience it's generally a guilty one . . .

He smokes with enjoyment.

God rest his soul.

BIEDERMANN You mean he's dead?

SCHMITZ Burnt to death with the whole shoot.

A grandfather clock strikes nine.

BIEDERMANN I can't think what's keeping that girl!

SCHMITZ I'm in no hurry. –

The two men happen suddenly to look into each other's eyes. And you haven't a bed free in the house, Herr Biedermann, the maid has already told me –

BIEDERMANN Why do you laugh?

SCHMITZ Unfortunately there isn't a bed free! That's what they all say the moment they see a homeless person – and I don't even want a bed.

BIEDERMANN No?

SCHMITZ I'm used to sleeping on the floor, Herr Biedermann. My father was a charcoal burner. I'm used to it . . .

He smokes.

No buts, Herr Biedermann, no buts, I say! You aren't one of those who talk big in pubs because they're scared stiff. I believe you. Unfortunately there isn't a bed free – that's what they all say – but you I believe, Herr Biedermann . . . Where shall we end up if nobody believes anyone else any more? That's what I always say, where shall we end up? Everybody thinks everybody else is a fire raiser, there's nothing but distrust in the world. Don't you agree? The whole pub could feel that, Herr Biedermann: you still believe in the good in man and in yourself. Don't you agree? You're the first person in this town who hasn't simply treated me like an arsonist –

BIEDERMANN   Here's an ash tray.

SCHMITZ   Don't you agree?
He carefully taps the ash off his cigar.
Most people nowadays believe in the Fire Brigade instead of in God.

BIEDERMANN   What do you mean by that?

SCHMITZ   The truth.
Anna brings a tray.

ANNA   We haven't any cold meat.

SCHMITZ   That'll do, Fräulein, that'll do – except that you've forgotten the mustard.

ANNA   Sorry!
Anna goes out.

BIEDERMANN   Tuck in! –
Biedermann fills the glasses.

SCHMITZ   You don't get this kind of reception everywhere, Herr Biedermann. I've had some nasty experiences, I can tell you. No sooner is a fellow like me across the threshold – a man without a tie, homeless and hungry – than they say, sit down, and ring the police behind my back. What do you think of that? I ask for a roof over my head, nothing more, an honest wrestler who has been wrestling all his life; some gentleman who has never wrestled comes along and takes me by the collar – What's the idea? I ask and I merely turn

round, just to have a look at him, and already his
shoulder's broken.

He takes the glass:

Cheers!

They drink and Schmitz starts eating.

BIEDERMANN Well, you know how things are these days. You
can't open a newspaper without reading of another
case of arson! And it's always the same story: a
hawker asks for shelter and next morning the
house goes up in flames . . . I simply mean I can
understand people being a bit distrustful.

He picks up his newspaper.

Here, look at this!

*He puts the open newspaper down beside Schmitz's
plate.*

SCHMITZ I've seen it.

BIEDERMANN A whole district.

He stands up to show Schmitz.

Here, read this!

Schmitz eats and reads and drinks.

SCHMITZ Beaujolais?

BIEDERMANN Yes.

SCHMITZ It would have been better with the chill off . . .

He reads across his plate:

' – It seems that the fire was planned and started
in the same manner as last time.'

They eye one another.

BIEDERMANN Isn't it incredible?

Schmitz puts the newspaper away.

SCHMITZ That's why I don't read the newspapers any
more.

BIEDERMANN How do you mean?

SCHMITZ Because it's always the same.

BIEDERMANN Yes, yes, of course, but – that's no solution, just
not reading the newspaper; I mean you have to
know what lies in store for you.

SCHMITZ Why?

BIEDERMANN Well, you just have to.

SCHMITZ It will come, Herr Biedermann, it will come.
He sniffs the sausage.
The judgment of God.
He cuts himself a slice of sausage.

BIEDERMANN Do you think so?
Anna brings the mustard.

SCHMITZ Thank you, Fräulein, thank you.

ANNA Is there anything else?

SCHMITZ Not today.
Anna remains by the door.
There's nothing I like better than mustard, you know.
He squeezes mustard out of the tube.

BIEDERMANN What do you mean, judgment of God?

SCHMITZ How should I know?
He eats and glances at the newspaper again.
' – It seems to the experts that the fire was planned and started in the same manner as last time.'
He laughs briefly, then fills his glass with wine.

ANNA Herr Biedermann?

BIEDERMANN What is it?

ANNA Herr Knechtling would like to speak to you.

BIEDERMANN Knechtling? Now? Knechtling?

ANNA He says –

BIEDERMANN I shouldn't dream of it.

ANNA He says he can't understand you –

BIEDERMANN Why does he have to understand me?

ANNA He has a sick wife and three children –

BIEDERMANN I shouldn't dream of it, I say!
He has jumped to his feet with impatience:
Herr Knechtling! Herr Knechtling! Damn it all, let Herr Knechtling leave me in peace or instruct a solicitor I'm taking an evening off. It's ridiculous. I won't put up with all this fuss, just because I gave him the sack! And never before in human history have we had such social insurance as we have today ... Yes, let him instruct a solicitor. I'll instruct a solicitor too. A share in his in-

vention! Let him put his head in the gas oven or instruct a solicitor – go ahead – if Herr Knechtling can afford to lose or win a case. Let him try!
He controls himself with a glance at Schmitz.
Tell Herr Knechtling I have a visitor.
Anna goes out.
My apologies!

SCHMITZ This is your house, Herr Biedermann.

BIEDERMANN Is the food all right?
He sits down and watches his guest enjoying himself.

SCHMITZ Who would have thought such a thing still existed nowadays?

BIEDERMANN Mustard?

SCHMITZ Humanity.
He screws the top back on the tube.
I mean who would have believed that you wouldn't grab me by the collar and chuck me out into the street – out into the rain! You see that's what we need, Herr Biedermann: humanity.
He takes the bottle and fills his glass.
God bless you for it.
He drinks with visible enjoyment.

BIEDERMANN You mustn't start thinking now that I'm inhuman, Herr Schmitz –

SCHMITZ Herr Biedermann!

BIEDERMANN That what's Frau Knechtling says!

SCHMITZ If you were inhuman, Herr Biedermann, you wouldn't be giving me shelter tonight, that's obvious.

BIEDERMANN Yes, isn't it?

SCHMITZ Even if it's only in the attic.
He puts down his glass.
Now our wine is just right.
The front door bell rings.
The police – ?

BIEDERMANN My wife –

SCHMITZ H'm.

The bell rings again.

BIEDERMANN Come this way ... But on one condition: No
noise! My wife has a weak heart –
*Women's voices are audible from outside and Bieder-
mann beckons to Schmitz to hurry and help him.
Taking the tray, glass and bottle with them they
tiptoe out right, where the Chorus is sitting.*

BIEDERMANN Excuse me.
He steps over the bench.

SCHMITZ Excuse me.
*He steps over the bench and they disappear, while
Frau Biedermann enters the room from the left
accompanied by Anna, who takes her things.*

BABETTE Where's my husband? We're not narrow-minded
you know, Anna. I don't mind your having a
sweetheart, but I won't have you hiding him in
the house.

ANNA I haven't got a sweetheart, Frau Biedermann.

BABETTE Then whose is that rusty bicycle by the front
door? I got the fright of my life –

ATTIC

*Biedermann switches on the light, revealing the
attic, and signs to Schmitz to come in. They con-
verse in whispers.*

BIEDERMANN Here's the switch ... If you're cold there's an old
sheep-skin rug somewhere, I think – but quiet,
for God's sake.... Take off your shoes!
Schmitz puts down the tray and takes off one shoe.
Herr Schmitz –

SCHMITZ Herr Biedermann?

BIEDERMANN Will you promise me that you're really not a fire
raiser?
Schmitz can't help laughing.
Sh!

He nods good night, goes out and shuts the door.
Schmitz takes off the other shoe.

ROOM

Babette has heard something and listens; she looks
horrified, then suddenly relieved; she turns to the
audience.

BABETTE My husband Gottlieb has promised me he will
personally go up into the attic every evening to
make sure there is no fire raiser there. I'm very
grateful to him. If he didn't go I should lie awake
half the night . . .

ATTIC

Schmitz goes to the switch, now in his socks, and
puts out the light.

. . . .

CHORUS Good people of our city, see
Us, guardians of innocence,
Still free from suspicion,
Filled with good will
Towards the sleeping city,
Sitting,
Standing –
CHORUS LEADER From time to time filling
A pipe to pass the time.
CHORUS Looking,

Listening,
That no fire shall blaze up
From homely roofs
To wipe out our well-beloved city.
A tower-clock strikes three.

CHORUS LEADER Everyone knows we are there and knows
That a call will suffice.
He fills his pipe.

CHORUS Who puts on the light
At this hour of the night?
O woe, I see
With nerves all on edge,
Distressed and sleepless,
The wife.
Babette appears in a dressing-gown.

BABETTE There's someone coughing! . . .
The sound of snoring.
Gottlieb! Can't you hear it?
The sound of coughing.
There's somebody there! . . .
The sound of snoring.
Men! As soon as there's trouble they take a sleep-
ing tablet.
A tower-clock strikes four.

CHORUS LEADER Four o'clock.
Babette puts out the light again.
But no call has come.
*He puts his pipe back in his pocket; the background
lights up.*

CHORUS Beams of the sun,
Lashes of the eye divine,
Day is once more breaking
Above the homely roofs of the city.
    Hail to us!
No ill has befallen the slumbering city,
No ill so far today . . .
    Hail to us!
The chorus sits down.

2

ROOM

Biedermann is standing with his hat and coat on, a leather briefcase under his arm, drinking his morning coffee and speaking to someone outside the room.

BIEDERMANN For the last time – he isn't a fire raiser!

VOICE How do you know?

BIEDERMANN I asked him myself . . . And anyhow, can't people think of anything else these days? It's enough to drive one crazy, you and your fire raisers the whole time –

Babette comes in with a milk jug.

Enough to drive one crazy!

BABETTE Don't shout at me.

BIEDERMANN I'm not shouting at you, Babette, I'm shouting at people in general.

She pours milk into his cup.

I must go!

He drinks his coffee, which is too hot.

If we take everyone for a fire raiser, where will it lead to?

We must have a little trust, Babette, a little trust –

He looks at his wrist watch.

BABETTE You're too good-natured. I'm not standing for it, Gottlieb. You let your heart speak, while I can't sleep all night long . . . I shall give him breakfast, but then I shall send him packing, Gottlieb.

BIEDERMANN Do that.

BABETTE In a perfectly friendly way, you know, without hurting his feelings.

BIEDERMANN Do that.

He puts his cup down.

I must go and see my solicitor.

He gives Babette a routine kiss. At this moment

Schmitz appears carrying a sheepskin rug; they don't see him at first.

BABETTE Why did you sack Knechtling?

BIEDERMANN Because I don't need him any more.

BABETTE You were always so satisfied with him.

BIEDERMANN That's what he's trying to make capital out of. A share in his invention! Knechtling knows perfectly well that our hair tonic is the result of salesmanship, not an invention at all. It's ridiculous! The good people who rub our hair tonic on their bald patches might just as well use their own urine –

BABETTE Gottlieb!

BIEDERMANN But it's true!
He makes sure he has everything in his briefcase.
I'm too kind-hearted, you're quite right. I shall twist this Knechtling's neck for him.
He is about to leave, when he sees Schmitz.

SCHMITZ Good morning, sir and madam!

BIEDERMANN Herr Schmitz –
Schmitz stretches out his hand to him.

SCHMITZ Call me Joe!
Biedermann does not take his hand.

BIEDERMANN – my wife will talk to you, Herr Schmitz. I have to go.
Unfortunately. But I wish you all the best . . .
He shakes Schmitz's hand.
All the best, Joe, all the best!
Biedermann leaves.

SCHMITZ All the best, Gottlieb, all the best!
Babette stares at him.
Your husband's name is Gottlieb, isn't it?

BABETTE How did you sleep?

SCHMITZ Cold, thank you. But I took the liberty of wrapping up in the sheepskin rug. – It reminded me of my youth in the charcoal burner's hut . . . Yes – I'm used to the cold . . .

BABETTE Your breakfast is ready.

SCHMITZ Madam!
> *She motions him to the chair.*
> This is too much!
> *She fills his cup.*

BABETTE You must have a good meal, Joe. I'm sure you
have a long journey in front of you.

SCHMITZ What do you mean?
> *She motions him to the chair again.*

BABETTE Would you like a soft-boiled egg?

SCHMITZ Two.

BABETTE Anna!

SCHMITZ You see, madam, I feel quite at home already . . .
I make so bold –
> *He sits down. Anna has come in.*

BABETTE Two soft-boiled eggs.

ANNA Very good.

SCHMITZ Three and a half minutes.

ANNA Very good.
> *Anna starts to go.*

SCHMITZ Fräulein!
> *Anna stands in the doorway.*
> Good morning!

ANNA Morning.
> *Anna goes out.*

SCHMITZ The way the young lady looks at me! My God, I
believe if it were up to her I should be outside in
the pouring rain!
> *Babette pours coffee.*

BABETTE Herr Schmitz –

SCHMITZ Yes?

BABETTE If I may speak frankly –

SCHMITZ You're trembling, madam!

BABETTE Herr Schmitz –

SCHMITZ What's worrying you?

BABETTE Here's some cheese.

SCHMITZ Thanks.

BABETTE Here's some jam.

SCHMITZ Thanks.

BABETTE Here's some honey.

SCHMITZ One at a time, madam, one at a time!

He leans back and eats his bread and butter, ready to listen.

BABETTE Not to mince matters, Herr Schmitz –

SCHMITZ Call me Joe.

BABETTE Not to mince matters –

SCHMITZ You want to get rid of me?

BABETTE No, Herr Schmitz, no! I wouldn't put it like that –

SCHMITZ Then how would you put it?

He helps himself to cheese.

There's nothing I like better than Tilsiter cheese.

He leans back again and eats, ready to listen.

So madam takes me for a fire raiser –

BABETTE Don't misunderstand me! What have I said? Nothing is further from my wishes, Herr Schmitz, than to hurt your feelings. Word of honour! You have got me all muddled up. Who said anything about fire raisers? I have no complaint whatever to make about your behaviour –

Schmitz puts down his knife and fork.

SCHMITZ I know, I have no manners.

BABETTE No, Herr Schmitz, it's not that –

SCHMITZ A man who makes a noise when he eats –

BABETTE Nonsense –

SCHMITZ They were always telling me that in the orphanage: Schmitz, they used to say, don't make such a din with your dinner!

She picks up the pot to pour coffee.

BABETTE Good heavens, you misunderstand me completely.

He holds his hand over his cup.

SCHMITZ I'm going.

BABETTE Herr Schmitz –

SCHMITZ I'm going.

BABETTE Another cup?

He shakes his head.

Half a cup?

He shakes his head.

You mustn't go like that, Herr Schmitz. I didn't mean to offend you. I didn't say a word about your making a noise when you eat!

He stands up.

Have I offended you?

He folds his table napkin.

SCHMITZ It's not madam's fault if I have no manners. My father was a charcoal burner. Where was I to learn manners? I don't mind hunger and cold, madam – but no education, no manners, madam, no culture . . .

BABETTE I understand.

SCHMITZ I'm going.

BABETTE Where to?

SCHMITZ Out into the rain . . .

BABETTE Oh dear.

SCHMITZ I'm used to it.

BABETTE Herr Schmitz . . . Don't look at me like that! – Your father was a charcoal burner, I see what you mean, Herr Schmitz, I'm sure you had a hard youth –

SCHMITZ No youth at all, madam.

He lowers his eyes and fingers his fingers.

No youth at all. I was seven years old when my mother died . . .

He turns away and wipes his eyes.

BABETTE Joe! – Please Joe . . .

Anna comes in bringing the soft-boiled eggs.

ANNA Anything else?

Anna receives no answer and goes out.

BABETTE I'm not sending you away, Herr Schmitz. I didn't say that at all. What did I say? You really misunderstand me, it's terrible. What can I do to make you believe me?

She hesitantly plucks at his sleeve.

Come on, Joe, eat!

Schmitz sits down at the table again.

What do you take us for? I haven't noticed that
you make a noise when you eat, word of honour!
And even if you did – we set no store by appear-
ances, Herr Schmitz, you must feel that, we're
not that type . . .

He takes the top off his egg.

SCHMITZ God bless you for it!

BABETTE Here's the salt.

He begins to eat the egg.

SCHMITZ It's quite true, madam didn't tell me to leave, not
a word about it, that's quite true. I apologize for
misunderstanding madam . . .

BABETTE Is the egg all right?

SCHMITZ A bit soft . . . I do apologize.

He eats the last spoonful.

What were you going to say, madam, earlier, when
you said: Not to mince matters!

BABETTE Yes, what was I going to say? . . .

He takes the top off the second egg.

SCHMITZ God bless you for it.

He eats the second egg.

Willie always says that private compassion doesn't
exist any more. There aren't any fine people left
nowadays. The State has taken over everything.
There aren't any human beings left. That's what
he says. And that's why the world is going to the
dogs! . . .

He puts salt in the egg.

He'll open his eyes wide when he gets a breakfast
like this, Willie will!

The front door bell rings.

Maybe that's him.

The front door bell rings again.

BABETTE Who is Willie?

SCHMITZ He has culture, madam, you'll see, he used to be
a waiter at the Metropol before it was burnt
down . . .

BABETTE Burnt down?

SCHMITZ Head waiter.
　　　　Anna has entered.
BABETTE Who is it?
　ANNA A gentleman.
BABETTE What does he want?
　ANNA From the Fire Insurance, he says; he has to look
　　　　at the house.
　　　　Babette stands up.
　　　　He's wearing tails.
　　　　*Babette and Anna go out, Schmitz pours himself
　　　　coffee.*
SCHMITZ That must be Willie!

．．．．．．．．．．．．．．．．．．．．．．．．．．．．．．．．．．．．．

　CHORUS But now there are two
　　　　　That arouse our suspicion,
　　　　　Bicycles, that is to say,
　　　　　Rusty ones, belong to someone,
　　　　　But who?
CHORUS LEADER One since yesterday, the other since today.
　CHORUS Woe!
CHORUS LEADER Once more it is night and we watch.
　　　　　A tower-clock strikes.
　CHORUS The faint-hearted sees much where there's
　　　　　nothing,
　　　　　Affright at the sight of his shadow,
　　　　　Falling over himself
　　　　　In excess of zeal.
　　　　　Thus in terror he lives
　　　　　Till it enters
　　　　　Into his very own room.

The tower-clock strikes.

CHORUS LEADER What am I to make of the fact
That these two remain in the house?

The tower-clock strikes.

CHORUS Blinder than blind is the faint-hearted,
Trembling with hope that the thing is not evil
He gives it a friendly reception,
Disarmed, tired out with terror,
Hoping for the best . . .
Until it's too late.

The tower-clock strikes.

CHORUS Woe!

The Chorus sits down.

3

ATTIC

*Schmitz, still in the clothes of a wrestler, and the
Other, who has taken off his tail coat and is wearing
only his white waistcoat, are busy rolling drums into
the attic, tin drums of the sort used to transport
petrol; they have both taken off their shoes and are
being as quiet as possible.*

THE OTHER Quietly! Quietly!

SCHMITZ Suppose it occurs to him to call the police?

THE OTHER Forward!

SCHMITZ What then?

THE OTHER Slowly! Slowly . . . Stop.

*They have rolled the last drum up to others already
standing in the half-light of early morning; the Other
takes cotton-waste and wipes his fingers.*

THE OTHER Why should he call the police?

SCHMITZ Why shouldn't he?

THE OTHER Because he has committed an offence himself.

The cooing of pigeons is heard.

I'm afraid it's day, let's turn in.
He throws away the cotton waste.
Strictly speaking, every citizen above a certain
level of income is guilty of some offence. Don't
worry! . . .
There is a knock on the bolted door.

BIEDERMANN Open up! Open up!
The door is banged and shaken.

THE OTHER That doesn't sound like breakfast.

BIEDERMANN Open the door, I say. Immediately!

SCHMITZ He's never been like that before.
*The banging gets louder and louder. The Other
puts on his tail coat. Without haste, but swiftly, he
straightens his tie and flicks of the dust, then he
opens the door. Biedermann enters in a dressing-
gown, not noticing the newcomer, who has taken up a
position behind the door.*

BIEDERMANN Herr Schmitz!

SCHMITZ Good morning, Herr Biedermann, good morning,
I hope that silly rumbling didn't wake you –

BIEDERMANN Herr Schmitz!

SCHMITZ It shan't happen again.

BIEDERMANN Leave my house.
Pause.
I said, leave my house!

SCHMITZ When?

BIEDERMANN At once.

SCHMITZ Why?

BIEDERMANN Or my wife will ring the police, and I can't and
won't stop her.

SCHMITZ H'm.

BIEDERMANN And at once!
Pause.
What are you waiting for?
Without speaking, Schmitz picks up his shoes.
I don't want any argument!

SCHMITZ I'm not saying anything.

BIEDERMANN If you think I'm going to put up with any old

thing, Herr Schmitz, just because you're a wrest-
ler – that rumbling all night long –
He points with outstretched arm to the door.
Out! Out! I say. Out!
Schmitz addresses the Other.

SCHMITZ He's never been like this before . . .
Biedermann turns round and is speechless.

THE OTHER My name is Eisenring.

BIEDERMANN Gentlemen –?

EISENRING Wilhelm Maria Eisenring.

BIEDERMANN How come there are suddenly two of you, gentle-
men?
Schmitz and Eisenring look at one another.
Without asking!

EISENRING You see?

BIEDERMANN What does that mean?

EISENRING I told you so. You can't do things like that, Joe,
you've got no manners. Without asking. What a
way to behave – suddenly there are two of us.

BIEDERMANN I'm beside myself.

EISENRING You see!
He turns to Biedermann.
I told him so!
He turns to Schmitz.
Didn't I tell you so?
Schmitz looks ashamed of himself.

BIEDERMANN What are you thinking of, gentlemen? I mean to
say, gentlemen, I am the householder. I ask you:
What are you thinking of?
Pause.

EISENRING Answer when the gentleman asks you a question!
Pause.

SCHMITZ Willie is a friend of mine.

BIEDERMANN So what?

SCHMITZ We went to school together, Herr Biedermann,
even as children . . .

BIEDERMANN Well?

SCHMITZ So I thought . . .

BIEDERMANN What?

SCHMITZ So I thought . . .
Pause.

EISENRING You didn't think at all!
He turns to Biedermann.
I understand your feelings perfectly well, Herr Biedermann, I mean, there's a limit to everything –
He shouts at Schmitz.
Do you imagine a householder has to put up with absolutely anything?
He turns to Biedermann.
Didn't Joe ask you at all?

BIEDERMANN Not a word!

EISENRING Joe –

BIEDERMANN Not a word!

EISENRING – and then you're surprised when people throw you out into the street?
He shakes his head and laughs as though over an imbecile.

BIEDERMANN It's not a laughing matter, gentlemen, I'm in deadly earnest. My wife has a weak heart –

EISENRING You see!

BIEDERMANN My wife was awake half the night. Because of the rumbling. And anyway, what are you up to here?
He looks around:
What the devil are these drums doing here?
Schmitz and Eiensring look towards a part of the attic where there are no drums.
Over here! Look! What's this?
He bangs a drum.
What's this?

SCHMITZ Drums.

BIEDERMANN Where did they come from?

SCHMITZ Do you know where they came from, Willie?

EISENRING They're imported, it says so on them.

BIEDERMANN Gentlemen –

EISENRING It says so on them somewhere!

Eisenring and Schmitz look for the label.

BIEDERMANN I'm speechless. What an idea! My whole attic full of drums – piled up, positively piled up!

EISENRING That's just it.

BIEDERMANN What do you mean by that?

EISENRING Joe miscalculated . . . Thirty-five by forty-five feet, you said. But the whole attic isn't more than a thousand square feet . . . I can't leave my drums out in the street, Herr Biedermann, you will understand that.

BIEDERMANN I don't understand anything –

Schmitz points to a label.

I'm speechless –

SCHMITZ It tells you here where they come from. Look, here.

BIEDERMANN – simply speechless.

He looks at the label.

DOWN BELOW

Anna conducts a policeman into the room.

ANNA I'll call him.

She goes. The policeman waits.

UP ABOVE

BIEDERMANN Petrol! –

DOWN BELOW

Anna comes back.

ANNA What is it about, sergeant?

POLICEMAN An official matter.

Anna goes. The policeman waits.

UP ABOVE

BIEDERMANN Is that true, gentlemen, is that true?

EISENRING That's what it says on the label. *He shows them the label.*

BEIDERMANN What do you take me for? I've never seen such a thing in my life. Do you imagine I can't read?
They look at the label.
I ask you!—
He speaks like an examining magistrate:
What's in these drums?

EISENRING Petrol.

BIEDERMANN Stop joking! I'm asking you for the last time, what's in these drums? You know as well as I do that an attic isn't the place for petrol –
He runs his finger over the drum:
There – just smell for yourselves!
He holds his finger under their noses:
Is that petrol or isn't it?
They sniff and look at each other.
Answer!

EISENRING It is.

SCHMITZ It is.

BOTH No doubt about it.

BIEDERMANN Are you crazy? My whole attic is full of petrol –

SCHMITZ That's why we aren't smoking, Herr Biedermann.

BIEDERMANN And at a time like this, when there's a warning in every newspaper you open. What are you thinking of? My wife will get a heart attack if she sees this.

EISENRING You see!

BIEDERMANN Don't keep saying, You see, all the time.

EISENRING You can't expect a woman to put up with that, Joe, a housewife. I know housewives –
Anna calls up the stairs.

ANNA Herr Biedermann! Herr Biedermann!
Biedermann shuts the door.

BIEDERMANN Herr Schmitz! Herr –

EISENRING   Eisenring.

BIEDERMANN   If you don't clear these drums out of the house this moment, but this moment, I say –

EISENRING   Then you'll call the police.

BIEDERMANN   Yes.

SCHMITZ   You see!
Anna calls up the stairs.

ANNA   Herr Biedermann!
Biedermann whispers.

BIEDERMANN   That was my last word.

EISENRING   Which one?

BIEDERMANN   I won't stand for petrol in my attic. Once and for all, I won't stand for it!
There is a knock at the door.
I'm coming!
He opens the door to go; a policeman enters.

POLICEMAN   There you are, Herr Biedermann, there you are. You needn't come down, I shan't keep you long.

BIEDERMANN   Good morning!

POLICEMAN   Good morning!

EISENRING   Morning . . .

SCHMITZ   Morning . . .
Schmitz and Eisenring bow.

POLICEMAN   It's about an accident –

BIEDERMANN   Good heavens!

POLICEMAN   An old man whose wife claims that he worked for you – as an inventor! – put his head in the gas oven last night.
He looks in his notebook.
Johann Knechtling, of 11 Horse Lane.
He puts the notebook away.
Did you know anyone of that name?

BIEDERMANN   I –

POLICEMAN   Perhaps you would rather discuss this in private, Herr Biedermann –

BIEDERMANN   Yes.

POLICEMAN   It's no concern of your staff.

BIEDERMANN   No –

He comes to a stop in the doorway.
If anybody asks for me, gentlemen, I shall be at the police station. All right? I shall be back in a few minutes.
Schmitz and Eisenring nod.

POLICEMAN Herr Biedermann –

BIEDERMANN Let's go.

POLICEMAN What have you got in those drums?

BIEDERMANN – I?

POLICEMAN If I may ask.

BIEDERMANN . . . Hair tonic . . .
He looks at Schmitz and Eisenring.

EISENRING HORMOFLOR.

SCHMITZ 'Fresh hope for men.'

EISENRING HORMOFLOR.

SCHMITZ 'Try it today.'

EISENRING 'Restore your hair the Hormoflor way.'

BOTH HORMOFLOR, HORMOFLOR, HORMOFLOR.
The policeman laughs.

BIEDERMANN Is he dead?
Biedermann and the policeman go.

EISENRING A charming fellow.

SCHMITZ Didn't I tell you so?

EISENRING But not a word about breakfast. . . .

SCHMITZ He's never been like that before.
Eisenring puts a hand in his trouser pocket.

EISENRING Have you got the primer?
Schmitz puts a hand in his trouser pocket.

SCHMITZ He's never been like that before . . .

. . . .

CHORUS Beams of the sun,
Lashes of the eye divine,

          Day is once more breaking
          Above the homely roofs of the city.

CHORUS LEADER Today as yesterday.

      CHORUS Hail to us!

CHORUS LEADER No ill has befallen the slumbering city.

      CHORUS Hail to us!

CHORUS LEADER No ill so far . . .

      CHORUS Hail to us!
          The sound of traffic, hooters, trams.

CHORUS LEADER Clever is man and master of many dangers.
          When he thinks
          Upon that which he sees.
          When his mind is alert he observes
          The signs of approaching disaster
          In time if he will.

      CHORUS But suppose he will not?

CHORUS LEADER He who, in order to know
          What danger threatens, reads papers,
          Each day at breakfast indignant
          Over some distant disaster,
          Each day given explanations
          That spare him the need to think,
          Each day informed of what happened the day
          before,
          He finds it hard to perceive what is happening
          now
          Beneath his own roof –

      CHORUS Unpublished!

CHORUS LEADER Manifest.

      CHORUS Scandalous!

CHORUS LEADER True.

      CHORUS Unwilling he is to see through it, for then –
          The Chorus Leader interrupts the Chorus with a
          gesture of the hand.

CHORUS LEADER Here he comes.
          The Chorus wheels round.

      CHORUS No ill has befallen the slumbering city,
          Today as yesterday,

As a means of forgetting
The danger that threatens
The citizen rushes,
Cleanly shaved,
To his office . . .
*Biedermann appears in overcoat and hat, his brief-
case under his arm.*

BIEDERMANN Taxi! . . . Taxi? . . . Taxi!
The Chorus blocks his path.
What's the matter?

CHORUS Woe!

BIEDERMANN What do you want?

CHORUS Woe!

BIEDERMANN You've said that already.

CHORUS Thrice woe!

BIEDERMANN What do you mean?

CHORUS LEADER Deeply suspicious, we think
The danger of fire is revealed
To our eyes as to yours.
How am I to construe
Drums full of fuel in the attic.
Biedermann yells.

BIEDERMANN Mind your own business!
Silence.
Let me pass. – I have to see my solicitor. – What
do you want with me? – I've done no wrong . . .
Biedermann appears to be frightened.
Is this a cross-examination?
Biedermann displays masterful self-assurance.
Stand aside.
The Chorus stands motionless.

CHORUS Never beseems it the Chorus
To sit in judgment upon
Citizens who take action.

CHORUS LEADER The Chorus sees from without
And thus more quickly perceives
The peril that threatens.

CHORUS Questioning merely, polite

    Even when danger dismays us,
    Warning merely, restrained
    In spite of our anguish,
    Helpless though watchful, the Chorus
    Offers its help till the fire
    Is beyond all hope of extinction.
    Biedermann looks at his wrist-watch.

BIEDERMANN I'm in a hurry.

CHORUS Woe!

BIEDERMANN I really don't know what you want.

CHORUS LEADER Biedermann Gottlieb, explain
    Why all those drums full of fuel
    In your loft you allow to remain.

BIEDERMANN Explain?

CHORUS LEADER Knowing full well how inflammable
    The world is, what did you think?

BIEDERMANN Think?
    He eyes the Chorus:
    Gentlemen, I am a free citizen. I can think what I
    like. What is the meaning of all these questions? I
    have a right not to think anything at all, gentle-
    men – quite apart from the fact that what happens
    under my roof is my business, I mean to say, I
    am the house-owner! . . .

CHORUS Sacred to us what is sacred,
    Property,
    Even if out of it springs
    A fire that we cannot extinguish
    That reduces us all to a cinder,
    Sacred to us what is sacred!

BIEDERMANN Very well, then. –
    Silence.
    Why don't you let me pass?
    Silence.
    People shouldn't always think the worst. Where
    will that lead? I want peace and quiet, that's all,
    and as to the two gentlemen – quite apart from the
    fact that I have other worries just now . . .

Enter Babette in hat and coat.
What are you doing here?

BABETTE Am I in the way?

BIEDERMANN I'm in conference with the Chorus.

Babette nods to the Chorus, then whispers in Biedermann's ear.

BIEDERMANN Of course with a ribbon! It doesn't matter what it costs so long as it's a wreath.

Babette nods to the Chorus.

BABETTE Excuse me, gentlemen.

Babette leaves.

BIEDERMANN In short, gentlemen, I've had enough of you and your fire raisers! I never go to the local any more, I'm fed up with it. Can't people find anything else to talk about nowadays? After all, I've only got one life. If we take everyone we meet, except ourselves, for a fire raiser, how are things ever going to improve? Damn it all, we must have a little trust, a little good will. That's what I think. We mustn't always look on the black side. Damn it all, not everybody is a fire raiser. That's what I think. A little trust, a little . . .

Pause.

I can't be scared the whole time!

Pause.

Do you think I slept a wink last night? I'm no fool. Petrol is petrol! The grimmest thoughts filled my mind – I climbed up onto the table to listen, and later even onto the cupboard to put my ear to the ceiling. They were snoring. Snoring! At least four times I climbed up onto the cupboard. Peacefully snoring! . . . But in spite of that, believe it or not, I once went out onto the landing, in my pyjamas – I was so furious. I was on the point of throwing the two scoundrels out into the street – along with their drums – with my own hands, ruthlessly, in the middle of the night!

CHORUS With your own hands?

BIEDERMANN Yes.

CHORUS Ruthlessly?

BIEDERMANN Yes.

CHORUS In the middle of the night?

BIEDERMANN I was just on the point of doing so, yes – if my
wife hadn't come out because she was afraid I
should catch cold – just on the point, I was!
He takes a cigar to hide his embarrassment.

CHORUS LEADER How am I to explain it?
He spent a sleepless night.
Did it cross his mind that they might
Abuse the citizen's kindness?
Seized with suspicion he was. Why was that?
Biedermann lights his cigar.

CHORUS What troubles beset the citizen
Who, though hard as nails in business,
Is elsewhere a charming fellow,
Anxious
To do good.

CHORUS LEADER When it suits him.

CHORUS Hoping that good will come
From good-natured actions,
A sadly mistaken assumption.

BIEDERMANN What do you mean?

CHORUS To us the place reeks of petrol.
Biedermann sniffs.

BIEDERMANN Well, gentlemen, I can't smell anything . . .

CHORUS Alas!

BIEDERMANN Nothing whatever.

CHORUS Alas!

CHORUS LEADER So used already is he
To evil stenches.

CHORUS Alas!

BIEDERMANN Don't be so defeatist all the time, gentlemen:
stop saying Alas! all the time.
A car hoots.
Taxi! – Taxi!
A car can be heard stopping.

Excuse me.
Biedermann hurries off.

CHORUS Citizen—where are you going?
A car is heard starting up.

CHORUS LEADER What is he planning to do,
The unhappy man?
Afraid and reckless,
I thought, and pale in the face,
He hurried away,
Afraid and determined – what is he planning to
do?
A car is heard hooting.

CHORUS So used already is he
To evil stenches!
The car is heard hooting in the distance.
Alas!

CHORUS LEADER Alack!
*The Chorus withdraws, with the exception of the
Leader, who takes out his pipe.*

CHORUS LEADER He who fears change
More than disaster,
What can he do to forestall
The threatening disaster?
He follows the Chorus.

4

ATTIC

*Eisenring, alone, is unwinding cord from a reel,
whistling Lili Marlene as he works. He stops
whistling to wet his index finger and hold it
up out of the skylight to test the direction of the
wind.*

ROOM

> *Enter Biedermann, followed by Babette. He takes off his coat and throws down the briefcase, a cigar in his mouth.*

BIEDERMANN Do as I tell you.

BABETTE A goose?

BIEDERMANN A goose.

> *He takes off his tie, the cigar in his mouth.*

BABETTE Why are you taking off your tie, Gottlieb?

> *He hands her the tie.*

BIEDERMANN If I report those two to the police, then I know I shall make enemies of them. What's the good of that? One match, and our whole house will be in flames. What's the good of that? But if I go up and invite them to supper – and they accept my invitation . . .

BABETTE What then?

BIEDERMANN Then we shall be friends. –

> *He takes off his jacket, hands it to his wife and goes out.*

BABETTE Anna, you won't be able to take this evening off. We're having visitors. Lay the table for four.

ATTIC

> *Eisenring is singing Lili Marlene, then there is a knock at the door.*

EISENRING Come in.

> *He goes on whistling, but no one comes in.*

Come in.

> *Enter Biedermann in shirtsleeves, his cigar in his hand.*

Morning, Herr Biedermann.

BIEDERMANN May I?

EISENRING How did you sleep?

BIEDERMANN Wretchedly, thank you.

EISENRING Me too. It's that south wind . . .
    He continues working with the cord and the reel.
BIEDERMANN I hope I'm not disturbing you.
EISENRING But of course not, Herr Biedermann, you're at home here.
BIEDERMANN I don't want to be in the way.
    The cooing of pigeons is heard.
    Where has our friend got to?
EISENRING Joe? At work, the lazy dog. He didn't want to go without breakfast! I sent him to get some wood-wool.
BIEDERMANN Wood-wool –?
EISENRING Wood-wool carries the sparks furthest.
    Biedermann laughs faintly as though at a poor joke.
BIEDERMANN What I was going to say, Herr Eisenring –
EISENRING Are you going to throw us out again?
BIEDERMANN In the middle of the night (my sleeping tablets are all gone) it suddenly occurred to me that you haven't a toilet up here –
EISENRING We have the gutter.
BIEDERMANN As you like, gentlemen, as you like. It just crossed my mind. All night long. Perhaps you'd like to wash or take a shower. Don't hesitate to use my bathroom. I told Anna to put out towels for you.
    Eisenring shakes his head.
    Why do you shake your head?
EISENRING Where on earth has he put it?
BIEDERMANN What?
EISENRING Have you seen a primer anywhere?
    He looks here and there.
    Don't worry about the bathroom, Herr Biedermann. Seriously. There was no bathroom in prison either, you know.
BIEDERMANN Prison?
EISENRING Didn't Joe tell you I had just come out of prison?
BIEDERMANN No.
EISENRING Not a word?

BIEDERMANN No.

EISENRING He talks of nothing but himself all the time. There are people like that. I mean, is it our fault that he had such a tragic youth? Did you have a tragic youth, Herr Biedermann? I didn't! – I could have gone to the university, Father wanted me to be a lawyer.

He stands at the skylight conversing with the pigeons: Grrr! Grrr! Grrr!

Biedermann re-lights his cigar.

BIEDERMANN Herr Eisenring, I didn't sleep all night. Tell me frankly, is there really petrol in those drums?

EISENRING Don't you trust us?

BIEDERMANN I'm only asking.

EISENRING What do you take us for, Herr Biedermann, tell me frankly, what do you take us for?

BIEDERMANN You mustn't think I have no sense of humour, my friend, but the kind of jokes you make are really a bit much.

EISENRING That's something we've learnt.

BIEDERMANN What is?

EISENRING Joking is the third best method of hoodwinking people. The second best is sentimentality. The kind of stuff our Joe goes in for – a childhood with charcoal burners in the forest, an orphanage, the circus and so on. But the best and safest method – in my opinion – is to tell the plain unvarnished truth. Oddly enough. No one believes it.

ROOM

Anna brings in Widow Knechtling all in black.

ANNA Sit down.

The Widow sits down.

But if you're Frau Knechtling, you're wasting your time. Herr Biedermann said he wouldn't have anything to do with you –

The Widow stands up.
Sit down.
The Widow sits down.
But I'm afraid you're going to be disappointed. . .
Anna goes out.

ATTIC

Eisenring is standing working, Biedermann is standing smoking.

EISENRING What on earth is keeping Joe so long? Wood-wool is easy enough to get hold of. I hope they haven't nabbed him.

BIEDERMANN Nabbed him?

EISENRING Why does that amuse you?

BIEDERMANN You know, when you talk like that, Herr Eisenring, you seem to me to come from another world. Nabbed! I find it fascinating. From another world! I mean, in the circles in which we move people hardly ever get nabbed –

EISENRING Because in such circles people don't steal wood-wool, that's obvious, Herr Biedermann, that's class distinction.

BIEDERMANN Nonsense!

EISENRING You don't mean, Herr Biedermann –

BIEDERMANN I don't believe in class distinctions! – You must have felt that, Eisenring, I'm not old-fashioned. On the contrary. I'm genuinely sorry that among the lower classes people still blather about class distinctions. Aren't we all creatures of one creator nowadays, whether we're rich or poor? The middle class too. Aren't we both flesh and blood, you and I? . . . I don't know, Herr Eisenring, whether you also smoke cigars?
He offers one, but Eisenring shakes his head.
I don't say all men are equal, of course; there will always be the competent and the incompetent,

thank God; but why don't we just shake hands?
A little good will, damn it all, a little idealism, a
little – and we could all live in peace, rich and
poor, don't you agree?

EISENRING If I may be frank, Herr Biedermann –

BIEDERMANN Please do.

EISENRING You won't take it amiss?

BIEDERMANN The franker the better.

EISENRING I mean, quite frankly, you ought not to smoke
here.

Biedermann starts and puts out his cigar.

It's not for me to tell you what to do here, Herr
Biedermann, after all this is your house, but you
understand –

BIEDERMANN Of course!

Eisenring bends down.

EISENRING There it is!

*He picks something up from the floor and blows it
clean before attaching it to the cord, once more
whistling Lili Marlene.*

BIEDERMANN Tell me, Herr Eisenring: What are you doing all
the time? If I may ask. And what's that thing?

EISENRING The primer.

BIEDERMANN –?

EISENRING And that's the fuse.

BIEDERMANN –?

EISENRING There are supposed to be even better ones now,
Joe says, new models. But they're not in the
arsenals yet, and it's out of the question for us
to buy them. Everything connected with war is
terribly expensive, nothing but the top quality.

BIEDERMANN Fuse, you say?

EISENRING Detonating fuse.

He gives Biedermann one end of the fuse:

Will you be so kind as to hold this end, Herr
Biedermann, so that I can measure it?

Biedermann holds the fuse.

BIEDERMANN Joking apart, my friend –

EISENRING Only for a moment!

He whistles Lili Marlene and measures the fuse.

Thanks, Herr Biedermann, thanks very much.

Biedermann bursts out laughing.

BIEDERMANN No, Willie, you can't kid me. Not me! But I must say you put a great deal of trust in people's sense of humour. A great deal! If you talk like that I can well believe you get arrested now and then. Not everyone has as much sense of humour as I have, my friend!

EISENRING We have to find the right people.

BIEDERMANN At the local, for instance, they fly off the handle if you so much as say you believe in the goodness in man.

EISENRING Ha.

BIEDERMANN And yet I donated a sum to our Fire Brigade so big I won't even tell you how much it was.

EISENRING Ha.

He lays the fuse.

The people who have no sense of humcur are just as lost when the balloon goes up; don't worry about that!

Biedermann has to sit down on a drum, sweating.

What's the matter, Herr Biedermann? You're quite pale!

He slaps him on the back.

I know, it's this smell, when you're not used to the smell of petrol it can upset you – I'll open a window.

Eisenring opens the door.

BIEDERMANN Thank you . . .

Anna calls up the stairs.

ANNA Herr Biedermann! Herr Biedermann!

EISENRING The police again?

ANNA Herr Biedermann!

EISENRING If this isn't a police state, what is it?

ANNA Herr Biedermann –

BIEDERMANN Coming!

In a whisper:
Herr Eisenring, do you like goose?

EISENRING Goose?

BIEDERMANN Goose, yes, goose.

EISENRING Like? Me? Why?

BIEDERMANN With chestnut stuffing?

EISENRING And red cabbage?

BIEDERMANN Yes ... What I meant to say was, my wife and I –
especially I – thought if you would like ... I
don't want to be a nuisance! – if you would like to
come to dinner, Herr Eisenring, you and Joe –

EISENRING Tonight?

BIEDERMANN Or would you rather come tomorrow?

EISENRING I don't think we shall be here tomorrow. But
tonight with pleasure, Herr Biedermann, with
pleasure!

BIEDERMANN Shall we say seven o'clock?
Anna calls up the stairs.

ANNA Herr Biedermann!
He shakes hands with Eisenring.

BIEDERMANN Is that a date?

EISENRING It's a date.
*Biedermann goes and stops once more in the door-
way, giving a friendly nod while he glances glumly
at the drums and fuse.* It's a date!
*Biedermann goes and Eisenring carries on with his
work, whistling. The Chorus steps forward as though
the scene were at an end; but just as the Chorus has
gathered by the footlights there is a crash in the
attic; something has fallen over.*

ATTIC

EISENRING You can come out, doctor.
*A Third crawls out from between the drums, a man
wearing glasses.*
You heard, didn't you? Joe and I have got to go

out to supper. You'll be on watch here. See no
one comes in and smokes. Got it? Before the
proper time.

*The Third polishes his glasses, silent and serious.
Eisenring laughs.*

I often wonder, doctor, what you're really doing
along with us, when you don't get any kick out of
a fine blaze, sparks and crackling flames, out of
sirens that are always too late, barking dogs and
human cries – and ashes.

*The Third puts on his glasses, silent and serious.
Eisenring laughs.*

World reformer!

*He whistles for a while to himself without looking
at the Doctor of Philosophy.*

I don't like you academic types, but you know that,
doctor, I told you so at the outset: there's no real
fun in it, you lot are always so ideological, so serious, to the point of treachery – there's no real
fun in it.

He continues working and whistling.

....

CHORUS	Ready are we,
	Carefully coiled are the hoses,
	In accordance with regulations,
	Polished and carefully greased and of brass
	Is each windlass.
	Everyone knows what his task is.
CHORUS LEADER	An ill wind is blowing –
CHORUS	Everyone knows what his task is,

Polished and carefully tested,
To make sure that we have full pressure,
And likewise of brass is our pump.

CHORUS LEADER And the hydrants?

CHORUS Ready are we. –
Babette enters carrying a goose, accompanied by the Ph.D.

BABETTE Yes, doctor, I know, but my husband – yes, doctor, I know it's urgent, yes, I'll tell him –
She leaves the doctor standing and moves forward to the footlights.
My husband has ordered a goose, look, here it is. And I'm supposed to roast it! So that we can get friendly with that lot up there.
The sound of church bells.
It's Saturday evening, as you can hear, and I can't get rid of a silly presentiment that maybe they're ringing for the last time, the bells of our city . . .
Biedermann shouts for Babette.
I don't know, ladies, whether Gottlieb is always right. This is what he once said: Of course they're scoundrels, but if I make enemies of them then it's all up with our hair restorer! And no sooner was he in the Party –
Biedermann shouts for Babette.
It's always the same! I know my Gottlieb. He's always too kind-hearted, just too kind-hearted!
Babette leaves with the goose.

CHORUS One wearing glasses.
A boy of good family doubtless,
Not given to envy,
But full of book-learning and pale,
No longer hopeful that good
Will come of good-nature,
But resolved to perform any action,
Convinced as he is that the end
Justifies fully the means,

Oh,
Hopeful he too . . . Man of good will and of ill.
Cleaning his glasses to lengthen his view
He sees in the drums full of fuel
Not fuel –
He sees the idea!
Till all's blazing.

PH.D. Good evening . . .

CHORUS LEADER Man the hoses!
Man the pumps!
Man the ladders!
The Firemen run to their places.
Good evening.
*To the audience, after calls of 'Be ready!' have
echoed from all sides:*
We are ready. –

5

ROOM

*Widow Knechtling is still there; she is standing.
The ringing of bells is heard very loud. Anna is
laying the table and Biedermann brings two chairs.*

BIEDERMANN – Because, as you can see, I haven't time, Frau
Knechtling, I haven't time to bother with the
dead – as I said: Get in touch with my solicitor.
Widow Knechtling goes.
One can't hear oneself speak, Anna, shut the
window!
Anna shuts the window; the ringing grows fainter.
I told you I wanted everything plain and simple,
a simple supper in a free and easy atmosphere.
What are these idiotic candelabra doing?

ANNA But we always have those, Herr Biedermann.

BIEDERMANN Plain and simple, free and easy, I said. No osten-

tation! – And these finger bowls, for God's sake, silver, nothing but silver and cut glass everywhere. What kind of an impression is that going to make?
He picks up the knife-rests and puts them in his pocket.
Can't you see I'm wearing my oldest jacket, Anna – And you . . . Leave the big poultry knife, Anna, we shall need that. But apart from that, away with all this silver! I want the two gentlemen to feel at home . . . Where's the corkscrew?

ANNA Here.

BIEDERMANN Haven't we something simpler?

ANNA In the kitchen, but it's rusty.

BIEDERMANN Bring it here!
He takes a silver bucket from the table.
What the hell's this for?

ANNA For the wine –

BIEDERMANN Silver!
He stares at the bucket and then at Anna:
Do we always have this?

ANNA Yes, you need it, Herr Biedermann.

BIEDERMANN Need! What do you mean, need? What we need is humanity, brotherhood. Away with it! – And what the hell have you got there?

ANNA Table napkins.

BIEDERMANN Damask!

ANNA We haven't any others.
He picks up the table napkins and puts them in the silver bucket.

BIEDERMANN There are whole tribes that live without table napkins, human beings like ourselves –
Enter Babette with a large wreath. Biedermann hasn't noticed her yet; he is standing by the table:
I ask myself what we need a tablecloth for at all –

BABETTE Gottlieb?

BIEDERMANN At all costs no class distinctions!
He sees Babette.
What's that wreath?

BABETTE It's the one we ordered. What do you think of that, Gottlieb, they've sent the wreath here. And yet I wrote out the address for them myself, Knechtling's address, in black and white. And they've got the ribbon and everything the wrong way round!

BIEDERMANN The ribbon? What do you mean?

BABETTE And the boy says they've sent the bill to Frau Knechtling.
She shows him the ribbon:

> TO OUR UNFORGETTABLE GOTTLIEB BIEDER-MANN.

He looks at the ribbon.

BIEDERMANN We're not accepting that. Certainly not! They'll have to change it –
He goes back to the table:
Don't worry me now, Babette, I've got other things to do. Damn it all, I can't be everywhere.
Babette goes with the wreath.
Right, get rid of the tablecloth! Give me a hand, Anna. And as I said, no waiting at table. Under no circumstances. Come in without knocking, just come straight in, and simply put the pan on the table –

ANNA The pan?
He removes the tablecloth.

BIEDERMANN That immediately creates a completely different atmosphere. You see? A bare wooden table, no fripperies, as at the Last Supper.
He gives her the tablecloth.

ANNA You mean I'm to bring the goose in the pan, Herr Biedermann?
She folds up the tablecloth.
What wine shall I bring, Herr Biedermann?

BIEDERMANN I'll fetch that myself.

ANNA Herr Biedermann!

BIEDERMANN What is it?

ANNA I haven't got a sweater like you said, Herr

Biedermann, a simple sweater that makes me look like one of the family.

BIEDERMANN   Borrow one from my wife!

ANNA   The yellow one or the red one?

BIEDERMANN   It doesn't matter. But I don't want any show – no cap and no apron. You understand? And as I said: Get rid of these candelabra! And see that things don't look so dreadfully neat and tidy here! . . . I'm going down to the cellar.

Biedermann goes out.

ANNA   'See that things don't look so dreadfully neat and tidy here' indeed!

After folding it, she hurls the tablecloth into a corner and stamps on it with both feet.

Anything you say!

Enter Schmitz and Eisenring, each carrying a rose.

BOTH   Good evening, Fräulein!

Anna goes out without looking at them.

EISENRING   Why no wood-wool?

SCHMITZ   Confiscated. By the police. As a safety measure. Anyone selling or possessing wood-wool without a police permit will be arrested. A precaution being taken throughout the country . . .

He combs his hair.

EISENRING   Have you any matches left?

SCHMITZ   Not me.

EISENRING   Nor me.

Schmitz blows through his comb.

SCHMITZ   We'll have to ask him for some.

EISENRING   Biedermann?

SCHMITZ   Mustn't forget.

He puts the comb away and sniffs.

M'm, it smells good! . . .

Biedermann comes to the footlights carrying a bottle.

BIEDERMANN   You can think what you like about me, gentlemen. But just answer one question:

The sound of raucous singing and laughter.

I tell myself: So long as they're bawling and boozing they're not doing anything else . . . The best bottles in my cellar – if anyone had told me a week ago –. Tell me the honest truth, gentlemen; When exactly did you know for sure that they were fire raisers? It doesn't come the way you think, gentlemen – it comes first slowly and then suddenly . . . Suspicion! I was suspicious from the beginning, one is always suspicious – but tell me honestly, gentlemen, what would you have done in my place, damn it all, and when?

He listens, There is silence.

I must go up!

He hurries away.

6

ROOM

The goose-dinner is in full swing; laughter, Bieder-mann especially (still carrying the bottle) cannot get over the joke that has just been made; only Babette is not laughing at all.

BIEDERMANN Cotton-waste! Did you hear that? Cotton-waste, he says, cotton-waste burns better still!

BABETTE What's funny about that?

BIEDERMANN Cotton-waste! – do you know what cotton-waste is?

BABETTE Yes.

BIEDERMANN You've no sense of humour, Babette.

He puts the bottle on the table.

What can you do, my friends, when a person has no sense of humour?

BABETTE All right, explain the joke to me.

BIEDERMANN Well, it's like this. Willie told me this morning he had sent Joe to steal wood-wool. Wood-wool, got it? Just now I asked Joe: How's the wood-wool? To which he replied that he hadn't been able to organize any wood-wool, but he'd picked up some cotton-waste. Got it? And Willie said: Cotton-waste burns far better!

BABETTE   I got that.

BIEDERMANN   Oh, you got that, did you?

BABETTE   And what's funny about it?
Biedermann gives up.

BIEDERMANN   Let's drink, gentlemen!
Biedermann uncorks the bottle.

BABETTE   Is it true, Herr Schmitz, that you have put cotton-waste in up our attic?

BIEDERMANN   You'll laugh, Babette, but this morning we actually measured the fuse together, Willie and I.

BABETTE   Fuse?

BIEDERMANN   Detonating fuse!
He fills the glasses.

BABETTE   But now seriously, gentlemen, what's all this about?
Biedermann laughs.

BIEDERMANN   Seriously, she says! Seriously! Did you hear that? Seriously! . . . Don't let them kid you, Babette; I told you, our friends have a way of joking – other circles, other jokes, I always say . . . They'll be asking me for matches next!
Schmitz and Eisenring exchange glances.
You know, the two gentlemen still take me for a nervous suburbanite with no sense of humour who can be scared – *He raises his glass:*
Cheers!

EISENRING   Cheers!

SCHMITZ   Cheers!
They rise and clink glasses.

BIEDERMANN   To our friendship.
They drink and sit down again.
We don't have anyone waiting at table in our house, gentlemen, just tuck in.

SCHMITZ   I simply can't eat any more.

EISENRING Go on, Joe, don't be shy. You're not in the orphanage now.
He helps himself to goose.
Your goose is first-class, madam.

BABETTE I'm glad.

EISENRING Goose and Pommard! – The only thing missing is a tablecloth.

BABETTE Did you hear that, Gottlieb?

EISENRING But we can manage without it – A white tablecloth, you know, damask with silver on it.

BIEDERMANN Anna!

EISENRING Damask with flowers in it, but white, you know, like frost flowers! – But we can manage without it, Herr Biedermann. We didn't have a tablecloth in prison either.

BIEDERMANN Anna!

BABETTE In prison –?

BIEDERMANN Where has she got to?

BABETTE Have you been in prison?
Anna comes; she is wearing a bright red sweater.

BIEDERMANN Bring a tablecloth at once!

ANNA Very good –

EISENRING And if you have something like finger bowls –

ANNA Very good –

EISENRING You may think it childish, madam, but that's what the common people are like. Take Joe, for instance who grew up among the charcoal burners and has never seen a knife-rest – the dream of his ruined life is a table laid with silver and cut-glass!

BABETTE Gottlieb, we have all that.

EISENRING But we can manage without it.

ANNA As you wish.

EISENRING And if you have table napkins, Fräulein, bring them here!

ANNA Herr Biedermann said –

BIEDERMANN Bring them here!

ANNA As you wish.
Anna brings everything back.

EISENRING   I hope you won't take it amiss, madam. When you
come out of prison, you know, after months with-
out civilization –
He takes the tablecloth and shows it to Schmitz :
Do you know what that is?
Speaking to Babette :
He's never seen such a thing before!
To Schmitz again :
That's damask.

SCHMITZ   Well, what am I supposed to do with it?
Eisenring ties the tablecloth round his neck.

EISENRING   Like this –
Biedermann tries to see the funny side and laughs.

BABETTE   And where are our knife-rests, Anna, where have
our knife-rests got to?

ANNA   Herr Biedermann –

BIEDERMANN   Bring them here!

ANNA   You said: Take them away.

BIEDERMANN   Bring them here, I say! Where are they, in
heaven's name?

ANNA   In your left trouser pocket.

EISENRING   Don't excite yourself.
Biedermann puts his hand in his pocket and finds them.

ANNA   It's not my fault.

EISENRING   Don't excite yourself, Fraulein –
Anna bursts out sobbing, turns and runs out.
It's this south wind that does it.
Pause.

BIEDERMANN   Drink, my friends, drink!
They drink in silence.

EISENRING   I used to eat goose every day, you know, when I
was a waiter. When you flit down the long corri-
dors with the dish on the palm of your hand. But
then, madam, where are we to wipe our fingers?
That's the problem. Where else but in our own
hair? – while other people have cut-glass finger
bowls for the purpose! That's what I shall never
forget.

He dips his fingers into the finger bowl.
Do you know what a trauma is?

BIEDERMANN No.

EISENRING They explained it all to me in prison . . .
He dries his fingers.

BABETTE Tell me, Herr Eisenring, what did you go to prison for?

BIEDERMANN Babette!

EISENRING What did I go to prison for?

BIEDERMANN One doesn't ask such questions!

EISENRING I ask myself . . . I was a waiter, as I told you, a little head-waiter, and suddenly they confused me with a big fire raiser.

BIEDERMANN H'm.

EISENRING Arrested me in my home.

BIEDERMANN H'm.

EISENRING I was so taken aback that I did as they told me.

BIEDERMANN H'm.

EISENRING I was lucky, madam, I had seven absolutely charming policemen. When I said, I had to go to work and had no time to spare, they said: Your restaurant has been burnt down.

BIEDERMANN Burnt down?

EISENRING Overnight, it seems, yes.

BABETTE Burnt down?

EISENRING Fine! I thought. Then I've got time on my hands. The restaurant was nothing but a smouldering skeleton. I saw it as I went past, you know, out of that little barred window in the prison van.
He drinks with the air of a connoisseur.
We used to have that too: Forty-nine! Cave de l'Echannon . . . What happened then? Joe must tell you about that. As I was sitting in the anteroom playing with the handcuffs, who should walk in but this fellow!
Schmitz beams.
Cheers, Joe!

SCHMITZ Cheers, Willie!

They drink.

BIEDERMANN Then what happened?

SCHMITZ Are you the fire raiser? they asked him and offered him a cigarette. Sorry, he said, I'm afraid I haven't any matches, superintendent, although you take me for a fire raiser – *They laugh uproariously and slap their thighs.*

BIEDERMANN H'm.

Anna has come in. She is wearing a cap and apron again, and hands Biedermann a visiting-card which he looks at.

ANNA It's urgent, he says.

BIEDERMANN But I have guests –

Schmitz and Eisenring clink glasses again.

SCHMITZ Cheers, Willie!

EISENRING Cheers, Joe!

They drink. Biedermann studies the visiting-card.

BABETTE Who is it, Gottlieb?

BIEDERMANN The Doctor of Philosophy . . .

Anna is busy at the sideboard.

EISENRING What's that other thing there, Fräulein, that silver thing?

ANNA The candelabra?

EISENRING Why are you hiding it?

BIEDERMANN Bring it here!

ANNA Herr Biedermann, you told me yourself –

BIEDERMANN Bring it here, I say!

Anna puts the candelabra on the table.

EISENRING Joe, what do you say to that? They have a candelabra and hide it! What more do you want? Silver with candles on it . . . Have you any matches?

He puts his hand in his trouser pocket.

SCHMITZ Me? No.

He puts his hand in his trouser pocket.

EISENRING I'm afraid we haven't any matches, Herr Biedermann, really we haven't.

BIEDERMANN I have.

EISENRING Give them here!

BIEDERMANN I'll do it. Leave it to me! I'll do it.
He lights the candles.

BABETTE What does the gentleman want?

ANNA I can't make out, madam. He can't keep silent any longer, he says, and he's waiting on the landing.

BABETTE Confidentially, he says?

ANNA Yes, he keeps saying he wants to make a disclosure.

BABETTE What disclosure?

ANNA I can't make that out, madam, however often he tells me. He says he wants to dissociate himself . . .
Many candles blaze.

EISENRING It creates a completely different impression all at once, don't you agree, madam? Candlelight.

BABETTE Oh yes.

EISENRING I like atmosphere.

BIEDERMANN You know, Herr Eisenring, I'm glad to hear that . . .
All the candles are lit.

EISENRING Schmitz, don't make such a din with your dinner!
Babette takes Eisenring on one side.

BABETTE Let him be!

EISENRING He has no manners, madam, I apologize; I find it terribly embarrassing. But where could he have learnt manners? From the charcoal burner's hut to the orphanage –

BABETTE I know!

EISENRING From the orphanage to the circus –

BABETTE I know!

EISENRING From the circus to the theatre.

BABETTE I didn't know that, no –

EISENRING Human destinies, madam, human destinies!
Babette turns to Schmitz.

BABETTE So you were in the theatre too?
Schmitz, gnawing a goose bone, nods.

Where was that?

SCHMITZ Backstage.

EISENRING And yet he's gifted – Joe as a ghost, have you ever seen that?

SCHMITZ But not now!

EISENRING Why not?

SCHMITZ I was only with the theatre for a week, madam, then it was burnt down –

BABETTE Burnt down?

EISENRING Come on! Don't be shy!

BIEDERMANN Burnt down?

EISENRING Don't be shy!

He unties the tablecloth which Schmitz has been wearing like a table napkin and throws it over Schmitz's head.

Go ahead!

Schmitz, covered by the white tablecloth, rises.

See? Doesn't he look like a ghost?

ANNA I'm frightened.

EISENRING Girlie!

He takes Anna in his arms; she covers her face with her hands.

SCHMITZ 'Can we?'

EISENRING That's theatrical language, madam, he learnt it during the rehearsals in a single week, before the theatre was burnt down, believe it or not!

BABETTE Don't keep talking about fires all the time!

SCHMITZ 'Can we?'

EISENRING Ready. –

All sit, Eisenring holding Anna to his breast.

SCHMITZ EVERYMAN! EVERYMAN!

BABETTE Gottlieb –?

BIEDERMANN Quiet!

BABETTE We saw that at Salzburg.

SCHMITZ BIEDERMANN! BIEDERMANN!

EISENRING I think it's wonderful the way he does that.

SCHMITZ BIEDERMANN! BIEDERMANN!

EISENRING You must ask: who are you?

BIEDERMANN Me?

EISENRING Otherwise he won't be able to get through his words.

SCHMITZ EVERYMAN! BIEDERMANN!

BIEDERMANN All right, then: who am I?

BABETTE No, you must ask who he is.

BIEDERMANN Oh, I see.

SCHMITZ DO YOU NOT HEAR ME?

EISENRING No, Joe, take it again from the beginning!
They take up fresh positions.

SCHMITZ EVERYMAN! BIEDERMANN!

BABETTE Are you – for example – death?

BIEDERMANN Tripe!

BABETTE What else can he be?

BIEDERMANN You must ask: Who are you? He might be Hamlet's ghost. Or the Stone Guest, you know. Or thingumyjig, what's his name: the chap who helped Macbeth . . .

SCHMITZ WHO CALLS ME?

EISENRING Carry on.

SCHMITZ GOTTLIEB BIEDERMANN!

BABETTE You ask him, he's talking to you.

SCHMITZ DO YOU NOT HEAR ME?

BIEDERMANN Who are you, then?

SCHMITZ I AM THE GHOST OF – KNECHTLING.
Babette jumps up and screams.

EISENRING Stop.
He tears the white tablecloth off Schmitz.
You're an idiot! You can't do that. Knechtling! That's impossible. Knechtling was buried today.

SCHMITZ Exactly.
Babette covers her face with her hands.

EISENRING It isn't really him.
He shakes his head over Schmitz.
How can you act in such bad taste?

SCHMITZ That was the only thing I could think of . . .

EISENRING Knechtling! Of all people. An old and faithful collaborator of Herr Biedermann's, just think of

that: buried today – he's still all there, as pale as a tablecloth, white and gleaming like damask, stiff and cold, but to set him up in front of us . . .
He takes Babette by the shoulder:
Word of honour, madam, it isn't really him.
Schmitz wipes away the sweat.

SCHMITZ Sorry.

BIEDERMANN Let's sit down.

ANNA Is that everything now?
They sit down. An embarrassed pause.

BIEDERMANN How about a little cigar, gentlemen?
He offers a box of cigars.

EISENRING Idiot! You can see how Herr Biedermann is trembling . . . Thank you, Herr Biedermann, thank you! . . . If you think that's funny. When you know perfectly well that Knechtling put his head in the gas oven, after our Gottlieb had done all he could for the man. For fourteen years he gave Knechtling work, and that's the thanks –

BIEDERMANN Don't let's talk any more about it.

EISENRING That's your thanks for the goose!
They prepare their cigars.

SCHMITZ Shall I sing something?

EISENRING What?

SCHMITZ 'Goosey, Goosey Gander –'
He sings at the top of his voice:
'Goosey, Goosey Gander, where shall I wander?'

EISENRING That's enough.

SCHMITZ 'Where shall I wander? Upstairs and downstairs –'

EISENRING He's drunk.

SCHMITZ 'And in my lady's chamber – pot.'

EISENRING Don't listen, madam.

SCHMITZ 'Where shall I wander?
Upstairs and downstairs,
And in my lady's chamber – pot!'

BIEDERMANN Chamber-pot, that's funny.

ALL THE MEN 'Goosey, Goosey Gander –'

They make a part song of it, singing sometimes very loud, sometimes very softly, alternating it in every possible way, with laughter and noisy bonhomie. There is a pause, but then it is Biedermann who leads the jollity, till they are all exhausted.

BIEDERMANN Well then – cheers!

They raise their glasses, and sirens are heard in the distance.

What was that?

EISENRING Sirens.

BIEDERMANN Joking apart! –

BABETTE Fire raisers! Fire raisers!

BIEDERMANN Don't yell.

Babette tears open the window and the sirens come closer, howling to chill the marrow, and race past.

BIEDERMANN At least it's not here.

BABETTE Where can it be?

EISENRING Where the south wind is blowing from.

BIEDERMANN At least it's not here . . .

EISENRING We generally do it like that. We get the fire engine off into some poor district on the outskirts, and later, when the balloon really goes up, they find the way back blocked.

BIEDERMANN No, gentlemen, joking apart –

SCHMITZ But that's how we do it, joking apart.

BIEDERMANN Stop this nonsense, please. Moderation in everything. Can't you see my wife's as white as a sheet?

BABETTE What about you?

BIEDERMANN And anyway, sirens are sirens, I can't laugh about that, gentlemen. Somewhere everything has come to a stop, somewhere the house is on fire, otherwise our fire engine wouldn't be going out.

Eisenring looks at his watch.

EISENRING We must go.

BIEDERMANN Now?

EISENRING I'm afraid so.

SCHMITZ 'Upstairs and downstairs . . .'

Sirens wail again.

BIEDERMANN   Make some coffee, Babette!

Babette goes out.

BIEDERMANN   And you, Anna, what are you standing there gaping for?

Anna goes out.

Between ourselves, gentlemen, enough is enough. My wife has a weak heart. Let's have no more joking about arson.

SCHMITZ   We're not joking. Herr Biedermann.

EISENRING   We're fire raisers.

BIEDERMANN   Gentlemen, quite seriously now –

SCHMITZ   Quite seriously.

EISENRING   Quite seriously.

SCHMITZ   Why don't you believe us?

EISENRING   Your house, Herr Biedermann, is very favourably situated, you must admit that: five ignition points like this round the gas-holders, which are unfortunately guarded, and a good south wind blowing –

BIEDERMANN   It isn't true.

SCHMITZ   Herr Biedermann, if you think we're fire raisers, why not say so straight out?

Biedermann looks like a whipped dog.

BIEDERMANN   I don't think you're fire raisers, gentlemen, it isn't true, you're being unfair to me, I don't think you're – fire raisers . . .

EISENRING   Cross your heart!

BIEDERMANN   No! No, no! No.

SCHMITZ   Then what do you think we are?

BIEDERMANN   My friends . . .

They slap him on the back and leave him standing.

Where are you going now?

EISENRING   It's time.

BIEDERMANN   I swear it, gentlemen, by God!

EISENRING   By God?

BIEDERMANN   Yes!

He slowly raises his right hand.

SCHMITZ Willie doesn't believe in God any more than you do, Herr Biedermann – you can swear till you're blue in the face.

They walk on towards the door.

BIEDERMANN What can I do to make you believe me?

He stands between them and the door.

EISENRING Gives us matches.

BIEDERMANN Do what?

EISENRING We've none left.

BIEDERMANN You want me to –

EISENRING Yes. If you don't think we're fire raisers.

BIEDERMANN Matches?

SCHMITZ As a sign of trust, he means.

Biedermann puts his hand in his pocket.

EISENRING He hesitates. You see? He hesitates.

BIEDERMANN Quiet! – but not in front of my wife . . .

Babette comes back.

BABETTE The coffee will be here in a minute.

Pause.

Do you have to go?

BIEDERMANN Yes, my friends – it's a pity, but there it is – the main thing is that you have come to feel – I don't want to make a song and dance about it, my friend but why don't we address each other by our first names?

BABETTE H'm.

BIEDERMANN Let's drink to our friendship!

He takes a bottle and the corkscrew.

EISENRING Tell your good husband not to open another bottle on that account, it's not worth it now.

Biederman uncorks the bottle.

BIEDERMANN Nothing is too much, my friends, nothing is too much, and if there's anything you want – anything at all . . .

He hurriedly fills the glasses and hands them round.

My friends, let's drink!

They clink glasses.
Gottlieb –
He kisses Schmitz on the cheek.

SCHMITZ Joe –

BIEDERMANN Gottlieb.
He kisses Eisenring on the cheek.

EISENRING Willie –
They stand and drink.
All the same, Gottlieb, we have to go now.

SCHMITZ Unfortunately.

EISENRING Madam –
Sirens wail.

BABETTE It was a delightful evening.
Alarm bells ring.

EISENRING Just one more thing, Gottlieb –

BIEDERMANN What is it?

EISENRING You know.

BIEDERMANN If there's anything you want –

EISENRING The matches.
Anna has come in with the coffee.

BABETTE What on earth's the matter?
Out at the back – the sky, Frau Biedermann,
from the kitchen window – the sky is on fire . . .
*The light has turned very red as Schmitz and Eisen-
ring bow and leave. Biedermann stands pale and
rigid.*

BIEDERMANN Thank goodness it isn't here. Thank goodness it
isn't here . . . Thank goodness –
Enter the Doctor of Philosophy.

BIEDERMANN What do you want?

PH.D. I can remain silent no longer.
*He takes a document from his breast pocket and
reads:*
'The undersigned, himself profoundly shocked
by the events now taking place, which even from
our standpoint, it seems to me, can only be char-
acterized as criminal, makes the following de-
claration to the public: –'

> *Many sirens wail. He reads out a lengthy text of*
> *which not a word is intelligible, dogs bark, alarm*
> *bells ring, there are shouts and sirens in the distance,*
> *the crackling of fire nearby; then he comes up to*
> *Biedermann and hands him the document.*
> I dissociate myself.

BIEDERMANN What of it?

PH.D. I have said what I have to say.

> *He takes off his glasses and folds them up.*

BIEDERMANN Herr Doktor –

> *The Ph.D. leaves.*

Herr Doktor, what am I supposed to do with this?

> *The Ph.D. steps over the footlights and sits down*
> *in the stalls.*

BABETTE Gottlieb –

BIEDERMANN He's gone.

BABETTE What was it you gave them? Did I see right? –
Were they matches?

BIEDERMANN Why not?

BABETTE Matches?

BIEDERMANN If they were really fire raisers, do you think they
wouldn't have matches? . . . Babette, Babette,
my dear little Babette! *The grandfather clock*
strikes, the light turns red and as the stage darkens
there are heard: alarm bells, the barking of dogs,
sirens, the crash of falling timber, hooting, the
crackling of fire and cries, until the Chorus moves
front stage.

. . . .

CHORUS   There is much that is senseless and nothing
More so than this story:
Which once it had started
Killed many, ah, but not all
And changed nothing.
First explosion.

CHORUS LEADER   That was a gas-holder.
Second explosion.

CHORUS   What all have foreseen
From the outset,
And yet in the end it takes place,
Is idiocy,
The fire it's too late to extinguish.
Called Fate.
Third explosion.

CHORUS LEADER   Another gas-holder.
A series of terrible explosions follows.

CHORUS   Woe! Woe! Woe!
Light in the auditorium.

Afterpiece

Characters

HERR BIEDERMANN
BABETTE
ANNA
BEELZEBUB
A FIGURE
A POLICEMAN·
A LONG-TAILED MONKEY
WIDOW KNECHTLING

THE CHORUS

        The stage has been cleared and is completely empty.
        Babette and Biedermann are standing as they were
        standing at the end of the previous scene.

BABETTE Gottlieb?

BIEDERMANN Quiet.

BABETTE Are we dead?
        A parrot screeches.
        What was that?
        The parrot screeches.

BIEDERMANN Why didn't you come down before the stairs
caught fire? I warned you. Why did you go back
into the bedroom?

BABETTE Because of my jewellery.

BIEDERMANN – Of course we're dead!
        The parrot screeches.

BABETTE Gottlieb?

BIEDERMANN Quiet now.

BABETTE Where are we now?

BIEDERMANN In heaven. Where else?
        A baby cries.

BABETTE What was that?
        The baby cries.
        To tell you the truth, Gottlieb, this isn't how I
pictured heaven –

BIEDERMANN Don't start losing your faith now!

BABETTE Is this how you pictured heaven?
        The parrot screeches.

BIEDERMANN That's a parrot.
        The parrot screeches.

BABETTE Gottlieb?

BIEDERMANN Don't start losing your faith now!

BABETTE We've been waiting for half an eternity already.
        The baby cries.
        And there goes that baby again!
        The parrot screeches.
        Gottlieb?

BIEDERMANN What is it?

BABETTE What's a parrot doing in heaven?
A doorbell rings.

BIEDERMANN Don't keep bothering me, Babette, please. Why
shouldn't a parrot go to heaven? If it's done no
wrong.
The doorbell rings.
What was that?

BABETTE Our doorbell.

BIEDERMANN Who on earth can it be?
*Doorbell, baby and parrot are all heard simultane-
ously.*

BABETTE If only that parrot wasn't here! And that baby!
I can't stand it, Gottlieb, a din like that going on
for all eternity – it's like a housing estate.

BIEDERMANN Quiet!

BABETTE They can't expect us to put up with that!

BIEDERMANN Calm down.

BABETTE We're not used to that sort of thing.

BIEDERMANN Why shouldn't we be in heaven? All our friends
are in heaven, even my solicitor. For the last time,
this can't be anything but heaven. What else
could it be? It must be heaven. What wrong have
we ever done?
The doorbell rings.

BABETTE Shouldn't we open the door?
The doorbell rings.
How did they get hold of our bell?
The doorbell rings.
Perhaps it's an angel . . .
The doorbell rings.

BIEDERMANN I've done no wrong! – I honoured my father and
mother, you know that, especially Mother, and
that often used to annoy you. All my life I've
kept the Ten Commandments, Babette. I've
never made myself a graven image, definitely not.
I've never stolen; we always had what we needed.
And I've never killed. I've never worked on

Sunday. I've never coveted my neighbour's house, or if I did covet it I bought it. I suppose one is allowed to buy! I'm not aware that I tell lies. I haven't committed adultery, Babette, really not – by comparison with other people! . . . You're my witness, Babette, if an angel comes: I had only one fault on earth, I was too kind-hearted, maybe, simply too kind-hearted.

The parrot screeches.

BABETTE Do you understand what it's calling out?

The parrot screeches.

BIEDERMANN Have you killed? I'm only asking. Did you go after other gods? Just that little bit of Yoga! . . . Did you commit adultery, Babette?

BABETTE Who with?

BIEDERMANN Precisely.

The doorbell rings.

We must be in heaven.

Enter Anna in cap and apron.

BABETTE What's Anna doing in heaven?

Anna wanders past; her hair is long and poison-green.

I hope she didn't see you give them the matches, Gottlieb. She's quite capable of reporting it.

BIEDERMANN Matches!

BABETTE I told you they were fire raisers, Gottlieb, the very first night –

Enter Anna and a policeman with small white wings.

ANNA I'll call him.

Anna goes out; the angel-policeman waits.

BIEDERMANN You see?

BABETTE What?

BIEDERMANN An angel.

The policeman salutes.

BABETTE I pictured angels differently.

BIEDERMANN We're not living in the Middle Ages.

BABETTE Didn't you picture angels differently?

The policeman turns round and waits.

Shall we kneel?

BIEDERMANN Ask him if this is heaven.

Biedermann encourages the hesitant Babette by nodding his head.

Tell him we've been waiting half an eternity already.

Babette approaches the policeman.

BABETTE My husband and I –

BIEDERMANN Tell him we're victims.

BABETTE My husband and I are victims.

BIEDERMANN Our villa is in ruins.

BABETTE My husband and I –

BIEDERMANN Tell him!

BABETTE – in ruins.

BIEDERMANN He simply can't imagine what we've been through Tell him! We've lost everything. Tell him! And yet we've done no wrong.

BABETTE You simply can't imagine.

BIEDERMANN What we've been through.

BABETTE All my jewellery was melted!

BIEDERMANN Tell him we've done no wrong –

BABETTE And yet we've done no wrong.

BIEDERMANN – compared with other people!

BABETTE – compared with other people.

The angel-policeman takes out a cigar.

POLICEMAN Have you any matches?

Biedermann turns pale.

BIEDERMANN I? Matches? Why?

A flame as tall as a man blazes up out of the ground.

POLICEMAN I've got a light here, thanks, this will do.

Babette and Biedermann stare at the jet of flame.

BABETTE Gottlieb –

BIEDERMANN Quiet!

BABETTE What's the meaning of that?

Enter a Long-tailed Monkey.

MONKEY What have we here?

POLICEMAN A few damned souls.

The monkey puts on glasses.

BABETTE Gottlieb, we know him, don't we?

BIEDERMANN Who is he?

BABETTE Our Doctor of Philosophy.

The monkey takes the report and leafs through it.

MONKEY How are you all up there?

POLICEMAN Mustn't complain, nobody knows where God lives, but we're all well, mustn't complain – thanks.

MONKEY Why have they been sent to us?

The policeman looks into the report.

POLICEMAN Freethinkers.

The monkey has ten rubber stamps and stamps each time.

MONKEY THOU SHALT HAVE NO OTHER GODS BEFORE ME . . .

POLICEMAN A doctor who gave the wrong injection.

MONKEY THOU SHALT NOT KILL.

POLICEMAN A company director with seven secretaries.

MONKEY THOU SHALT NOT LUST.

POLICEMAN An abortionist.

MONKEY THOU SHALT NOT KILL

POLICEMAN A drunken driver.

MONKEY THOU SHALT NOT KILL.

POLICEMAN Refugees.

MONKEY What was their sin?

POLICEMAN Here: 52 potatoes, 1 umbrella, 2 blankets.

MONKEY THOU SHALT NOT STEAL.

POLICEMAN An income tax adviser.

MONKEY THOU SHALT NOT BEAR FALSE WITNESS . . .

POLICEMAN Another drunken driver.

The monkey stamps without speaking.

Another freethinker.

The monkey stamps without speaking.

Seven partisans. They went to heaven by mistake, and now it turns out that they looted, before they were captured and put against the wall and shot. Looted without uniforms.

MONKEY THOU SHALT NOT STEAL.

POLICEMAN Another abortionist.

MONKEY THOU SHALT NOT KILL.

POLICEMAN And those are the rest.

MONKEY THOU SHALT NOT COMMIT ADULTERY.
The monkey stamps at least thirteen reports.
Once again nothing but middle-class people! The
Devil will be furious. Once again nothing but
teenagers! I scarcely dare tell the Devil. Again
not a single public figure! Not a single cabinet
minister, not a single field-marshal –

POLICEMAN Uhuh.

MONKEY Take the people down below, our Beelzebub has
already heated the place, I think, or he's just doing
so.
The policeman salutes and goes.

BABETTE Gottlieb – we're in hell!

BIEDERMANN Don't shout!

BABETTE Gottlieb –
Babette bursts out sobbing.

BIEDERMANN Herr Doktor?

MONKEY What can I do for you?

BIEDERMANN It must be a mistake . . . It's quite impossible . . .
The situation must be rectified . . . Why are we
in hell, my wife and I?
To Babette:
Compose yourself, Babette, it must be a mis-
take –
To the monkey:
Can I speak to the Devil?

BABETTE Gottlieb –

BIEDERMANN Can I speak to the Devil?
*The monkey gestures into the emptiness, as if there
were chairs.*

MONKEY Take a seat.
Biedermann and Babette see no chairs.
What's the trouble?
Biedermann produces documents.
What's this?

BIEDERMANN My driving licence.

MONKEY We don't need that.
The monkey returns the documents without looking at them.
Your name is Biedermann?

BIEDERMANN Yes.

MONKEY Gottlieb Biedermann.

BIEDERMANN Businessman.

MONKEY Millionaire.

BIEDERMANN How do you know?

MONKEY Of 33 Roseway.

BIEDERMANN Yes . . .

MONKEY The Devil knows you.
Babette and Biedermann exchange glances.
Take a seat!
Two fire-blackened chairs come down onto the stage.
Do sit down.

BABETTE Gottlieb – our chairs!

MONKEY Do sit down.
Biedermann and Babette sit down.
Do you smoke?

BIEDERMANN Not any more.

MONKEY Your own cigars, Herr Biedermann . . .
The monkey takes a cigar.
You were burnt out?

BIEDERMANN Yes.

MONKEY Were you surprised?
Seven flames as tall as a man shoot up out of the ground.
I've got matches, thanks.
The monkey lights the cigar and smokes.
To come back to the point, what can I do for you?

BIEDERMANN We are homeless.

MONKEY Would you like a slice of bread?

BABETTE – Bread?

MONKEY Or a glass of wine?

BIEDERMANN We're homeless!
The monkey calls.

MONKEY Anna!
The monkey smokes.

BABETTE We don't want bread and wine –

MONKEY Don't you?

BABETTE We're not beggars –

BIEDERMANN We're victims.

BABETTE We don't want charity!

BIEDERMANN We aren't used to it.

BABETTE We don't need it!
Enter Anna.

ANNA You called?

MONKEY They don't want charity.

ANNA Very good.
Anna goes.

BIEDERMANN We want our rights.

BABETTE We had a home of our own.

BIEDERMANN Our simple rights.

BABETTE Our simple home.

BIEDERMANN We demand restitution!
The monkey walks away in the manner of a secretary, without a word.

BABETTE What did he mean when he said the Devil knew you?

BIEDERMANN No idea . . .
A grandfather clock strikes.

BABETTE Gottlieb – our grandfather clock!
The grandfather clock has struck nine.

BIEDERMANN We have a claim to everything that was burnt. We were insured. Believe me, I shan't rest until everything has been restored just as it was.
The monkey comes back from the left.

MONKEY One moment. One moment.
The monkey goes out right.

BIEDERMANN The devils are putting on airs!

BABETTE Sh.

BIEDERMANN Well it's true! Next thing we know they'll be

taking finger-prints. As at a consulate. Simply to give us a guilty conscience.

Babette rests her hand on his arm.

I haven't got a guilty conscience, don't worry, I shan't get excited, Babette, I shall keep strictly to the point, strictly to the point.

The parrot screeches.

Strictly to the point!

BABETTE Suppose they ask you about the matches?

BIEDERMANN I gave them. What of it? Everyone gave matches. Almost everyone. Otherwise the whole city wouldn't have burnt down. I saw how the fire blazed up out of every roof. Including the Hofmanns'! Including Karl's! Including Professor Mohr's! – Quite apart from the fact that I acted in good faith!

BABETTE Don't get excited.

BIEDERMANN I ask you, if we, you and I, hadn't given matches, do you think it would have made any difference to the disaster?

BABETTE I didn't give any.

BIEDERMANN And anyhow, they can't throw everybody into hell if everybody did the same thing!

BABETTE Why not?

BIEDERMANN After all, they're bound to show some mercy . . .

The monkey comes back.

MONKEY I'm afraid the Lord of the Underworld isn't here yet. Unless the lady and gentleman would like to speak to Beelzebub?

BABETTE Beelzebub?

MONKEY He's here.

BIEDERMANN Beelzebub?

MONKEY But he stinks. You know, he's the one with the cloven foot and the goat's tail and the horns. You know him. But he can't help you much, not a poor devil like Joe.

BIEDERMANN – Joe?

Babette has jumped up.

Sit down!

BABETTE Didn't I tell you straight away, Gottlieb, the very first night –

BIEDERMANN Keep quiet!

Biedermann gives Babette a look that makes her sit down.

My wife had a weak heart.

MONKEY Oh.

BIEDERMANN My wife was often unable to sleep. Then you hear ghosts of all kinds. But by daylight, Herr Doktor, we had no grounds for any suspicion, I swear to you, not for a second . . .

Babette gives Biedermann a look.

BIEDERMANN Well, I didn't.

BABETTE Then why were you going to throw them out into the street, Gottlieb, with your own hands and in the middle of the night?

BIEDERMANN I didn't throw them out!

BABETTE That's just the trouble.

BIEDERMANN And why the devil didn't you throw him out?

BABETTE Me?

BIEDERMANN Instead of giving him breakfast with marmalade and cheese, you and your soft-boiled eggs, yes, you!

The monkey smokes the cigar.

In short, Herr Doktor, we had no idea at the time of what was going on in our house, no idea whatever –

A fanfare of trumpets.

MONKEY That'll be him now.

BABETTE Who?

MONKEY The Lord of the Underworld.

A fanfare of trumpets.

He's been on a visit to heaven and he may be very bad tempered. We expected him yesterday. There seems to have been some tough negotiating again.

BIEDERMANN About me?

MONKEY About the last amnesty . . .

    The monkey whispers in Biedermann's ear.

BIEDERMANN So I read.

  MONKEY What do you say to that?

    The monkey whispers in Biedermann's ear.

BIEDERMANN I don't follow you.

    The monkey whispers in Biedermann's ear.

    How do you mean?

    The monkey whispers in Biedermann's ear.

    Do you think so?

  MONKEY If heaven doesn't keep the Ten Command-
    ments –

BIEDERMANN H'm.

  MONKEY Without heaven there can be no hell!

BIEDERMANN H'm.

  MONKEY That's what the negotiations are about.

BIEDERMANN About the Ten Commandments?

  MONKEY About the principle.

BIEDERMANN H'm.

  MONKEY If heaven thinks hell is going to put up with
    absolutely anything –

    The monkey whispers in Biedermann's ear.

BIEDERMANN Strike –!

    The monkey whispers in Biedermann's ear.

    Do you think so?

  MONKEY I don't know, Herr Biedermann, I'm just saying
    it's possible. Very possible. Depending on the
    result of these negotiations –

    Fanfare of trumpets.

    He's coming.

    The monkey goes.

  BABETTE What did he say?

BIEDERMANN It's possible, he says, very possible, that no one
    else will be let into hell. From today on. Do you
    understand: no one at all.

  BABETTE Why?

BIEDERMANN Because hell is going on strike.

    The doorbell rings.

    He says the devils are beside themselves. They

feel cheated, they were hoping for a whole lot of public figures, and it seems that heaven has pardoned them. Under these circumstances they refuse to keep hell going any longer. There's talk of a crisis in hell.

Anna comes in from the left and goes out from the right.

Why is Anna in hell?

BABETTE She stole a pair of stockings from me. I didn't dare tell you at the time. A new pair of nylon stockings.

Anna comes in leading Widow Knechtling.

ANNA Take a seat. But if you're Widow Knechtling you're wasting your time: your husband is a suicide. Take a seat! But you're wasting your time.

Anna goes, and Widow Knechtling stands; there is no chair.

BABETTE What does she want here?

Biedermann nods to her with sour friendliness.

She means to denounce us, Gottlieb . . .

Babette nods to her with sour friendliness.

BIEDERMANN Let her!

More fanfares, now closer than the first time.

That's nonsense. Damn it all, why didn't Knechtling wait for a week and talk it over with me at a favourable opportunity? Damn it all, I wasn't to know that Knechtling would really put his head in the gas oven, because he'd been given notice . . .

Fanfares closer still.

So I'm not frightened.

Fanfares closer still.

Matches! Matches!

BABETTE Perhaps nobody saw.

BIEDERMANN I won't have all this fuss about a disaster. There have always been disasters! – And anyhow, just look at our city! All glass and chrome! To be quite frank, I must say it's a blessing it was burnt down,

a positive blessing, from a town-planning point
of view –

*Fanfares, then an organ. A gorgeous figure dressed
somewhat, but only somewhat, like a bishop appears
with splendid and solemn bearing. Biedermann and
Babette kneel beside the footlights. The figure stands
in the centre.*

FIGURE Anna?

The Figure slowly takes off his violet gloves.

I have just come from heaven.

BIEDERMANN Did you hear?

FIGURE It's hopeless.

The Figure throws down the first glove.

Anna!

The Figure slowly takes off the other glove.

I doubt whether what I saw was the true heaven;
they said it was, but I doubt it . . . They wear
medals and decorations and there's a smell of incense coming from every loudspeaker. I saw a
Milky Way of decorations, a gala performance that
was enough to make the Devil's blood run cold. I
saw all my clients, all my mass-murderers, and the
little angel's circle round their bald heads; people
greet one another, they wander round drinking
and crying Hallelujah, they giggle over all this
clemency – the saints are strikingly silent, because they are made of stone or wood, gifts on
loan, and the Princes of the Church (I mixed with
the Princes of the Church to find out where God
lives) are also silent, although they are not made
of stone or wood . . .

The Figure throws down the glove.

Anna?

The Figure removes his headgear. It is Eisenring.

I disguised myself. It's the powerful who are up
there and they spend their time pardoning one
another and lo and behold, they didn't recognize
me: – I gave them my blessing.

Enter Anna and the monkey, who bow.
Let me be disrobed!
The Figure, still with splendid bearing, stretches out both arms so that the four silken robes may be unbuttoned, the first silver-white, the second gold, the third violet, the fourth blood-red. The organ falls silent. Biedermann and Babette kneel by the footlights.
Let my tails be brought!

ANNA Very good.

FIGURE And my head-waiter's wig.
They take off the first robe.
I doubt whether it was God who received me. – He knows everything and when he raises his voice he says exactly what is in the newspapers, word for word.
The parrot screeches.
Where is Beelzebub?

MONKEY At the boilers.

FIGURE Let him appear before me.
The light suddenly turns very red.
Why this firelight?

MONKEY He is heating. A few damned souls have just arrived – nobody well known, just the usual small fry . . .
They take off the second robe.

FIGURE Tell him to put out the boilers.

MONKEY Put them out?

FIGURE Put them out.
The parrot screeches.
How's my parrot?
The Figure notices Biedermann and Babette.
Ask those people why they're praying.

MONKEY They're not praying.

FIGURE But they're kneeling –

MONKEY They want their home back.

FIGURE They want what?

MONKEY Restitution.

> *The parrot screeches.*

FIGURE I love my parrot. The only living creature that doesn't change its slogans! I found it once in a burning house. A faithful bird! I shall set it on my right shoulder next time I go down to earth.
> *They take off the third robe.*
And now, girlie, my tails!

ANNA Very good.

FIGURE And you, doctor, fetch the bicycles. You remember? The two rusty bicycles.
> *The monkey and Anna bow and go.*

BIEDERMANN Willie! – It is Willie, isn't it? . . . I'm Gottlieb, your friend – Willie, don't you remember me?
> *The Figure takes off the fourth and last robe.*

BABETTE We've done no wrong, Herr Eisenring. Why have we been sent to you, Herr Eisenring? We're victims, Herr Eisenring. All my jewellery has been melted –
> *The Figure stands in shirt and socks.*

BIEDERMANN Why does he pretend not to know us?

BABETTE He feels embarrassed, don't look!
> *Anna brings the dress trousers.*

FIGURE Thanks, girlie, thanks very much.
> *Anna turns to go.*
Anna!

ANNA At your service.

FIGURE Bring two velvet cushions.

ANNA Very good.

FIGURE For the lady and gentleman who are kneeling.

ANNA Very good.
> *Anna goes out and the Figure climbs into the dress trousers.*

BIEDERMANN Willie –

BABETTE You remember us, Herr Eisenring, I'm sure, my goose was first-class, you said so yourself.

BIEDERMANN Goose and Pommard.

BABETTE With chestnut stuffing.

BIEDERMANN And red cabbage.

BABETTE And candlelight, Herr Eisenring, candlelight!

BIEDERMANN And the way we sang together –

BABETTE Oh yes.

BIEDERMANN Do you really not remember?

BABETTE It was a delightful evening.

BIEDERMANN Forty-nine, Willie, Cave de l'Echannon! The best bottle in my cellar. Willie, didn't I give you everything so that we should be friends?

The Figure flicks specks off the dress trousers.

You're my witness, Babette: Didn't I give everything I had in the house?

BABETTE Even the matches.

Anna brings two red velvet cushions.

Anna takes the cushions to Biedermann and Babette.

ANNA Anything else?

Biedermann and Babette kneel on the red cushions.

FIGURE My waistcoat, girlie, my white waistcoat!

ANNA Very good.

FIGURE And the wig!

Anna goes and the Figure knots his tie.

Cave de l'Echannon –?

Biedermann nods and beams with confidence.

I remember it all, Gottlieb, very clearly, as only the Devil can remember. You clinked glasses and drank to our friendship, and you went so far – it was pretty embarrassing! – as to kiss the Devil's cheek.

The parrot screeches.

BIEDERMANN We didn't know you were devils, Willie. Cross my heart! If we had known you were really devils –

Enter Joe as Beelzebub with a cloven foot, a goat's tail and horns; in addition he is carrying a large coal shovel.

BEELZEBUB What's the matter?

FIGURE Don't bellow.

BEELZEBUB Why are you changing your clothes?

FIGURE We've got to go down to earth again, Joe.

Anna brings the white waistcoat.

Thanks, girlie, thanks very much.
The Figure puts on the waistcoat.
Did you put out the boilers?

BEELZEBUB No.

FIGURE Do as I tell you.
The firelight becomes brighter than before.

BEELZEBUB The coal is in! . . .
Anna brings the jacket.

FIGURE Just a minute, girlie, just a minute!
The Figure buttons up the waistcoat.
I've been in heaven –

BEELZEBUB What happened?

FIGURE I bargained and bargained, I tried everything and
achieved nothing. They won't hand over a single
one. It's hopeless.

BEELZEBUB Not one?

FIGURE Not one.
Anna is holding the jacket.
Doctor!

MONKEY At your service.

FIGURE Call the Fire Brigade.
The monkey bows and goes.

BEELZEBUB They won't hand over a single one!

FIGURE Whoever wears a uniform or did wear a uniform
when he killed, or whoever promises to wear a
uniform when he kills or orders others to kill, is
saved.

BEELZEBUB Saved?

FIGURE Don't bellow.

BEELZEBUB Saved!
The echo is heard from above.

ECHO Saved.

FIGURE Do you hear?

ECHO Saved. Saved. Saved.
Beelzebub gazes upwards.

FIGURE Take your clobber off, Joe, we must go back to
work.
Enter the Chorus.

CHORUS	Woe! Woe! Woe!
BABETTE	Gottlieb!
BIEDERMANN	Quiet!
BABETTE	What are they doing here?
CHORUS	Good people of our city, see

        Us as we helpless stand.
Once the guardians of the city,
Trained to extinguish fires,
Splendidly equipped, oh
Now we are condemned
Forever to stand by and watch
The fires of hell,
Full of goodwill towards the frying citizen,
Helpless.

FIGURE Gentlemen, extinguish hell!

The Chorus is speechless.

I've no intention of running a hell for stuffed shirts and intellectuals, pickpockets, adulterers, servants who have stolen nylon stockings, and conscientious objectors – I shouldn't dream of it!

The Chorus is speechless.

What are you waiting for?

CHORUS Ready are we.

Carefully coiled are the hoses
In accordance with regulations,
Polished and carefully greased and of brass
Is each windlass.
Everyone knows what his task is,
Polished too and carefully tested,
To make sure that we have full pressure,
Is our pump,
Likewise of brass.

CHORUS LEADER And the hydrants?

CHORUS Everyone knows what his task is.

CHORUS LEADER We are ready. –

The Figure straightens his dress-suit.

FIGURE Go ahead.

The firelight has become very bright again.

CHORUS LEADER Man the hoses!
Man the pump!
Man the ladders!
The firemen run to their places and shout:

CHORUS Ready.

CHORUS LEADER We are ready.

FIGURE Go ahead.
The hissing of hydrants; the firelight dies down.

MONKEY Well, Herr Biedermann, it's as I foresaw –

FIGURE Doctor!

MONKEY Yes, sir?

FIGURE Our bicycles!

MONKEY Very good.

FIGURE And my wig, girlie, my wig!

ANNA Very good.

FIGURE And my parrot!
The monkey and Anna go.

BEELZEBUB My childhood faith! My childhood faith!
Thou shalt not kill, ha, and I believed it.
What are they making of my childhood faith!
The Figure cleans his finger nails.

I, the son of a charcoal burner and a gypsy woman, who couldn't read but knew the Ten Commandments off by heart, I'm possessed by the Devil. Why? Simply because I scorned all commandments. Go to hell, Joe, you're possessed by the Devil everyone said to me, and I went to hell. I lied, because then everything went better, and I became possessed by the Devil. I stole whatever took my fancy and became possessed by the Devil. I whored with whatever came my way, married or unmarried, because I had the urge to, and I felt fine when I gave way to my urge, and became possessed by the Devil.

And they feared me in every village, for I was stronger than all of them, because I was possessed by the Devil. I tripped them up on their

way to church, because I felt the urge, I set fire
to their stables while they were praying and singing, every Sunday, because I felt the urge, and I
laughed at their God who did not lay hold of me.
Who felled the fir tree that killed my father in
broad daylight? And my mother, who prayed for
me, died of worry over me, and I entered the
orphanage to set fire to it, and the circus to set
fire to it, because I felt the urge more and more,
and I started fires in every town simply in order
to be possessed by the Devil. – Thou shalt!
Thou shalt not! Thou shalt! Because we had no
newspapers and no radio out there in the forest,
we had only a Bible, and therefore I believed that
one became possessed by the Devil if one killed
and ravished and murdered and mocked every
commandment and destroyed whole cities – that's
what I believed! . . .
The Figure laughs.
It's no laughing matter, Willie!
Anna brings the wig.

FIGURE   Thanks, girlie, thanks very much.
The monkey brings two rusty bicycles.

BEELZEBUB   It's no laughing matter. I feel like vomiting when
I see the way things are going. What are they
making of my childhood faith! I can't eat as much
as I want to vomit.
The Figure has put on the wig.

FIGURE   Get ready!
The Figure takes a rusty bicycle.
I'm burning to see my old customers again, the
fine people who never come to hell, I'm burning
to serve them afresh! . . . Once again sparks and
crackling flames, sirens that are always too late,
the barking of dogs and smoke and human cries
– and ashes!
Beelzebub unbuckles his goat's tail.
Are you ready?

BEELZEBUB One moment –

> *The Figure swings himself up onto the saddle and rings the bell.*

I'm just coming.

> *Beelzebub unbuckles his cloven foot.*

CHORUS LEADER Stop pump!

Down hoses!

Off water!

> *The red firelight disappears completely.*

FIGURE Ready?

> *Beelzebub takes the other bicycle.*
>
> *Beelzebub swings himself up onto the saddle and rings the bell.*

What about your horns?

> *Beelzebub has to stop and take off his horns.*

Anna?

ANNA Yes, sir?

FIGURE Yes, sir?

FIGURE Thanks, girlie, thanks very much for all your services. Why are you so glum all day long? I've only seen you laugh once. Do you remember – when we sang the song about Goosey, Goosey Gander and the chamber-pot?

> *Anna laughs.*

We'll sing it again!

ANNA Oh please!

> *Enter the Chorus.*

CHORUS Good people of our city, see –

FIGURE Keep it short!

CHORUS – hell is extinguished.

FIGURE Thank you. –

> *The Figure puts his hand in his trouser pocket.*

Have you any matches?

BEELZEBUB Not me.

FIGURE Nor me.

BEELZEBUB It's always the same!

FIGURE People will give us some . . .

> *The monkey brings the parrot.*

My parrot!

The Figure places the parrot on his right shoulder.

Before I forget, doctor: we're not accepting any
more souls here. Tell the good people hell is on
strike. And if an angel comes to look for us, say
we're on earth.

Beelzebub rings his bell.

Off we go.

Schmitz and Eisenring cycle off, waving.

BOTH   So long, Gottlieb, all the best!

The Chorus comes to the front of the stage.

CHORUS   Beams of the sun,
Lashes of the eye divine,
Day is once more breaking –

CHORUS LEADER   Over the resurrected city.

CHORUS   Hallelujah!

The parrot screeches in the distance.

BABETTE   Gottlieb?

BIEDERMANN   Quiet now.

BABETTE   Are we saved?

BIEDERMANN   Don't start losing your faith now.

Widow Knechtling goes.

CHORUS   Hallelujah!

BABETTE   Frau Knechtling has gone.

CHORUS   Finer than ever,
Risen again from rubble and ashes
Is our city,
Cleared away without trace and forgotten
The rubble,
Forgotten too
Those who were burnt to a cinder
And their cries from the flames –

BIEDERMANN   Life goes on.

CHORUS   History they have become
And are silent.

CHORUS LEADER   Hallelujah!

CHORUS   Finer than ever,
Richer than ever,

Tall, modern buildings,
Gleaming with glass and with chrome,
But at heart just the same as before,
Hallelujah,
Risen again is our city!
An organ strikes up.

BABETTE Gottlieb?

BIEDERMANN What is it?

BABETTE Do you think we are saved?

BIEDERMANN It looks like it . . .

The organ swells, Biedermann and Babette kneel, the curtain comes down.

Andorra

A Play in Twelve Scenes

translated by

Michael Bullock

Andorra. The Andorra of this play has nothing to do with the real small state of this name, nor does it stand for another real small state; Andorra is the name of a model.

Names. The following names have the stress on the final syllable: Barblín, Andrí, Pradér, Ferrér, Fedrí. In the name Peider the stress falls on the first syllable.

Costumes. Costumes should not be traditional. The Andorrans wear modern ready-made clothes; it will be sufficient if their hats are peculiar to them, and they almost always wear hats. An exception is the Doctor, whose hat is in keeping with international fashion. Andri wears blue jeans. Barblin wears a ready-made costume, even when taking part in the procession, but over it she wears a shawl decorated with Andorran embroidery. All the men wear white shirts and nobody wears a tie, with the exception once more of the Doctor. Unlike all the others, the Señora is smartly, but unostentatiously, dressed. The uniform of the Andorran soldiers is olive-grey. Any resemblance to uniforms of the past is to be avoided in the uniform of the Blacks.

Types. Some of the parts might lead to caricature. This should under all circumstances be avoided. It is enough that they are types. They should be played in such a way that the spectator at first likes, or at least tolerates, them, since they all appear innocuous, and that he always sees them in their true light rather too late, as in real life.

Setting. The basic setting for the whole play is the square in Andorra. This should be a square typical of any southern country, not picturesque, bare, white with a few touches of colour (shutters, Shell posters etc.) beneath a gloomy blue sky. The stage should be as empty as possible. A vista at the back indicates how Andorra is to be imagined; nothing but what the actors require should be present in the acting-area. All those scenes that do not take place in the square are to be set in front of it. No curtain between scenes, only the displacement of the light onto the forestage. No anti-illusionism need be demonstrated, but the spectator should be continuously reminded that a model is being shown, as in fact is always the case in the theatre.

First performed on 2 November 1961 at the Schauspielhaus,
Zürich, and directed by Kurt Hirschfeld.

Characters

Speaking
ANDRI
BARBLIN
THE TEACHER
THE MOTHER
THE SEÑORA
THE PRIEST
THE SOLDIER
THE INNKEEPER
THE CARPENTER
THE DOCTOR
THE JOURNEYMAN
THE SOMEBODY

Silent
AN IDIOT
THE SOLDIERS IN BLACK UNIFORMS
THE JEW DETECTOR
THE ANDORRAN PEOPLE

Outside an Andorran house. Barblin is whitewashing the high, narrow wall with a brush on a long stick. An Andorran soldier in olive-grey is leaning against the wall.

BARBLIN If you could take your eyes off my legs for a minute you could see what I'm doing. I'm whitewashing. Because tomorrow is St George's Day, in case you've forgotten. I'm whitewashing my father's house. And what do you soldiers do? You just hang about the streets with your thumbs in your belts, squinting into our blouses when we bend down.
The Soldier laughs.
Anyway, I'm engaged.

SOLDIER Engaged!

BARBLIN What are you laughing at?

SOLDIER Is he pigeon-chested?

BARBLIN Why should he be?

SOLDIER Because you never let us see him.

BARBLIN Leave me alone!

SOLDIER Or flat-footed?

BARBLIN Why should he be flat-footed?

SOLDIER Anyhow, he doesn't dance with you.
Barblin whitewashes.
Perhaps he's an angel!
The Soldier laughs.
That's why I've never seen him.

BARBLIN I'm engaged!

SOLDIER Well, I don't see any ring.

BARBLIN I'm engaged.
She dips the brush in the bucket.
And anyway – I don't like you.
On the forestage right stands a juke box, by which – as Barblin whitewashes – there appear the Carpenter, a corpulent man, and behind him Andri as a kitchen-boy.

CARPENTER Where's my stick?

ANDRI Here, sir.

CARPENTER A bloody nuisance, these tips all the time. No sooner
have you taken your hand out of your pocket –

*Andri gives him his stick and receives a tip which he drops
into the juke box so that music starts up, while the Carpenter
walks across the front of the stage, forcing Barblin to move
her bucket out of his way. Andri dries a plate, moving in
time to the music, and then goes out as the music stops.*

BARBLIN Are you still there?

SOLDIER I'm on leave.

BARBLIN What else do you want to know?

SOLDIER Who is your fiancé supposed to be?

Barblin whitewashes.

They're all whitewashing their father's houses, because
tomorrow is St George's Day, and the coal-sack is
tearing around on his bicycle. Whitewash, you virgins,
whitewash your father's houses, so that we have a white
Andorra, you virgins, a snow-white Andorra!

BARBLIN The coal-sack – who on earth is that?

SOLDIER Are you a virgin?

The Soldier laughs.

So you don't like me.

BARBLIN No.

SOLDIER A lot of women have told me that, but I've had them just
the same, if I liked their legs and their hair.

Barblin puts out her tongue at him.

And their red tongue too!

The Soldier takes out a cigarette and looks up at the house.

Which is your room?

Enter a Priest pushing a bicycle.

PRIEST That's how I like to see it, Barblin, that's how I like to
see it. We shall have a white Andorra, you virgins, a
snow-white Andorra, so long as there isn't a cloudburst
during the night.

The Soldier laughs.

Is your father at home?

SOLDIER So long as there isn't a cloudburst during the night! The fact is, his church isn't as white as he pretends, we know that now; his church is also only made of earth, and the earth is red, and when there's a cloudburst it washes off the whitewash and leaves a mess as if a pig had been slaughtered on it, and there's nothing left of your snow-white church.

The Soldier stretches out his hand to see if it is raining.

So long as there isn't a cloudburst during the night!

The Soldier laughs and strolls away.

PRIEST What was he doing here?

BARBLIN Is it true, Father, what people say? They'll attack us, the Blacks across the frontier, because they're jealous of our white houses. Early one morning they'll come with a thousand black tanks, and they'll roll in all directions over our fields, and they'll drop from the sky with parachutes like grey locusts.

PRIEST Who says that?

BARBLIN Peider, the soldier.

Barblin dips her brush in the bucket.

Father isn't at home.

PRIEST I might have guessed.

Why has he been drinking so much lately? And then he swears at everyone. He forgets who he is. Why does he always talk such rubbish?

BARBLIN I don't know what Father says in the inn.

PRIEST He sees ghosts. Wasn't everyone in this country horrified about the Blacks across the frontier when they behaved like Herod during the Massacre of the Innocents? Didn't they collect clothes for the refugees? Now he's saying we're no better than the Blacks. Why does he keep saying that all the time? People take offence and I'm not surprised. A teacher shouldn't talk like that. And why does he believe every rumour that gets about in the inn?

Pause.

Nobody is persecuting your Andri –

Barblin stops and listens.

– nobody has yet hurt a hair of your Andri's head.

Barblin goes on whitewashing.

I see you take your work seriously, you're not a child any more, you work like a grown-up girl.

BARBLIN I'm nineteen.

PRIEST And not engaged yet?

Barblin says nothing.

I hope that Peider doesn't have any luck with you.

BARBLIN No.

PRIEST He has dirty eyes.

Pause.

Did he frighten you? To make himself important. Why should they attack us? Our valleys are narrow, our fields are stony and steep, our olives are no juicier than elsewhere. What should they want from us? Anyone who wants our rye must reap it with the sickle, must bend down and cut it step by step. Andorra is a beautiful country, but a poor country. A peaceful country, a weak country – a pious country, so long as we fear God, and we do fear Him, my child, don't we?

BARBLIN And suppose they come all the same?

A vesper bell, brief and monotonous.

PRIEST We shall see one another tomorrow, Barblin. Tell your father St George doesn't want to see him drunk.

The Priest mounts his bicycle.

On second thoughts, don't tell him anything, it will only irritate him, but keep an eye on him.

The Priest rides silently away.

BARBLIN And suppose they come all the same, Father?

Front stage, right, by the juke box. The Somebody appears with Andri behind him as a kitchen-boy.

SOMEBODY Where's my hat?

ANDRI Here, sir.

SOMEBODY A heavy evening, I think there's a storm in the air . . .

Andri gives him his hat and receives a tip, which he drops into the juke box; he doesn't press the button, however, but only whistles and studies the record selector, while the Somebody walks across the front of the stage and comes to a stop before Barblin, who is whitewashing and hasn't noticed that the Priest has cycled away.

BARBLIN Is it true, Father, what people say? They say: When the Blacks come everyone who is a Jew will be taken away. He will be tied to a stake, they say, and shot in the back of the neck. Is that true or is it a rumour? And if he has a sweetheart she will have her head shaved, they say, like a mangy dog.

SOMEBODY That's a nice way to talk!

BARBLIN *turns round and starts with fright.*

SOMEBODY Good evening.

BARBLIN Good evening.

SOMEBODY A fine evening today.

BARBLIN *takes the bucket.*

SOMEBODY But heavy.

BARBLIN Yes.

SOMEBODY There's something in the air.

BARBLIN What do you mean by that?

SOMEBODY A storm. Everything is waiting for wind, the leaves and the dust and the curtains. And yet I can't see a cloud in the sky, but you can feel it. Such a hot stillness. The gnats can feel it too. Such a dry and stagnant heat. I think there's a storm in the air, a violent storm, it will do the land good . . .

Barblin goes indoors, the Somebody saunters on, Andri sets the juke-box going, the same record as before, and leaves drying a plate. The square of Andorra is seen. The Carpenter and the Teacher are sitting outside the inn. The music has stopped.

TEACHER Prader, it's my son I'm talking about.

CARPENTER I said, fifty pounds.

TEACHER My foster-son, I mean.

CARPENTER I still say, fifty pounds.

The Carpenter bangs on the table with a coin.

I must go.

The Carpenter bangs again.

Why does he want to be a carpenter of all things? It isn't easy to become a carpenter, you know, if it's not in your blood. And how could it be in his blood? You know what I mean. Why doesn't he become a stockbroker?

Why don't you put him on the Stock Exchange? You
know what I mean . . .

TEACHER Prader, how did that stake get there?

CARPENTER What are you talking about?

TEACHER Look, there!

CARPENTER Are you feeling all right?

TEACHER I'm talking about a stake!

CARPENTER I can't see any stake.

TEACHER There!

The Carpenter has to turn round.

Is that a stake or isn't it?

CARPENTER Why shouldn't it be a stake?

TEACHER It wasn't there yesterday.

The Carpenter laughs.

Don't laugh, Prader, you know exactly what I mean.

CARPENTER You're seeing ghosts.

TEACHER What's it there for?

CARPENTER *bangs on the table with a coin.*

TEACHER I'm not drunk. I can see it, you can all see it.

CARPENTER I must go.

The Carpenter throws a coin on the table and stands up.

I've told you: Fifty pounds.

TEACHER Is that your last word?

CARPENTER My name is Prader.

TEACHER Fifty pounds?

CARPENTER I don't haggle.

TEACHER Oh no, you're above that sort of thing, we all know that
. . . Prader, that's extortion, fifty pounds for a carpenter's
apprenticeship, that's extortion. It's ridiculous, Prader,
and you know it. I'm just an ordinary schoolmaster, living on a schoolmaster's salary, not a master carpenter
– I haven't got fifty pounds, quite simply, I haven't
got it!

CARPENTER Then there's no more to be said.

TEACHER Look, Prader –

CARPENTER I said, fifty pounds.

The Carpenter goes.

TEACHER Some day I'll tell them the truth – the bastards! I'll make them see themselves as they really are, that'll wipe the grins off their faces.

Enter the Innkeeper.

INNKEEPER What's the matter?

TEACHER I need a brandy.

INNKEEPER Trouble?

TEACHER Fifty pounds for a carpenter's apprenticeship!

INNKEEPER I heard him.

TEACHER I shall scrape it together.

The Teacher laughs.

If it isn't in your blood!

The Innkeeper wipes the table with a cloth.

They'll find out what their own blood is like.

INNKEEPER It's no good getting angry with your own people, it upsets you and doesn't change them. Of course it's extortion! The Andorrans are easy-going people, but, as I've always said, when it's a question of money, they're like the Jews.

The Innkeeper turns to go.

TEACHER How do you know what a Jew is like?

INNKEEPER Listen –

TEACHER How do you know?

INNKEEPER – I have nothing against your Andri. What do you think I am? Otherwise I shouldn't have taken him on as a kitchen-boy. What are you looking at me like that for? Anyone will bear me out. Haven't I always said, Andri is an exception?

TEACHER I'm not going to discuss it!

INNKEEPER A real exception –

The tolling of bells.

TEACHER Who put that stake there?

INNKEEPER What stake?

TEACHER I'm not always drunk, as the Reverend Father thinks. A stake is a stake. Somebody put it there. It wasn't there yesterday. A stake doesn't just grow up out of the ground, does it?

INNKEEPER I don't know.

TEACHER What's it there for?

INNKEEPER I don't know, perhaps the surveyor's department, something to do with the roads perhaps, they've got to do something with the taxes, maybe a by-pass, you never know, maybe the drains –

TEACHER Maybe.

INNKEEPER Or the telephone –

TEACHER And maybe not.

INNKEEPER What's eating you?

TEACHER And what's the rope for?

INNKEEPER How should I know?

TEACHER I'm not mad, I'm not seeing ghosts, what I see is a stake that could be used for all sorts of things –

INNKEEPER What of it?

The Innkeeper goes into the inn. The Teacher is alone. More pealing of bells. The Priest hurries across the square in a chasuble followed by the little servers, whose censers leave a powerful smell of incense behind. The Innkeeper comes with the brandy.

INNKEEPER He wants fifty pounds, does he?

TEACHER I shall scrape it together.

INNKEEPER How?

TEACHER Somehow.

The Teacher drinks the brandy.

Sell land.

The Innkeeper sits down with the Teacher.

Somehow . . .

INNKEEPER How much land have you?

TEACHER Why?

INNKEEPER I'm always ready to buy land. If it's not too expensive! I mean, if you've got to raise money.

Noise outside the inn.

I'm coming!

The Innkeeper seizes the Teacher's arm.

Think it over, Can, in peace and quiet, but I can't pay more than fifty pounds –

The Innkeeper goes.

TEACHER 'The Andorrans are easy-going people, but when it's a question of money they're like the Jews.'

The Teacher puts the empty glass to his lips again, while Barblin, dressed for the procession, appears beside him.

BARBLIN Father!

TEACHER Why aren't you in the procession?

BARBLIN Father, you promised not to drink on St George's Day –

TEACHER *lays a coin on the table.*

BARBLIN They're coming past here.

TEACHER Fifty pounds for a carpenter's apprenticeship!

Now loud, high-pitched singing is heard, and the ringing of bells. The procession passes in the background. Barblin kneels down, the Teacher remains seated. People have gathered in the square. They all kneel down and above the heads of the kneeling people appear flags; the Virgin Mary is carried past accompanied by fixed bayonets. All cross themselves; the Teacher stands up and goes into the inn. The procession is slow and long and beautiful; the high-pitched singing is lost in the distance, the ringing of bells remains. Andri comes out of the inn, while the people in the square join the end of the procession; he stands on one side and whispers:

ANDRI Barblin!

BARBLIN *crosses herself.*

ANDRI Can't you hear me?

BARBLIN *stands up.*

ANDRI Barblin?

BARBLIN What is it?

ANDRI I'm going to be a carpenter!

Barblin tags on to the end of the procession; Andri is left alone.

The sun is shining green in the trees today. Today the bells are ringing for me too.

He takes off his apron.

I shall always remember this happiness. And yet I'm only taking off my apron. It's so quiet. I should like to throw my name in the air like a cap, and yet I'm only standing here rolling up my apron. This is happiness. I shall never forget the way I stood here today . . .

Uproar from the inn.

Barblin, we shall marry!
Andri goes.

INNKEEPER Get out! He's completely canned, then he always talks such rubbish. Get out!
The Soldier staggers out with the drum.
You're not having another drop.

SOLDIER I'm a soldier.

INNKEEPER We can see that.

SOLDIER My name is Peider.

INNKEEPER We know that.

SOLDIER Well then.

INNKEEPER Stop making such a row!

SOLDIER Where is she?

INNKEEPER There's no sense in it, Peider. If a girl's willing she's willing, if she isn't, she isn't. Shut up. Put your drumsticks away! You're tight. Think of the reputation of the Army!
The Innkeeper goes back inside the inn.

SOLDIER Gutless bastards! They're not worth my fighting for. But I shall fight. Don't you worry. To the last man, don't you worry, rather dead than a slave, so I'm telling you: Watch out – I'm a soldier and I've got my eye on her . . .
Enter Andri, putting on his jacket.
Where is she?

ANDRI Who?

SOLDIER Your sister.

ANDRI I haven't got a sister.

SOLDIER I said: Where is she?

ANDRI Why?

SOLDIER I'm off duty and I fancy her, that's why . . .
Andri has put on his jacket and tries to walk on; the Soldier sticks out his leg so that Andri trips up; the Soldier laughs.
A soldier isn't a scarecrow. Got that? Walking past as if I wasn't here. I'm a soldier, and you're a Jew.
Andri stands up without speaking.
You are a Jew, aren't you?
Andri says nothing.
But you're lucky, damned lucky, not every Jew is a

lucky as you are – you've got the chance to make yourself popular.

Andri brushes the dust from his trousers.

Did you hear what I said? I said you can make yourself
popular.

ANDRI Who with?

SOLDIER With the Army.

ANDRI You stink.

SOLDIER What did you say?

ANDRI Nothing. Nothing.

SOLDIER I stink?

ANDRI At seven paces and against the wind.

SOLDIER Take care what you say.

The Soldier tries to smell his own breath.

I can't smell anything.

Andri laughs.

It's no laughing matter being a Jew, it's no laughing
matter, a Jew has to make himself popular.

ANDRI Why?

SOLDIER *bawls:*

'When a man's in love,
And when a man's a soldier,
It's on the floor
And shut the door
And take your knickers off, girl – '

Stop staring at me as if you were a gentleman!

'When a man's in love,
And when a man's a soldier.'

ANDRI Can I go now?

SOLDIER Gentleman!

ANDRI I'm not a gentleman.

SOLDIER All right, then kitchen-boy.

ANDRI Ex-kitchen boy.

SOLDIER They wouldn't have your sort in the Army.

ANDRI Do you know what that is?

SOLDIER Money?

ANDRI My wages. I'm going to be a carpenter now.

SOLDIER Doesn't it make you sick!

ANDRI What do you mean?

SOLDIER I said, doesn't it make you sick.

The Soldier knocks the money out of his hand and laughs.
There!

Andri stares at the Soldier.

You Jews think of nothing but money all the time.

Andri controls himself with difficulty, then bends down and picks up the money from the pavement.

So you don't want to make yourself popular?

ANDRI No.

SOLDIER You're sure?

ANDRI Yes.

SOLDIER And we're supposed to fight for people like you? To the last man – do you know what that means, one battalion against twelve battalions, that's how it works out, rather dead than a slave, that's for sure, but not for you!

ANDRI What's for sure?

SOLDIER Andorrans aren't cowards. Let them come with their parachutes like the locusts from the sky, they won't get through, as true as my name is Peider, not past me. That's for sure. Not past me. They'll get the shock of their lives.

ANDRI Who will get the shock of their lives?

SOLDIER Not past me.

Enter an Idiot who can only grin and nod.

Did you hear that? He thinks we're scared. Because he's scared himself! We shan't fight to the last man, he says, we shan't die because we're outnumbered, we shall put our tails between our legs, we'll be in a blue funk, he dares to say that to my face, to the Army's face!

ANDRI I didn't say a word.

SOLDIER I ask you: Did you hear him?

IDIOT *nods and grins.*

SOLDIER An Andorran isn't scared!

ANDRI You've said that already.

SOLDIER But you're scared!

ANDRI *says nothing.*

SOLDIER Because you're a coward.

ANDRI Why am I a coward?

SOLDIER Because you're a Jew.

IDIOT *grins and nods.*

SOLDIER All right, now I'm going . . .

ANDRI You leave Barblin alone!

SOLDIER What red ears he's got!

ANDRI Barblin is my fiancée.

SOLDIER *laughs.*

ANDRI That's true.

SOLDIER *bawls*:

> 'It's on the floor
> And shut the door – '

ANDRI Go to hell!

SOLDIER Fiancée, he said!

ANDRI Barblin will turn her back on you.

SOLDIER Then I'll take her from behind!

ANDRI You're a pig.

SOLDIER What did you say?

ANDRI I said you're a pig.

SOLDIER Say that again. He's trembling! Say that again. But loudly, so the whole square can hear. Say that again.
Andri goes.
What did he say?

IDIOT *grins and nods.*

SOLDIER A pig? I'm a pig?

IDIOT *grins and nods.*

SOLDIER He's not making himself popular with me . . .

FORESTAGE

The Innkeeper, now without his apron, enters the witness-box

INNKEEPER I admit that we were all wrong over this business. At the time. Naturally I believed what everyone believed at the time. He believed it himself right up to the last minute. A Jewish kid our teacher saved from the Blacks across the frontier, that's what everybody thought, and we all thought it was marvellous the way the teacher looked after him like his own son. Anyhow, I thought it was marvellous. Did I tie him to the stake? None of us could have known that Andri really was his son, our teacher's son. When he was my kitchen-boy, did I treat him badly? It wasn't my fault that things turned out as they did. That's all I can say about the business after all this time. It wasn't my fault.

2

Andri and Barblin on the threshold outside Barblin's room.

BARBLIN Andri, are you asleep?

ANDRI No.

BARBLIN Why don't you give me a kiss?

ANDRI I'm awake, Barblin, I'm thinking.

BARBLIN All night long.

ANDRI Is it true what they say?
Barblin, who has been lying with her head in his lap, now sits up and undoes her hair.
Do you think they're right?

BARBLIN Don't start that again!

ANDRI Perhaps they're right.
Barblin busies herself with her hair.
Perhaps they're right.

BARBLIN You've made me all rumpled.

ANDRI They say my kind have no feelings.

BARBLIN Who says that?

ANDRI Lots of people.

BARBLIN Just look at my blouse!

ANDRI Everybody.

BARBLIN Shall I take it off?
Barblin takes off her blouse.

ANDRI They say my kind are lecherous, but heartless, you know –

BARBLIN Andri, you think too much!
Barblin lies down with her head in his lap again.

ANDRI I love your hair, your red hair, it's light, warm, it tastes

bitter, Barblin, I shall die if I lose it.
Andri kisses her hair.
You ought to be asleep.

BARBLIN *listens.*

ANDRI What was that?

BARBLIN The cat.

ANDRI *listens.*

BARBLIN I saw it.

ANDRI Was that the cat?

BARBLIN They're all asleep . . .
Barblin lays her head in his lap again.
Kiss me!

ANDRI *laughs.*

BARBLIN What are you laughing at?

ANDRI I ought to be grateful!

BARBLIN I don't know what you're talking about.

ANDRI Your father. He saved my life, he would think me very
ungrateful if I seduced his daughter. I'm laughing, but
it's no laughing matter always having to be grateful to
people for being alive.
Pause.
Perhaps that's why I'm not cheerful.

BARBLIN *kisses him.*

ANDRI Are you quite sure you want me, Barblin?

BARBLIN Why do you keep asking me that?

ANDRI The others are more fun.

BARBLIN The others!

ANDRI Perhaps they're right. Perhaps I am a coward, otherwise
I should go to your father and tell him we're engaged.
Do you think I'm a coward?
The sound of raucous singing in the distance.

ANDRI They're still singing.
The raucous singing dies away.

BARBLIN I never go out of the house now, so that they shall leave
me in peace. I think of you, Andri, all day long, when
you're at work, and now you're here and we're alone –
I want you to think of me, Andri, not of the others. Do
you hear? Only of me and of us. And I want you to be

proud, Andri, gay and proud, because I love you above
all the others.

ANDRI I'm frightened when I feel proud.

BARBLIN And now I want you to kiss me.

Andri gives her a kiss.

No, kiss me properly!

Andri thinks.

I don't think of the others, Andri, when you hold me in
your arms and kiss me, believe me, I don't think of them.

ANDRI But I do.

BARBLIN You and your 'others' all the time!

ANDRI I was tripped up again.

A tower-clock strikes.

I don't know in what way I'm different from everyone
else. Tell me. In what way? I can't see it . . .

Another tower-clock strikes.

It's three o'clock already.

BARBLIN Let's go to sleep!

ANDRI I'm boring you.

Barblin says nothing.

Shall I put out the candle? . . . You can sleep, I'll wake
you at seven.

Pause.

It isn't a superstition, oh no, there are people like that,
people with a curse on them. I'm like that. It doesn't
matter what I do, the others only have to look at me and
suddenly I'm what they say I am. That's what evil is.
Everyone has it in him, nobody wants it, so where is it
to go to? Into the air? It is in the air, but it doesn't stay
there long, it has to enter into a human being, so that
one day they can seize it and kill it . . .

Andri takes hold of the candle.

Do you know a soldier named Peider?

Barblin mumbles sleepily

He's got his eye on you.

BARBLIN Him!

ANDRI I thought you were already asleep.

Andri blows out the candle.

FORESTAGE

The Carpenter enters the witness-box.

CARPENTER I admit that I asked fifty pounds for his apprenticeship because I didn't want his sort in my workshop, and I knew there would be trouble. Why didn't he want to be a salesman? I thought that would come naturally to him. Nobody could have known that he wasn't one. You know what I mean. I can only say that fundamentally I meant well by him. It's not my fault that things turned out as they did.

3

The sound of a lathe; a carpenter's shop. Andri and a journeyman carpenter, each with a finished chair.

ANDRI I've played outside left too, when there wasn't anyone else. I'd love to play, if your team will have me.
JOURNEYMAN Have you any football boots?
ANDRI No.
JOURNEYMAN Well, you can't play without them.
ANDRI How much do they cost?
JOURNEYMAN I've got an old pair, I'll sell them to you. Of course, you'll also need black shorts, and a yellow jersey, and yellow socks.
ANDRI I'm better on the right, but I can play on the left. I'm not bad at corners.
  Andri rubs his hands.
  That'll be smashing, Fedri, if it comes off.
JOURNEYMAN Why shouldn't it come off?
ANDRI That's smashing.
JOURNEYMAN I'm the captain and you're my friend.
ANDRI I'll go into training.

JOURNEYMAN But don't keep rubbing your hands together, otherwise
you'll have the crowd laughing at you.
Andri puts his hands in his trouser pockets.
Have you got a fag? Then give us one. He won't bawl
me out! If he did he'd be scared of his own voice. Have
you ever heard him bawl me out?
The Journeyman lights a cigarette.

ANDRI I'm glad you're my friend, Fedri.

JOURNEYMAN This your first chair?

ANDRI What do you think of it?
*The Journeyman takes Andri's chair and tries to pull the
leg off. Andri laughs.*
You won't pull those out.

JOURNEYMAN That's what he does.

ANDRI Go on, try!

CARPENTER [*off*] They said what?
The Journeyman tries in vain.

ANDRI He's coming.

JOURNEYMAN You're lucky.

ANDRI What do you mean lucky? Every proper chair is mortised.
Only those that are just stuck together fall apart.
Enter the Carpenter.

CARPENTER ... Write to them – tell them my name is Prader. A
chair by Prader doesn't collapse, every child knows that.
A chair by Prader is a chair by Prader. And anyhow,
paid is paid. In a word: I don't haggle.
To the two:
Are you on holiday?
The Journeyman dodges away fast.
Who has been smoking in here?
Andri doesn't answer.
I can smell it.
Andri says nothing.
Andri, if only you had the guts –

ANDRI Today is Saturday.

CARPENTER What has that to do with it?

ANDRI My apprenticeship test. You said, on the last Saturday
of the month. Here's my first chair.

The Carpenter takes the chair.

Not that one, Mr Prader, the other one.

CARPENTER It isn't easy to become a carpenter, it isn't easy at all if you don't have it in your blood. And how could it be in your blood? I told your father before you started. Why don't you go into selling? It's not easy if you haven't grown up with timber, you see, with our timber – you people may praise your cedars of Lebanon, but in this country we work in Andorran oak, my lad.

ANDRI That's beech.

CARPENTER Are you trying to teach me my job?

ANDRI I thought you were testing me.

CARPENTER *tries to pull out a leg of the chair.*

ANDRI Mr Prader, that isn't mine!

CARPENTER There –

The Carpenter pulls out the first leg.

What did I say?

The Carpenter pulls out the other three legs.

– Like frog's legs, like frog's legs. And I'm supposed to sell rubbish like that? A chair by Prader, do you know what that means? – There –

The Carpenter throws the debris down at his feet.

– just look at it!

ANDRI You're making a mistake.

CARPENTER Now, there's a chair!

The Carpenter sits on the other chair.

Fifteen stone I weigh, more's the pity, fifteen stone, but a proper chair doesn't groan when a real man sits on it, and it doesn't wobble. Does this chair groan?

ANDRI No.

CARPENTER Does it wobble?

ANDRI No.

CARPENTER There you are!

ANDRI That's my chair.

CARPENTER Then who made this rubbish?

ANDRI I told you at the beginning.

CARPENTER Fedri! Fedri!

The lathe stops.

I have nothing but trouble with you, that's the thanks I get for taking your kind into the shop. I knew what it would be like.

Enter the Journeyman.

Now, Fedri, are you a journeyman or what are you?

JOURNEYMAN I –

CARPENTER How long have you been with Prader & Son?

JOURNEYMAN Five years.

CARPENTER Which chair did you make?
This one or that rubbish over there? Answer.
The Journeyman looks at the débris.
Answer me frankly, which chair?

JOURNEYMAN I . . .

CARPENTER Did you mortise or didn't you?

JOURNEYMAN Every proper chair is mortised . . .

CARPENTER Do you hear that?

JOURNEYMAN Only those that are just stuck together fall apart . . .

CARPENTER You can go.

JOURNEYMAN *starts in alarm.*

CARPENTER Into the workshop, I mean.
The Journeyman hurries out.
Let that be a lesson to you. I knew your place wasn't in a workshop.
The Carpenter sits down and fills his pipe.
A pity about the wasted timber.

ANDRI *says nothing.*

CARPENTER Have to use that for firewood.

ANDRI No.

CARPENTER *lights his pipe.*

ANDRI That's a dirty trick.

CARPENTER *lights his pipe.*

ANDRI I won't take back what I said. You're sitting on my chair, I tell you, you lie whenever it suits you and light your pipe. You, yes, you! I'm afraid of you, yes, I'm trembling. Why have I no rights in your eyes? I'm young, I thought to myself: I must be humble. There's no sense in it, you take no notice of proof. You're sitting on my chair. You don't give a damn about that. It makes no difference

what I do, you always twist it against me, and there's no
end to your scorn. I can't keep silent any longer, it's
burning me up. You're not even listening to me. You sit
there sucking at your pipe and I tell you to your face:
You're lying. You know perfectly well what a dirty
trick you're playing. A rotten low-down trick. You're
sitting on the chair I made and lighting your pipe. What
harm have I done you? You don't want to admit that I'm
any good. Why do you insult me? You all insult and jeer
at me the whole time. How can you be stronger than the
truth? You know very well what the truth is, you're
sitting on it.

The Carpenter has at last lit his pipe.

You have no shame.

CARPENTER It's no good trying to get round me, lad.

ANDRI You look like a toad!

CARPENTER In the first place this isn't a Wailing Wall.

*The Journeyman and two others give away their presence by
giggling.*

Do you want me to get rid of the lot of you?

The Journeyman and the two others disappear.

In the first place this isn't a Wailing Wall, in the second
place I never said I was going to dismiss you. I didn't
say that at all. I've got another job for you. Take off your
apron! I'll show you how to write out orders. Are you
listening when your master is speaking? For every order
you bring in I'll give you ten shillings. Let's say a pound
for three orders! That's what your kind have in their
blood, believe me, and everyone should do what he has
in his blood . . . There's lots of money to be made,
Andri, lots of money . . .

Andri stands motionless.

Agreed?

The Carpenter stands up and slaps Andri on the back.

I've got your interests at heart.

The Carpenter goes. The lathe starts up again.

ANDRI But I wanted to be a carpenter . . .

FORESTAGE

*The Journeyman Carpenter, now in a motor-cyclist's jacket,
enters the witness box.*

JOURNEYMAN I admit that it was my chair and not his. At the time.
I wanted to explain to him afterwards, but by then he
was in such a state that it was impossible to talk to him.
Afterwards I couldn't stand him either, I admit. He
didn't even say good morning to us any more. I don't say
he deserved it, but it was partly his fault, otherwise it
would never have happened. When we asked him again
about joining the team, he thought himself too good for
us. It wasn't my fault that later they came and took him
away.

4

*A room in the Teacher's house. Andri is sitting being exam-
ined by a doctor, who is holding his tongue down with a spoon.
Beside him the Mother.*

ANDRI Aaaandorra.
DOCTOR But louder, my friend, much louder!
ANDRI Aaaaaaandorra.
DOCTOR Have you a longer spoon?
The Mother goes out.
How old are you?
ANDRI Twenty.
DOCTOR *lights a small cigar.*
ANDRI I've never been ill before.
DOCTOR You're a strong lad, I can see that, a good lad, a healthy
lad, I like that, mens sana in corpore sano, if you know
what that means.
ANDRI No.
DOCTOR What's your trade?
ANDRI I wanted to be a carpenter –

DOCTOR Let's have a look at your eyes!

The Doctor takes a magnifying glass out of his waistcoat pocket and examines Andri's eyes.

Now the other one!

ANDRI What's that thing you were talking about – a virus?

DOCTOR I used to know your father twenty years ago. I didn't know he had a son. The bull, we used to call him. Always charging straight at the wall. He got himself talked about in those days, a young teacher who tore up the school books; he wanted different ones and when he didn't get different ones he taught the Andorran children to underline page by page in beautiful red pencil everything in the Andorran school books that isn't true. And they couldn't contradict him. What a fellow he was! Nobody knew what he was really after. A hell of a fellow. The ladies were very keen on him – oh, thank you very much –

Enter the Mother with a longer spoon.

I like your son!

The examination continues.

Carpentry is a fine trade, an Andorran trade; there are no carpenters anywhere in the world as good as the Andorrans, that's well known.

ANDRI Aaaaaaaaaaandorra!

DOCTOR Again.

ANDRI Aaaaaaaaaaandorra!

MOTHER Is it serious, Doctor?

DOCTOR What do you mean, Doctor! My name is Ferrer.

The Doctor takes Andri's pulse.

Professor, to be exact, not that I attach any importance to titles, dear lady. The Andorran is sober and simple, they say, and there's some truth in it. The Andorran doesn't bow and scrape. I could have had titles by the dozen. Andorra is a republic. Take an example from her! With us everyone is valued for himself. I've said that all over the world. Why do you think I came back here again after twenty years?

The Doctor stops talking in order to count Andri's pulse.

H'm.

MOTHER Is it serious, Professor?

DOCTOR Dear lady, when a man has been around the world as I have he knows the meaning of the word home. This is my place, title or no title, this is where my roots are.
Andri coughs.
How long has he been coughing?

ANDRI Since you lit your cigar.

DOCTOR Andorra is a small country, but a free country. Where else will you find that nowadays? No fatherland in the world has a more beautiful name, and no people in the world is so free. – Open your mouth, my friend, open your mouth! Let's have another look at that throat.
The Doctor looks into Andri's throat again, then he takes out the spoon.
A bit inflamed.

ANDRI Me?

DOCTOR Headache?

ANDRI No.

DOCTOR Insomnia?

ANDRI Sometimes.

DOCTOR Aha.

ANDRI But not because of that.
The Doctor pushes the spoon down his throat again.

DOCTOR Tongue down.

ANDRI Aaaaaaaa-Aaaaaaaaaaaaaaaaandorra.

DOCTOR That's right, my friend, that's how it must ring out, so that every Jew sinks into the ground when he hears the name of our fatherland.
Andri winces.
Don't swallow the spoon!

MOTHER Andri . . .

ANDRI *has stood up.*

DOCTOR Well, there's nothing much to worry about, a slight inflammation, he'll soon get over it, a pill before every meal –

ANDRI Why – should every Jew – sink into the ground?

DOCTOR Where did I put them?
The Doctor rummages in his little bag.

You ask that, my young friend, because you haven't been out into the world. I know Jews. Wherever you go you find them already there, knowing everything better, and you, simple Andorran that you are, can pack up and go. That's the way it is. The worst thing about Jews is their ambition. In every country in the world they occupy all the university chairs, I know that from experience, and there's nothing left for us but our homeland. Mark you, I've nothing against Jews. I'm not in favour of atrocities. I saved the lives of Jews, although I can't stand the sight of them. And what thanks did I get? You can't change them. They occupy all the university chairs in the world. You can't change them.

The Doctor holds out the pills.

Here are your pills.

Andri doesn't take them but goes.

What's the matter with him all of a sudden?

MOTHER Andri! Andri!

DOCTOR Simply turning on his heel and going . . .

MOTHER You shouldn't have said that about Jews, Professor.

DOCTOR Why not?

MOTHER Andri is a Jew.

DOCTOR What!

Enter the Teacher, carrying exercise books.

TEACHER What's the matter?

MOTHER Nothing, don't excite yourself, nothing at all.

DOCTOR I wasn't to know that –

TEACHER Know what?

DOCTOR How is it that your son is a Jew?

TEACHER *says nothing.*

DOCTOR I must say, simply turning on his heel and going. I gave him medical treatment, even chatted with him, I explained to him what a virus is –

TEACHER I have work to do.

Silence.

MOTHER Andri is our foster-son.

TEACHER Goodbye.

DOCTOR Goodbye.

The Doctor takes his hat and bag.

I'm going.

The Doctor goes.

TEACHER What happened this time?

MOTHER Don't excite yourself!

TEACHER How did he get in here?

MOTHER He's the new medical officer.

Enter the Doctor again.

DOCTOR Let him take the pills just the same.

The Doctor takes off his hat.

I'm sorry about what happened.

The Doctor puts on his hat again.

What did I say . . . just because I said . . . I was joking, of course, they can't take a joke, I can see that. Did anyone ever meet a Jew who could take a joke? Anyway I never did . . . all I said was: I know Jews. I suppose one is still allowed to speak the truth in Andorra . . .

TEACHER *says nothing.*

DOCTOR Where did I put my hat?

TEACHER *goes up to the Doctor, takes his hat from his head, opens the door and throws out the hat.*

There's your hat.

The Doctor goes.

MOTHER I told you not to excite yourself. He'll never forgive you for that. You quarrel with everybody and that doesn't make things easier for Andri.

TEACHER Tell him to come here.

MOTHER Andri! Andri!

TEACHER That's the last straw. That man the medical officer. I don't know what it is, but everything nowadays seems to take the worst possible turn . . .

Enter Barblin and Andri.

Andri, you're not to take any notice of them. I'm not going to put up with any injustice, you know that, Andri.

ANDRI Yes, Father.

TEACHER If that new medical officer of ours opens his stupid mouth again, that pedant, that useless failure, that smuggler's son – I used to smuggle too, like every Andorran,

but I don't stick titles in front of my name – if he opens
his stupid mouth again he'll be thrown down the steps
himself and not just his hat.

To the Mother:

I'm not afraid of them!

To Andri:

And you're not to be afraid of them either, understand?
If we stick together, you and me, like men, Andri, like
friends, like father and son – or haven't I treated you like
a son? Have I ever neglected you? If I have, say to my
face. Have I treated you differently from my daughter?
Tell me so to my face. I'm waiting.

ANDRI What do you want me to say, Father?

TEACHER I can't bear it when you stand there like a choir boy who
has been caught stealing or something, so well behaved –
is it because you're afraid of me? I know I fly off the
handle sometimes, I suppose I'm unjust. I haven't made
a note of all my mistakes as an educator.

MOTHER *lays the table.*

TEACHER Has your Mother ever treated you heartlessly?

MOTHER What are you making a speech for? Anyone would think
you were addressing a meeting.

TEACHER I'm speaking to Andri.

MOTHER I see.

TEACHER Man to man.

MOTHER Supper's ready.

The Mother goes out.

TEACHER That's really all I wanted to say to you.

BARBLIN *finishes laying the table.*

TEACHER If he's such a big noise abroad, why doesn't he stay there,
this professor who didn't even manage to get his doctorate at any university in the world? This patriot who's
now our medical officer because he can't construct a
single sentence without using the words homeland and
Andorra? Whose fault is it if his ambition came to
nothing, whose fault could it be if not the Jews? – Jew!
I'm sick of the word. I never want to hear it again.

MOTHER *brings the soup.*

TEACHER And you're not to use that word either, Andri. Understand? I won't tolerate it. You don't know what you're saying, and I don't want you to end up by believing what they say. Just remember, there's nothing in it. Once and for all. Understand? Once and for all.

MOTHER Have you finished?

TEACHER There's nothing in it.

MOTHER Then cut the bread for us.

TEACHER *cuts the bread.*

ANDRI I wanted to ask you something else . . .

MOTHER *ladles out the soup.*

ANDRI Perhaps you know already. Nothing has happened, there's no need for you to worry. I don't know the right way to say a thing like this. – I'm almost twenty-one and Barblin is nineteen . . .

TEACHER What of it?

ANDRI We want to get married.

TEACHER *drops the bread.*

ANDRI Yes. I've come to ask – I meant to do it when I had passed my carpentry test, but you know what happened about that. – We want to become engaged now, so that the others know and don't keep running after Barblin wherever she goes.

TEACHER Married!

ANDRI I am asking you, Father, for the hand of your daughter.

TEACHER *rises like a prisoner upon whom sentence has been passed.*

MOTHER I've seen it coming, Can.

TEACHER Quiet!

MOTHER It's no reason to get so upset.
The Mother picks up the bread from the floor.
They love each other.

TEACHER Be quiet!
Silence.

ANDRI But that's the way it is, Father, we love each other. It's hard to talk about it. Ever since we shared the green bedroom as children we have talked about getting married. At school we felt embarrassed because everyone laughed at us. You can't do that, they said, because you're brother

and sister! Once we made up our minds to poison ourselves, because we were brother and sister, with deadly
nightshade, but it was winter and there wasn't any deadly
nightshade. And we cried, until Mother noticed – till you
came, Mother, and comforted us and told us we were not
brother and sister. And the whole story, how father
smuggled me across the frontier, because I'm a Jew. And
I was very happy about it and told them at school and
everywhere. Since then we haven't slept in the same
room; we're not children any more.
The Teacher remains silent as though turned to stone.
It is time we were married, Father.

TEACHER Andri, that's impossible.

MOTHER Why?

TEACHER Because it's impossible!

MOTHER Don't shout.

TEACHER No – No – No . . .

BARBLIN *bursts into tears.*

MOTHER And don't you start howling straight away!

BARBLIN I shall kill myself.

MOTHER And don't talk rubbish!

BARBLIN Or I shall go to the soldiers, I shall.

MOTHER Then may God punish you!

BARBLIN Let him.

ANDRI Barblin?

BARBLIN *runs out.*

TEACHER Let her go. She's a silly goose. There are lots of other
girls.
Andri tears himself away from him.
Andri – !

ANDRI She may do something crazy.

TEACHER Stay here.
Andri stays.
I've never had to say no to you before, Andri.
The Teacher holds both hands over his face.
No!

MOTHER I don't understand you, Can, I don't understand you.
Are you jealous? Barblin is nineteen and someone is

going to come along. Why not Andri, whom we know? That's the way of the world. Why do you stare into space and shake your head? I think we're very lucky. Why won't you give your daughter to Andri? You say nothing. Do you want to marry her yourself? You keep silent because you're jealous, Can, jealous of the youngsters and of life in general, because now it is going on without you.

TEACHER   What do you know about it!

MOTHER   I'm only asking.

TEACHER   Barblin is still a child –

MOTHER   That's what all fathers say. A child! – To you, Can, but not to Andri.

TEACHER   *says nothing.*

MOTHER   Why do you say No?

TEACHER   *says nothing.*

ANDRI   Because I'm a Jew.

TEACHER   Andri –

ANDRI   Go on, say it.

TEACHER   Jew! Jew!

ANDRI   That's it.

TEACHER   Jew! Every third word I hear is Jew, every second word, there's not a day without Jew, not a night without Jew, I hear Jew when someone snores, Jew, Jew, not a joke without Jew, not a business deal without Jew, not a curse without Jew, I hear Jew where there is no Jew, Jew and Jew and again Jew, in school the children play Jew when I turn my back, everyone babbles it after everyone else, the horses neigh it in the streets: Jeeeew, Jeew, Jew . . .

MOTHER   You're exaggerating.

TEACHER   Aren't there any other reasons any more?

MOTHER   Then tell us them.

TEACHER   *says nothing, then takes his hat.*

MOTHER   Where are you going?

TEACHER   Where I can find peace and quiet.
He goes, slamming the door behind him.

MOTHER   Now he'll drink till midnight again.
Andri walks slowly across to the other side.
Andri? – Now they're all parted.

5

*The square of Andorra. The Teacher is sitting alone outside
the inn. The Innkeeper brings the brandy which he has
ordered but which he does not at first pick up.*

INNKEEPER What's new?

TEACHER Another brandy.

The Innkeeper goes.

Because I'm a Jew!

He now drains the brandy.

Some day I shall tell them the truth – at least that's what
one says; but a lie is a leech, it sucks the truth dry. It
grows. I shall never shake it off. It grows and is full of
blood. It looks at me like a son, flesh and blood, a Jew,
my son . . . What's new? – I lied and you fondled him,
so long as he was still a child, but now he is a man, now
he wants to marry, wants to marry his sister. – That's
something new! . . . I know already what you will think:
Even a Jew-rescuer thinks his own child too good for a
Jew! I can already see your grins.

Enter the Somebody, who sits down with the Teacher.

SOMEBODY What's new?

TEACHER *says nothing.*

SOMEBODY *opens his newspaper.*

TEACHER What are you grinning at?

SOMEBODY They're threatening again.

TEACHER Who?

SOMEBODY The people across the border.

The Teacher rises; the Innkeeper comes out.

INNKEEPER Where are you off to?

TEACHER Where I can find peace and quiet.

The Teacher goes into the inn.

SOMEBODY What's got into him? If he carries on like that, he'll come
to a sticky end, if you ask me . . . I'll have a beer.

The Innkeeper goes.
At least you can get some peace here now that lad's gone.
He was always wasting his tips on that juke box.

6

Outside Barblin's room. Andri is sleeping on the threshold.
Candlelight. A large shadow appears on the wall: the Sol-
dier. Andri snores. The Soldier takes fright and hesitates.
A tower-clock strikes the hour. The Soldier sees that Andri
does not stir and ventures to the door, hesitates again, opens
the door. Another clock strikes the hour. The Soldier now
steps over the sleeping Andri and, having got so far, enters
the darkened room. Barblin tries to scream, but the Soldier
puts his hand over her mouth. Silence. Andri wakes.

ANDRI Barblin? . . .
Now it's quiet again outside, they've finished boozing
and bawling, they've all gone home to bed.
Silence.
Are you asleep, Barblin? What time is it? I've been
asleep. Four o'clock? The night is like milk, Barblin,
like blue milk. Soon the birds will start. Like a Flood
of milk . . .
A sound.
Why are you bolting the door?
Silence.
Let your father come up, let him find me on his daugh-
ter's threshold. I don't care! I shan't give up, Barblin,
I shall sit here every night, even if he drinks himself to
death over there, every night.
He takes a cigarette.
I'm wide awake again now.
He sits and smokes.
I don't slink about like a begging dog any more. I hate.
I don't shed any tears now. I laugh. The meaner they

behave towards me, the more comfortable I feel in my
hate. And the more confident. Hate makes plans. I feel
good every day now because I have a plan and no one
knows about it, and if I walk about timidly I'm only pre-
tending. Hate makes you cunning. Hate makes you
proud. One day I'll show them. Since I have hated them
there are times when I feel like whistling and singing,
but I don't do it. Hate makes you patient. Hate makes
you hard. I hate their country that we are going to leave,
and I hate their faces. I love one single person, and that
is enough.

He listens.

The cat's awake too!

He counts coins.

I made thirty shillings today, Barblin, thirty shillings in
a single day. I'm saving now. I don't go to the juke-box
any more.

He laughs.

If they could see how right they are: I'm always counting my money!

He listens.

There goes another one shuffling off home.

The twittering of birds.

I saw that Peider yesterday, you know, the one who
fancies you, the one who tripped me up; he grins every
time he sees me now, but I don't care –

He listens.

He's coming up!

Footsteps in the house.

We've got forty-one pounds now, Barblin, but don't tell
anyone. We'll get married. Believe me, there's another
world where nobody knows us, where nobody will trip
me up; that's where we'll go, Barblin. He can yell himself hoarse here if he wants to.

He smokes.

I'm glad you have bolted the door.

Enter the Teacher.

TEACHER My son!

ANDRI   I'm not your son.

TEACHER   Andri, I've come to tell you the truth, before the night's
           over . . .

ANDRI   You've been drinking.

TEACHER   Only on your account, Andri, only on your account.
           Andri laughs.
           My son –

ANDRI   Stop that!

TEACHER   Are you listening to me?

ANDRI   Hang onto a lamp-post, not me, I can smell you.
         Andri frees himself.
         And don't keep saying 'My son!' all the time. It's only
         because you're tight.

TEACHER   *staggers.*

ANDRI   Your daughter has bolted her door, don't worry.

TEACHER   Andri –

ANDRI   You can't stand up.

TEACHER   I'm worried.

ANDRI   There's no need.

TEACHER   Very worried . . .

ANDRI   Look, Mother is crying, she's waiting up for you.

TEACHER   I didn't reckon with that . . .

ANDRI   What didn't you reckon with?

TEACHER   That you would refuse to be my son.
           Andri laughs.
           I must sit down . . .

ANDRI   Then I'm going.

TEACHER   So you won't listen?

ANDRI   *takes the candle.*

TEACHER   All right, then don't.

ANDRI   I owe you my life. I know. If you attach importance to
         it I can repeat it once a day: I owe you my life. Twice a
         day if you like: I owe you my life. Once in the morning,
         once in the evening: I owe you my life, I owe you my
         life.

TEACHER   Andri, I've been drinking, all night long, so that I could
           come and tell you the truth – I know I've had too
           much . . .

ANDRI That's what I think too.

TEACHER Andri, you do owe me your life.

ANDRI Thank you for it.

TEACHER You don't understand what I mean . . .

ANDRI *says nothing*.

TEACHER Don't just stand there like that! – I wanted to tell you
about my life . . .
Cocks crow.
But you're not interested in my life.

ANDRI I'm interested in my own life.
Cocks crow.
It's morning already.

TEACHER *staggers*.

ANDRI Don't pretend you can still think.

TEACHER You despise me, don't you?

ANDRI I'm just looking at you. That's all. I used to respect you.
Not because you saved my life, but because I thought
you weren't like all the others; you didn't think their
thoughts, you had courage. I relied on you. And then I
found out the truth, and now I'm looking at you.

TEACHER What is the truth?

ANDRI *says nothing*.

TEACHER I don't think their thoughts, Andri. I tore up their school
books. I wanted them to have others –

ANDRI Everyone knows that.

TEACHER Do you know what I did?

ANDRI I'm going.

TEACHER I asked you if you knew what I did . . .

ANDRI You tore up their school books.

TEACHER I lied.
Pause.
You refuse to understand me . . .
Cocks crow.

ANDRI At seven I have to be in the shop, selling chairs, selling
tables, selling cupboards, rubbing my hands.

TEACHER Why do you have to rub your hands?

ANDRI 'Could you find a better chair? Does it wobble? Does it
creak? Could you find a cheaper chair?'

The Teacher stares at him.

I have to make money.

TEACHER Why do you have to make money?

ANDRI Because I'm a Jew.

TEACHER My son – !

ANDRI Stop that!

TEACHER *staggers.*

ANDRI You're disgusting.

TEACHER Andri –

ANDRI Stop snivelling.

TEACHER Andri –

ANDRI Push off.

TEACHER What did you say?

ANDRI It's coming out of your eyes; if you can't hold your drink, then go to bed.

TEACHER Do you hate me?

ANDRI *says nothing.*

The Teacher goes.

He has gone, Barblin, I didn't want to hurt his feelings. But things get worse and worse. Did you hear him? He doesn't know what he's saying any more, and then you'd think he really was crying – Barblin – are you asleep?

He listens at the door.

Barblin! Barblin!

He shakes the door, then tries to break it open. He starts to run at it again, but at this moment the door is opened from inside: in the doorway stands the Soldier, lit by the candle, barefoot, the belt of his trousers undone, naked to the waist.

Barblin . . .

SOLDIER Beat it.

ANDRI That can't be true . . .

SOLDIER Beat it, or I'll smash your face in.

FORESTAGE

The Soldier, now in civilian clothes, enters the witness box.

SOLDIER I admit I never liked him. I didn't know that he wasn't
one, everybody said he was one. As a matter of fact I
still think he was one. I didn't like him from the start.
But I didn't kill him. I only did my duty. Orders are
orders. What would the world come to if orders weren't
carried out? I was a soldier.

7

Sacristy, the Priest and Andri

PRIEST Andri, we must have a talk together. Your foster-mother
is very worried about you . . . Sit down!

ANDRI *says nothing.*

PRIEST Do sit down, Andri!

ANDRI *says nothing.*

PRIEST You won't sit down?

ANDRI *says nothing.*

PRIEST I can understand, this is the first time you've been here.
More or less. I remember they once sent you to fetch
your football from behind the altar when it came sailing
in.
The Priest laughs.

ANDRI What do you want to talk about, Father?

PRIEST Sit down!

ANDRI *says nothing.*

PRIEST You don't want to sit down?

ANDRI *says nothing.*

PRIEST Very well then.

ANDRI Is it true, Father, that I am different from everyone
else?
Pause.

PRIEST Andri, I want to tell you something.

ANDRI I'm insolent, I know.

PRIEST I understand your distress. But you must know that we like you, Andri, just as you are. Hasn't your foster-father done everything he could for you? I hear he sold land so that you could become a carpenter.

ANDRI But I'm not going to become a carpenter.

PRIEST Why not?

ANDRI My sort think of nothing but money all the time, people say, so my place isn't in the workshop, says the carpenter, but in the salesroom. I'm going to be a salesman, Father.

PRIEST Very well then.

ANDRI But I wanted to be a carpenter.

PRIEST Why don't you sit down?

ANDRI I think you're mistaken, Father, people don't like me. The innkeeper says I'm insolent, and the carpenter thinks so too, I believe. And the doctor says I'm ambitious, and my sort have no backbone.

PRIEST Sit down!

ANDRI Do you think I've no backbone, Father?

PRIEST It may be that there is something restless about you, Andri.

ANDRI And Peider says I'm a coward.

PRIEST A coward? Why?

ANDRI Because I'm a Jew.

PRIEST Fancy paying attention to Peider!

ANDRI *says nothing*.

PRIEST Andri, I want to tell you something.

ANDRI I know – I shouldn't keep thinking of myself all the time. But I can't help it, Father. I can't help wondering all the time whether what people say about me is true: that I'm not like them, not gay, not jolly, just not like them. And you too think there is something restless about me, Father, you've just said so. I can quite understand that nobody likes me. I don't like myself when I think about myself.

The Priest stands up.

Can I go now?

PRIEST Now listen to me!

ANDRI What do people want from me, Father?

PRIEST Why are you so suspicious?

ANDRI They all put their hands on my shoulder.

PRIEST Do you know what you are, Andri?
The Priest laughs.
You don't know, so I shall tell you.
Andri stares at him.
A splendid fellow! In your own way. A splendid fellow!
I have been watching you, Andri, for years!

ANDRI Watching?

PRIEST Of course.

ANDRI Why does everyone watch me?

PRIEST I like you, Andri, more than all the others, yes, precisely
because you are different from all the others. Why do you
shake your head? You are cleverer than they are. Indeed
you are. I like that about you, Andri, and I'm glad that
you have come to see me and that I have had the chance
to tell you so.

ANDRI It's not true.

PRIEST What isn't true?

ANDRI I'm not different. I don't want to be different. And even
if he's three times stronger than me, that Peider, I'll beat
the daylight out of him in front of everybody in the
square; I've sworn that to myself –

PRIEST As far as I'm concerned you're welcome to.

ANDRI I've sworn to do it –

PRIEST I don't like him either.

ANDRI I don't want to be popular. I shall stand up for myself.
I'm not a coward – and I'm not cleverer than the others,
Father; I don't want you to say that.

PRIEST Will you listen to me now?

ANDRI No.
Andri draws away.
I don't like having everyone's hands on my shoulders
the whole time.
Pause.

PRIEST You really don't make it easy for one.
Pause.

> To be brief, your foster-mother came to see me. She was
> here for more than four hours. The good woman is very
> unhappy. You don't come home to meals any more, she
> says, and you won't talk to anyone. She says you don't
> believe that people are thinking of your wellbeing.

ANDRI Everyone is thinking of my wellbeing!

PRIEST Why do you laugh?

ANDRI If he's thinking of my wellbeing, Father, why is he
willing to give me everything, but not his own daughter,
why?

PRIEST It is his right as a father –

ANDRI But why? Why? Because I'm a Jew.

PRIEST Don't shout!

ANDRI *says nothing.*

PRIEST Haven't you any other idea in your head? I have told
you, Andri, as a Christian, that I love you – but you have
one unfortunate habit, I'm afraid I must say, all of you:
whatever difficulties you come up against in life, you
attribute absolutely everything to the fact that you are
Jews. You really don't make things easy for one with
your over-sensitiveness.

ANDRI *says nothing.*

PRIEST You're crying.

ANDRI *sobs, covering his face with his hands.*

PRIEST What has happened? Answer me. What's the matter?
I'm asking you what has happened. Andri! Why don't
you speak, Andri? You're shivering. You've lost your
senses. How can I help you if you don't speak? Pull yourself together, Andri! Do you hear? Andri! Remember
you're a man! Well, I don't know.

ANDRI Barblin!
*Andri lets his hands fall from his face and stares in front
of him.*
She can't love me, no one can, I can't love myself . . .
Enter a sacristan with a chasuble.
Can I go now?
The Sacristan unbuttons the Priest.

PRIEST You can stay.

The Sacristan dresses the Priest for Mass.

You've said it yourself: how can other people love us if we don't love ourselves? Our Lord said: Love thy neighbour as thyself. He said: As thyself. We must accept ourselves, and that is what you don't do, Andri. Why do you want to be like the others? You're cleverer than they, believe me, you're more alert. Why won't you admit that? There is a spark in you. Why do you play football like all those boneheads, and rush about the field shouting, simply in order to be an Andorran? They don't like you, I know. And I know why. There's a spark in you. You think. Why shouldn't there also be some among God's creatures who have more intelligence than feeling? I tell you, that is exactly what I admire about you people. Why do you look at me like that? There is a spark in all of you. Think of Einstein! And all the rest of them, whatever their names are. Think of Spinoza!

ANDRI Can I go now?

PRIEST No man can change his skin, Andri, no Jew and no Christian. Nobody. God wants us to be as he created us. Do you understand me? And when they say to you: Jews are cowards, then know that you are not a coward if you accept being a Jew. On the contrary. You are different from us. Do you hear me? I say: You are not a coward. Only if you try to be like all Andorrans, then you are a coward . . .

An organ starts to play.

ANDRI Can I go now?

PRIEST Think over what you yourself said, Andri: How can the others accept you, if you don't accept yourself?

ANDRI Can I go now . . .

PRIEST Andri, have you understood me?

FORESTAGE

The Priest kneels.

PRIEST Thou shalt not make unto thee any graven image of the Lord, thy God, nor of men who are his creatures. I too was guilty at that time. I wanted to meet him with love when I spoke with him. I too made an image of him, I too put fetters on him. I too bound him to the stake.

8

The square of Andorra. The Doctor is the only one sitting; the others are standing: the Innkeeper, the Soldier, the Journeyman, the Somebody.

SOLDIER I say it's disgusting

DOCTOR I say, keep calm!

SOLDIER Why can't Andorra be attacked?

DOCTOR *lights a small cigar.*

SOLDIER I say it's disgusting.

INNKEEPER Was I to say there isn't a decent room in Andorra? I'm an innkeeper. You can't turn a foreigneress away from your door –

SOMEBODY *laughs.*

INNKEEPER What else could I do? A Señora stands there and asks if there's a decent room – .

SOLDIER A Señora, listen to him!

CARPENTER A woman from over the border?

SOLDIER Any trouble and we'll fight to the last man – and he puts her up!
He spits on the asphalt.
I say it's disgusting!

DOCTOR Don't get excited.
He smokes.
I've been around the world and I know. I'm an Andorran, everyone knows that, an Andorran body and soul. Other-

wise I shouldn't have come back home, you good people;
otherwise your professor wouldn't have renounced all
the university chairs in the world –

SOMEBODY *laughs.*

INNKEEPER What is there to laugh about?

SOMEBODY Who is going to fight to the last man?

SOLDIER I am.

SOMEBODY In the Bible it says, the last shall be first, or the other
way round, I don't remember, the first shall be last.

SOLDIER What does he mean by that?

SOMEBODY I'm only asking.

SOLDIER To the last man, that's an order. Rather dead than a
slave, that's pasted on the wall in every barracks. That's
an order. Let them come, they'll get the shock of their
lives . . .
Brief silence.

CARPENTER Why can't Andorra be attacked?

DOCTOR I am aware that the situation is tense.

CARPENTER Tenser than it's ever been before.

DOCTOR It's been that for years.

CARPENTER Why have they massed troops on the frontier?

DOCTOR What I was going to say was this: I've been around in
the world. One thing you can take from me: there is no
people in the whole world so universally beloved as we
are. That's a fact.

CARPENTER True enough.

DOCTOR Bearing that fact in mind, let us ask ourselves, what
can happen to a country like Andorra? Quite object-
ively.

INNKEEPER That's right, that's right.

SOLDIER What's right?

INNKEEPER No country is so much loved as we are.

CARPENTER True enough.

DOCTOR Loved isn't the word for it. I have met people who had
no idea where Andorra was, but every child in the world
knows that Andorra is a sanctuary, a sanctuary of peace
and freedom and human rights.

INNKEEPER Very true.

DOCTOR   Andorra is an idea, the incarnation of an idea, if you know what that means.
He smokes.
I say, they won't dare.

SOLDIER   Why not, why not?

INNKEEPER   Because we are the incarnation of an idea.

SOLDIER   But they outnumber us!

INNKEEPER   Because we are so loved.
The Idiot brings a lady's suitcase and puts it down.

SOLDIER   Just look at that!
The Idiot leaves again.

CARPENTER   What does she want here?

JOURNEYMAN   A spyess!

SOLDIER   What else?

JOURNEYMAN   A spyess!

SOLDIER   And he's putting her up!

SOMEBODY   *laughs.*

SOLDIER   What are you grinning at?

SOMEBODY   Spyess is rich.

SOLDIER   What else can she be?

SOMEBODY   The word isn't spyess, but spy, even if the situation is tense and if the individual is female.

CARPENTER   I wonder what she has come for really.
The Idiot brings a second lady's suitcase.

SOLDIER   Just look at that!

JOURNEYMAN   Let's kick her stuff to pieces!

INNKEEPER   That would be the last straw.
The Idiot leaves again.
Instead of taking the luggage upstairs, the idiot runs off and leaves it, and it attracts everybody's attention –

SOMEBODY   *laughs.*

INNKEEPER   I'm not a traitor, am I, Professor? That's not true. I'm an innkeeper. I should be the first to throw a stone. Indeed I should! There's still a law of hospitality in Andorra, an ancient and sacred law. Isn't that so, Professor, isn't that so? An innkeeper can't say no, however tense the situation may be, and certainly not when it's a lady.

SOMEBODY *laughs.*

JOURNEYMAN And when she has dough!

SOMEBODY *laughs.*

INNKEEPER The situation is no laughing matter.

SOMEBODY Spyess.

INNKEEPER Leave her luggage alone!

SOMEBODY Spyess is very good.

The Idiot brings a lady's coat and puts it down.

SOLDIER Just look at that!

The Idiot leaves again.

CARPENTER Why do you think Andorra can't be attacked?

DOCTOR You aren't listening to me.

He smokes.

I thought you were listening to me.

He smokes.

They won't dare, I say. No matter how many tanks they have, and parachutes on top of that, they simply can't afford to. Or as Perin, our great poet, once said: Our weapon is our innocence. Or the other way round: Our innocence is our weapon. Where else in the world is there a republic which can say that? I ask you: Where? A people like us, who can appeal to the conscience of the world like no other, a people without guilt –

Andri appears in the background.

SOLDIER There he goes slinking around again!

Andri withdraws, because everyone is looking at him.

DOCTOR Andorrans, let me tell you something. No nation in the world has ever been attacked unless there was some offence it could be reproached with. What can they reproach us with? The only thing that could happen to Andorra would be an injustice, a crude and blatant injustice. And they won't dare to do that. They won't dare tomorrow any more than yesterday. Because the whole world would defend us. In a flash. Because the conscience of the whole world is on our side.

SOMEBODY In a flash.

INNKEEPER Will you keep your trap shut for a change!

SOMEBODY *laughs.*

DOCTOR Who are you, anyhow?

SOMEBODY A man with a sense of humour.

DOCTOR Your sense of humour is out of place.

JOURNEYMAN *kicks the cases.*

INNKEEPER Stop!

DOCTOR What's the idea?

INNKEEPER For heaven's sake!

SOMEBODY *laughs.*

DOCTOR What a stupid thing to do. That's just what they're waiting for. Interference with travellers in Andorra! So that they have an excuse to attack us. What a stupid thing to do! Just when I'm telling you to keep calm! We wo n't give them an excuse – spy or no spy.

INNKEEPER *puts the cases straight again.*

SOLDIER I say it's disgusting!

INNKEEPER *wipes the cases clean.*

DOCTOR It's a good job no one saw . . .

Enter the Señora. Silence. The Señora sits down at an empty table. The Andorrans eye her as she slowly takes off her gloves.

Here's what I owe you? I'm off.

CARPENTER So am I.

The Doctor rises and leaves, raising his hat to the lady as he goes; the Carpenter signs to the Journeyman to follow him too.

SEÑORA Has something been happening here?

SOMEBODY *laughs.*

SEÑORA Can I have something to drink?

INNKEEPER With pleasure, Señora –

SEÑORA What do people drink in this country?

INNKEEPER Anything you like, Señora –

SEÑORA I'd really prefer a glass of cold water.

INNKEEPER Señora, we have everything.

SOMEBODY *laughs.*

INNKEEPER The gentleman has a sense of humour.

SOMEBODY *goes.*

SEÑORA The room is very nice, innkeeper, very nice.

INNKEEPER *bows and leaves.*

SOLDIER And a whisky for me!

*The Soldier stays and sits down in order to stare at the
Señora. On the forestage right, by the juke-box, Andri appears and drops in a coin.*

INNKEEPER You're always at that damned juke-box!

ANDRI I pay.

INNKEEPER Don't you ever think of anything else?

ANDRI No.

*While the same record goes on playing: The Señora writes
a note; the Soldier stares; she folds the note and speaks to
the Soldier, without looking at him.*

SEÑORA Aren't there any women in Andorra?

The Idiot comes back.

Do you know a teacher named Can?

The Idiot grins and nods.

Take him this note, please.

Enter three other soldiers and the Journeyman.

SOLDIER Did you hear that? Aren't there any women in Andorra,
she asked me.

JOURNEYMAN What did you say?

SOLDIER No, but there are men!

JOURNEYMAN Did you say that?

SOLDIER I asked her if she came to Andorra because there aren't
any men across the border.

JOURNEYMAN Did you say that?

SOLDIER That's what I said.

They grin.

Here he comes. As white as chalk! He wants to beat me
up. Did you know that?

Enter Andri. The music has stopped.

How's your fiancée?

ANDRI *seizes the Soldier by the collar.*

SOLDIER What's the idea.

The Soldier frees himself.

Some old rabbi has been telling him about David and
Goliath; now he wants to play David.

They grin.

Let's go.

ANDRI Fedri –

JOURNEYMAN How he stammers!

ANDRI Why did you betray me?

SOLDIER Let's go.

Andri knocks the Soldier's cap off his head.

Now you watch it!

The Soldier picks the cap up from the ground and dusts it.

If you think I'm going to get put in the glasshouse because of you –

JOURNEYMAN What the hell does he want?

ANDRI Now smash my face in.

SOLDIER Let's go.

The Soldier puts on his cap, Andri knocks it off again, the others laugh, the Soldier suddenly gives him an uppercut and Andri goes down.

Where's your sling, David?

Andri gets up.

Now watch our David cut loose!

Andri suddenly gives the Soldier an uppercut, and the Soldier goes down.

You damn Jew – !

SEÑORA No! No! All against one. No!

The other soldiers have seized hold of Andri, so that the Soldier gets away. The Soldier lashes out at Andri while the others are holding him. Andri defends himself silently, then suddenly breaks loose. The Journeyman kicks him from behind. When Andri turns round the Soldier attacks him from behind. Andri falls. The four soldiers and the Journeyman kick him from all sides, until they notice the Señora, who has come up to them.

SOLDIER That's the last straw, making us look ridiculous in front of a foreigner . . .

The Soldier and the others make off.

SEÑORA Who are you?

ANDRI I'm not a coward.

SEÑORA What's your name?

ANDRI They're always saying I'm a coward.

SEÑORA No, no, don't touch the wound!

Enter the Innkeeper with a carafe and glass on a tray.

INNKEEPER What's happened?

SEÑORA Get a doctor.

INNKEEPER And in front of my hotel – !

SEÑORA Give me that.

The Señora takes the carafe and her handkerchief and kneels down beside Andri, who tries to sit up.

They kicked him with their boots.

INNKEEPER Impossible, Señora!

SEÑORA Don't just stand there, fetch a doctor.

INNKEEPER Señora, this sort of thing isn't usual here . . .

SEÑORA I'm only cleaning it.

INNKEEPER It's your own fault. Why do you always come when the soldiers are here . . . ?

SEÑORA Look at me!

INNKEEPER I've warned you.

SEÑORA Luckily it's missed your eye.

INNKEEPER It's his own fault, Señora, he's always going to the juke-box, I've warned him. He gets on people's nerves . . .

SEÑORA Will you please fetch a doctor?

The Innkeeper goes.

ANDRI Now they're all against me.

SEÑORA Is it hurting you?

ANDRI I don't need a doctor.

SEÑORA It's gone right down to the bone.

ANDRI I know the doctor.

Andri stands up.

I can walk, it's only my forehead.

SEÑORA *stands up.*

ANDRI I'm sorry, I've spoilt your handkerchief.

SEÑORA Take me to your father.

The Señora takes Andri's arm and they walk slowly away while the Innkeeper and the Doctor come.

DOCTOR Arm in arm?

INNKEEPER They kicked him with their boots, I saw it with my own eyes, I was inside.

DOCTOR *lights a small cigar.*

INNKEEPER He's always going to the juke-box, I've told him about it. He gets on people's nerves.

DOCTOR Blood?

INNKEEPER I saw it coming.

DOCTOR *smokes.*

INNKEEPER Why don't you say anything?

DOCTOR A nasty business.

INNKEEPER He started it.

DOCTOR I have nothing against these people, but I feel uncomfortable the moment I set eyes on one of them. However you behave, it's wrong. What did I say? They can't leave well alone, they're always asking us to prove ourselves by our attitude to them. As though we had nothing else to do! No one likes to have a guilty conscience, but that's what they bank on. They want us to do them an injustice. That's all they're waiting for . . .

He turns to go.

Wash that little bit of blood away. And don't gossip! There's no need to tell people what you saw.

FORESTAGE

The Teacher and the Señora outside the white house as at the beginning.

SEÑORA You said our son was a Jew.

TEACHER *says nothing.*

SEÑORA Why did you put that lie into the world?

TEACHER *says nothing.*

SEÑORA One day an Andorran peddlar came by. He was very talkative. To praise Andorra he told everyone the touching story of a teacher from here, who had saved a Jewish child at the time of the great murder and now cares for him as if he were his own son. I immediately sent a letter: Are you this teacher? I wrote. I demanded an answer. Why do you say he is a Jewish child? I asked: Do you know what you have done? I waited for an answer. It didn't come. Perhaps you never got my letter. I couldn't believe what I feared. I wrote a second letter,

and a third. I waited for an answer. So time passed . . .
Why did you put that lie into the world?

TEACHER Why, why, why!

SEÑORA You hated me when the child was born because I was a
coward, because I was afraid of my people. When you
came to the frontier, you said it was a Jewish child whom
you had saved from us. Why? Because you too were a
coward when you returned home. Because you too were
afraid of your people.
Pause.
Wasn't it like that?
Pause.
Perhaps you wanted to show that you Andorrans are
quite different from us. Because you hated me. But the
people here are not different, you can see that, not very
different.

TEACHER *says nothing.*

SEÑORA He must know the truth. Which of us is going to tell
him?

TEACHER I will, I'll tell him.

SEÑORA And will you tell them?

TEACHER Yes, I'll tell them that he is my son, our son, their own
flesh and blood.

SEÑORA Why don't you go and tell them?

TEACHER Suppose they don't want the truth?

Interval

9

*A room in the Teacher's house. The Señora is seated, Andri
standing.*

SEÑORA   *puts on one glove.*
    Noise in the street.

SEÑORA   I'm glad to have seen you.

ANDRI   Are you leaving us, Señora?

SEÑORA   I have been asked to go.

ANDRI   If you say no country is worse and no country is better
than Andorra, why don't you stay here?

SEÑORA   Would you like me to? Do you know that you are hand-
some?
    Noise in the street.
They have treated you badly, Andri, but that will stop
now. The truth will put them right; and you are the only
one here who need not fear the truth.

ANDRI   What truth?
    Noise in the street.

SEÑORA   I must go. I'm from the other side of the frontier, you
can hear how I exasperate them. A Black! That's what
they call us here, I know . . .
    She puts on the other glove.
There are lots of other things I should like to tell you,
and a lot of things I should like to ask. I should like to
have a long talk with you. But we shall see each other
again, I hope . . .
    She is ready.
We shall see each other again.
    She looks round once more.
So this is where you grew up?

ANDRI   Yes.
    Noise in the street.

SEÑORA   I ought to go now.
    She remains seated.
When I was your age – that time goes very quickly, Andri,
you're twenty now and can't believe it: people meet,

love, part, life is in front of you, and when you look in
the mirror, all of a sudden it is behind you. You don't
seem to yourself very different, but suddenly it is other
people who are twenty ... When I was your age – my
father, who was in the army, had been killed in the war.
I knew how he thought, and I didn't want to think like
him. We wanted a different world. We were young like
you, and what we were taught was murderous, we knew
that. And we despised the world as it is, we saw through
it and dared to want another one. And we tried to create
another one. We wanted not to be afraid of people. Not
for anything in the world. We didn't want to lie. When
we saw that we were merely keeping silent about our fear,
we hated each other. Our new world didn't last long. We
crossed the frontiers again, back to where we had come
from when we were as young as you ...
She rises.
Do you understand what I'm saying?

ANDRI No.

SEÑORA *goes up to Andri and kisses him.*

ANDRI Why did you do that?

SEÑORA I must go.
Noise in the street.
Shall we see each other again?

ANDRI I should like that, Señora.

SEÑORA I always wished I had never known my father and mother.
No one, when he sees the world they have left behind for
him, can understand his parents.
Enter the Teacher and the Mother.
I'm going, yes, I'm just going.
Silence.
So I'll say goodbye.
Silence.
I'm going, yes, now I'm really going ...
The Señora goes out.

TEACHER Andri, you go with her! But not across the square, take
her round the back way.

ANDRI Why round the back?

TEACHER Just do as I say.
　　　　Andri goes out.
　　　　The Priest will tell him. Don't ask me about it now! I
　　　　never told you, because you've never understood me.
　　　　He sits down.
　　　　Now you know.

MOTHER What will Andri say?

TEACHER He doesn't believe me.
　　　　Noise in the street.
　　　　I hope the mob will leave her alone.

MOTHER I understand more than you think, Can. You loved *her*,
　　　　but you married *me*, because I am an Andorran. You
　　　　have betrayed us all, but Andri more than anyone. Don't
　　　　curse the Andorrans, you are one yourself.
　　　　Enter the Priest.
　　　　You have a difficult task in this house, Reverend Father.
　　　　You explained to Andri what it means to be a Jew and
　　　　that he should accept it. Now he has accepted it. And
　　　　now you must tell him what an Andorran is and that he
　　　　should accept that.

TEACHER Now leave us!

MOTHER May God guide you, Father Benedict.
　　　　The Mother goes out.

PRIEST I tried, but it was no use, it's impossible to talk to them,
　　　　every reasonable word exasperates them. I told them to
　　　　go home and mind their own business. Not one of them
　　　　knows what they really want.
　　　　Andri comes back.

TEACHER Why are you back so soon?

ANDRI She said she wanted to go alone.
　　　　He shows his hand.
　　　　She gave me this.

TEACHER Her ring?

ANDRI Yes.

TEACHER *says nothing, then stands up.*

ANDRI Who is this Señora?

TEACHER I'll go with her.
　　　　The Teacher goes.

PRIEST What are you laughing about?

ANDRI He's jealous!

PRIEST Sit down.

ANDRI What's the matter with you all?

PRIEST It's no laughing matter, Andri.

ANDRI But it's ludicrous.

Andri looks at the ring.

You know, I think this is a topaz.

PRIEST Andri, we must have a talk.

ANDRI Again?

Andri laughs.

Everyone is behaving today like puppets when the strings are tangled, including you, Father.

Andri takes a cigarette.

I believe she was once his mistress.

Andri smokes.

She's a fantastic woman.

PRIEST Andri, I have something to tell you.

ANDRI Can't I stand while you say it?

Andri sits down.

I have to be in the shop by two. Isn't she a fantastic woman?

PRIEST I'm glad you like her.

ANDRI Everyone is behaving so strangely.

Andri smokes.

You're going to tell me that you shouldn't go up to a soldier and knock his cap off when you know you're a Jew, one shouldn't do that at all, and yet I'm glad I did it. I learnt something from it, even if it's no use to me. As a matter of fact not a day passes now, since our talk, without my learning something that is no use to me, Reverend Father, no more use to me than your kind words. I'm sure you mean well, you are a Christian by profession, but I am a Jew by birth, and that's why I am going to emigrate.

PRIEST Andri –

ANDRI If I can.

Andri puts out his cigarette.

I didn't mean to tell anyone that.

PRIEST Stay where you are!

ANDRI This ring will help me.

The Priest says nothing.

Please don't repeat what I've just told you, that's the only thing you can do for me now.

Andri stands up.

I must go.

Andri laughs.

You're quite right, there is something restless about me, Father . . .

PRIEST Are you doing the talking or am I?

ANDRI I'm sorry.

Andri sits down.

I'm listening.

PRIEST Andri –

ANDRI You're so solemn!

PRIEST I have come to redeem you.

ANDRI I'm listening.

PRIEST I knew nothing about it either, Andri, when we talked together last time. For years the story has always been that he rescued a Jewish child, a Christian deed, so why shouldn't I have believed it? But now, Andri, your mother has come –

ANDRI Who has come?

PRIEST The Señora.

ANDRI *jumps up.*

PRIEST Andri – you're not a Jew.

Silence.

Don't you believe me?

ANDRI No.

PRIEST So you think I'm lying?

ANDRI Father, one feels a thing like that.

PRIEST What does one feel?

ANDRI Whether one is a Jew or not.

The Priest stands up and approaches Andri.

Don't touch me! Keep your hands off me! I don't want any more of that.

PRIEST Don't you hear what I say?

ANDRI *says nothing.*

PRIEST You're his son.

ANDRI *laughs.*

PRIEST Andri, that is the truth.

ANDRI How many truths have you got?
Andri takes a cigarette, which he then forgets.
You can't do that with me any more . . .

PRIEST Why don't you believe me?

ANDRI My belief is used up.

PRIEST I swear to you by my soul's salvation, Andri: You are
his son, our son, and there can be no question of your
being a Jew.

ANDRI There's been plenty of question of it up to now . . .
Noise in the street.

PRIEST What's going on?
Silence.

ANDRI Ever since I have been able to hear, people have told me
I'm different, and I watched to see if what they said was
true. And it is true, Father: I am different. People told
me my kind have a certain way of moving, and I looked
at myself in the mirror almost every evening. They are
right: I do move like this and like this. I can't help it.
And I watched to see whether it was true that I'm always
thinking of money, when the Andorrans watch me and
think, now he's thinking of money; and they were right
again: I am always thinking of money. It's true. And
I have no guts, I've tried, it's no use: I have no guts,
only fear. And people told me that my kind are cowards.
I watched out for this too. Many of them are cowards,
but I know when I'm being a coward. I didn't want to
admit what they told me, but it's true. They kicked me
with their boots, and it's true what they say: I don't feel
like they do. And I have no country. You told me,
Father, that one must accept that, and I have accepted it.
Now it's up to you, Reverend Father, to accept your Jew.

PRIEST Andri –

ANDRI Now, Father, I'm doing the talking.

PRIEST – do you want to be a Jew?

ANDRI I am a Jew. For a long time I didn't know what it meant. Now I know.

PRIEST *sits down helplessly.*

ANDRI I don't want to have a father and mother, for their death to come over me with anguish and despair, nor my death over them. And no sister and no sweetheart. Soon everything will be torn to pieces, then neither our promises nor our fidelity will help. I want it to happen soon. I'm old. My trust has fallen out, one piece after the other, like teeth. I used to be happy, the sun shone green in the trees, I threw my name in the air like a cap that belonged to nobody but me, and down fell a stone that killed me. I have been wrong, all the time, though not in the way they thought. I wanted to be right and to rejoice. But my enemies were right, even if they were unjust, no matter how much I understand I still can't feel that I am right. I don't need enemies any more, the truth is enough. I take fright the moment I begin to hope. I have never been able to hope. I take fright when I laugh, and I can't weep. My affliction raises me above everyone, and therefore I must fall. My eyes are big with melancholy, my blood knows everything, and I wish I were dead. But I have a horror of dying. There is no grace –

PRIEST Now you are committing a sin.

ANDRI Look at the old teacher, the way he is going downhill, and he was once a young man, he says, with great ideals. Look at Barblin. And all of them, all of them, not only me. Look at the soldiers. Damned. Look at yourself. You already know, Father, what you will do when they take me away, a Jew, in front of your kind eyes, and that's why they stare at me so, your kind, kind eyes. You will pray. For me and for yourself. Your prayers won't even help you, you will betray me in spite of them. Grace is an everlasting rumour, the sun will shine green in the trees even when they take me away.

Enter the Teacher, his clothes torn.

PRIEST What has happened?

TEACHER *collapses.*

PRIEST What has happened?

Two men bring in the dead Señora, lay her down and go.

ANDRI The Señora – ?

PRIEST How did that happen?

TEACHER A stone.

PRIEST Who threw it?

TEACHER They say Andri did. The innkeeper saw it with his own eyes.

ANDRI *tries to run out; the Teacher holds him back.*

TEACHER He was here, you are his witness.

FORESTAGE

The Somebody enters the witness box.

SOMEBODY I admit there's no proof as to who threw the stone at the foreign woman that time. I personally wasn't in the square when it happened. I don't want to put the blame on anyone; I'm not the judge of the universe. As to the young lad – of course I remember him. He used to spend all his tips on the juke-box, and when they took him away I felt sorry for him. I don't know what the soldiers did to him after they took him away, we only heard him screaming ... There must come a time when we are allowed to forget, I think.

10

The square of Andorra. Andri is sitting alone.

ANDRI People are looking at me from all round, I know. Let them look ...

He takes a cigarette.

I didn't throw the stone!

He smokes.

Let them come out, if they saw it with their own eyes,
let them come out of their houses, if they dare, and point
their fingers at me.

VOICE *whispers.*

ANDRI Why are you whispering behind the wall?

VOICE *whispers.*

ANDRI I can't hear a word when you whisper.

He smokes.

I've been sitting here for an hour. It's like a dead town.
There's no one about. They're all in their cellars. It
looks strange. Only the sparrows on the wires.

VOICE *whispers.*

ANDRI Why should I hide?

VOICE *whispers.*

ANDRI I didn't throw the stone.

He smokes.

Since dawn I've been sauntering through your streets.
All alone. All the shutters were down, every door shut.
There is nothing left but dogs and cats in your snow-
white Andorra . . .

*The rumbling of a loudspeaker van is heard, loud and rever-
berating; the words are unintelligible.*

You're not supposed to carry a rifle. Did you hear? It's
all over.

The Teacher appears, a rifle on his arm.

TEACHER Andri –

ANDRI *smokes.*

TEACHER We've been looking for you all night –

ANDRI Where is Barblin?

TEACHER I was up in the forest –

ANDRI What would I be doing in the forest?

TEACHER Andri – the Blacks are here.

ANDRI Really?

He listens.

TEACHER Listen.

He releases the safety catch of his rifle.

ANDRI Only the sparrows.

The twittering of birds.

TEACHER You can't stay here.

ANDRI Where can I stay?

TEACHER It's senseless, what you're doing, it's madness –
He takes Andri's arm.
Now come along!

ANDRI I didn't throw the stone –
He tears himself away.
I didn't throw the stone!
A sound.

TEACHER What was that?

ANDRI Shutters.
He stamps out his cigarette.
People behind shutters.
He takes another cigarette.
Have you a light?
Drums in the distance.

TEACHER Was that gunfire?

ANDRI It's quieter than it has ever been.

TEACHER What's happening now?

ANDRI The shock of their lives.

TEACHER What did you say?

ANDRI Rather dead than a slave.
Again the rumble of the loudspeaker van.
NO ANDORRAN HAS ANYTHING TO FEAR. Did you hear that?
CALM AND ORDER – ALL BLOODSHED – IN THE NAME OF
PEACE – ANYONE CARRYING OR CONCEALING ARMS – THE
COMMANDER IN CHIEF – NO ANDORRAN HAS ANYTHING TO
FEAR . . .
Silence.
In fact it's exactly what I expected. Exactly.

TEACHER What are you talking about?

ANDRI Your surrender.
Three men without rifles cross the square.
You're the last one with a rifle.

TEACHER Scum!

ANDRI No Andorran has anything to fear.
The twittering of birds.
Haven't you got a light?

TEACHER   *stares after the men.*

ANDRI   Did you see how they were walking? They didn't look
at one another. And they were very quiet! A point comes
when everyone realizes how many things he never really
believed. That's why they're walking about in that
strange way. Like men who have been lying.

Two men without rifles cross the square.

TEACHER   My son –

ANDRI   Don't start that again!

TEACHER   You're lost if you don't believe me.

ANDRI   I'm not your son.

TEACHER   Andri, no one can choose his father. What else can I do
to make you believe me? What else can I do? I tell you
at every possible moment. I've even told the children at
school that you are my son. What else can I do? Do you
want me to hang myself to make you believe it? I'm not
leaving you, Andri.

He sits down beside Andri.

Andri –

ANDRI   *looks up at the houses.*

A black flag is hoisted.

ANDRI   They simply can't wait.

TEACHER   Where did they get the flags from?

ANDRI   All they need now is a scapegoat.

A second flag is hoisted.

TEACHER   Andri, come home!

ANDRI   It's no use telling me all over again, Father. Your fate is
not mine, Father, nor mine yours.

TEACHER   The only witness I had is dead.

ANDRI   Don't talk about her!

TEACHER   You're wearing her ring –

ANDRI   What you have done, no father would do.

TEACHER   How can you know?

ANDRI   *listens.*

TEACHER   An Andorran, they say, has nothing to do with a woman
from over the border and certainly doesn't have a child
by her. I was afraid of them, yes, afraid of Andorra,
because I was a coward –

ANDRI People are listening.

TEACHER That's why I said it – because I was a coward. It was easier, at that time, to have a Jewish child. It was something to be admired. At first they used to fondle you, because it flattered them not to be like the people across the frontier.

ANDRI *listens.*

TEACHER Andri, do you hear your father talking to you?
The sound of a shutter.
Let them listen!
The sound of a shutter.
Andri –

ANDRI They don't believe you.

TEACHER Because you don't believe me!

ANDRI *smokes.*

TEACHER You with your innocence, yes, you didn't throw the stone, say it again, you didn't throw the stone, yes, you with your enormous innocence, look at me like a Jew, but you are my son, yes, my son, and if you don't believe it you are beyond help.

ANDRI I am beyond help.

TEACHER You want me to be guilty!

ANDRI *looks at him.*

TEACHER Go on, say it!

ANDRI What?

TEACHER Tell me to hang myself.
Military music in the distance.

ANDRI They are coming with music.
He takes another cigarette.
I'm not the first one who has been beyond help. There is no point in talking the way you are. I know who my forbears are. Thousands and hundreds of thousands have died at the stake, their fate is mine.

TEACHER Fate!

ANDRI You don't understand that, because you are not a Jew –
He looks into the street.
Now leave me!

ANDRI They're throwing their rifles away.

*Enter the Soldier, disarmed and carrying only a drum. The
sound of rifles being thrown into a pile can be heard. The
Soldier speaks over his shoulder.*

SOLDIER But tidily, I said! Like in the Army!
He goes up to the Teacher.
Hand over your rifle.

TEACHER No.

SOLDIER Orders are orders.

TEACHER No.

SOLDIER No Andorran has anything to fear.
*Enter the Doctor, the Innkeeper, the Carpenter, the Journey-
man, the Somebody, all without rifles.*

TEACHER Scum! All of you! Scum! To the last man. Scum!
*The Teacher releases the safety catch of his rifle and is about
to fire upon the Andorrans, but the Soldier intervenes; after
a brief, soundless struggle the Teacher is disarmed and looks
round.*

TEACHER My son! Where is my son?
The Teacher rushes out.

SOMEBODY What's got into him?
*On the forestage right, by the juke-box, Andri appears and
drops in a coin so that his tune plays, then slowly walks
away.*

FORESTAGE

*While the juke-box is playing, two soldiers in black uni-
forms, each carrying a sub-machine gun, march to and fro
on sentry-go, passing one another.*

11

*Outside Barblin's room. Andri and Barblin. Drums in the
distance.*

ANDRI How often did you sleep with him?

BARBLIN Andri.

ANDRI How often did you sleep with him, while I was sitting here talking. About going away with you –

BARBLIN *says nothing.*

ANDRI You remember, he stood right here – great hairy chest.

BARBLIN Don't!

ANDRI A real man!

BARBLIN *says nothing.*

ANDRI How often did you sleep with him?

BARBLIN *says nothing.*

ANDRI You don't say anything ... Then what are we to talk about all night? I mustn't think about that now, you say. I should think about my future, but I haven't got a future, so I should like to know how many times you slept with him?

BARBLIN *sobs.*

ANDRI And will it carry on?

BARBLIN *sobs.*

ANDRI Why do I want to know anyhow? What's it matter now? Just to be able to feel something for you again.
Andri listens.

BARBLIN Andri ...

ANDRI Ssh!

BARBLIN It wasn't like that.

ANDRI I wonder how near they are.

BARBLIN You're not fair.

ANDRI I shall apologize when they come ...

BARBLIN *sobs.*

ANDRI Why not fair? I thought we loved each other. I'm only asking what it's like to have a real man. Don't be shy. Surely you could tell me that, now that you think of yourself as my little sister.
Andri strokes her hair.
I have waited too long for you.
Andri listens.

BARBLIN They mustn't hurt you!

ANDRI You try and stop them!

BARBLIN I shall stay with you!
Silence.

ANDRI Barblin, now I'm frightened again –

BARBLIN Brother!

ANDRI Suddenly. If they know I'm in the house and they can't find me, they set fire to the house, that's well known, and wait down below till the Jew jumps out of the window.

BARBLIN Andri – you aren't a Jew!

ANDRI Then why do you want to hide me?
Drums in the distance.

BARBLIN Come into my room!

ANDRI *shakes his head.*

BARBLIN Nobody knows there's another room up here.

ANDRI Except Peider.
The drums disappear into the distance.
All wiped out.

BARBLIN What did you say?

ANDRI What is coming has all happened before. I said: All wiped out. My head in your lap. Do you remember? There's no end to it. My head in your lap. Was I in your way? I can't imagine that. So what? I can imagine it. What rubbish did I talk when I wasn't there any more? Why didn't you laugh? You didn't even laugh. All wiped out, all wiped out! And I didn't even feel it when Peider was there, your hair in his hands. So what? It has all happened before . . .
Drums near by.
You see, they know where fear is.

BARBLIN They're going past.

ANDRI They're surrounding the house.
The drums suddenly fall silent.
It's me they're after, you know that very well. I'm not your brother. Lies won't help. There have been too many already.
Silence.
Go on, kiss me!

BARBLIN No.

ANDRI Take your clothes off!

BARBLIN No, Andri.

ANDRI Kiss me, put your arms round me!

BARBLIN *struggles.*

ANDRI What's it matter now?

BARBLIN *struggles.*

ANDRI Don't act so pure, you –
The tinkling of a broken window.

BARBLIN What was that?

ANDRI They know where I am.

BARBLIN Put out the candle!
The tinkling of a second window.

ANDRI Kiss me!

BARBLIN No. No . . .

ANDRI Can't you do with me what you can do with anyone,
merry and naked? I shan't let go of you. Why is it different with others? Go on, tell me. Why is it different?
I shall kiss you, soldier's sweetheart! One more or less,
don't be so fussy. Why is it different with me? Tell me!
Is your hair bored when I kiss it?

BARBLIN Brother –

ANDRI Why do you only feel ashamed with me?

BARBLIN Now let go of me!

ANDRI Now, yes, now and never again, yes, I want you, yes,
merry and naked, yes, little sister, yes, yes, yes –

BARBLIN *screams.*

ANDRI Remember the deadly nightshade.
Andri undoes her blouse as if she were lying unconscious.
Remember our deadly nightshade –

BARBLIN You're out of your mind!
The doorbell rings.
Did you hear that, Andri? You're lost if you don't believe
us. Hide! Hide, Andri!
The doorbell rings.

ANDRI Why didn't we poison ourselves, Barblin, while we were
still children. Now it's too late . . .
Blows on the front door.

BARBLIN Father won't open the door.

ANDRI How slow. How slow they are.
Blows on the front door.

BARBLIN Oh Lord, our God, who art, who art, Lord, Almighty

God, who art in heaven, Lord, Lord, who art – Lord . . .
The front door cracks.

ANDRI   Leave me quickly. If they find you with me that won't
be good. Take your blouse. Quickly. Think of your hair.
*Voices in the house. Barblin puts out the candle; the tramp-
ing of boots. The Soldier appears with the drum and two
soldiers in black uniforms equipped with a searchlight: Barblin, without a blouse, alone outside the room.*

SOLDIER   Where is he?

BARBLIN   Who?

SOLDIER   Our Jew.

BARBLIN   There isn't any Jew.

SOLDIER   *pushes her aside and goes up to the door.*

BARBLIN   Don't you dare!

SOLDIER   Open up!

BARBLIN   Help! Help!

ANDRI   *opens the door and steps out.*

SOLDIER   That's him.

ANDRI   *is bound.*

BARBLIN   Don't touch him, he is my brother –

SOLDIER   We shall see about that at the Jew Inspection.

BARBLIN   The Jew Inspection?

SOLDIER   All right, get going.

BARBLIN   What's that?

SOLDIER   You too. Everybody has to appear at the Jew Inspection.
Come on.
Andri is led away.
Jew's whore!

FORESTAGE

The Doctor enters the witness box.

DOCTOR   I shall try to be brief, although there are a great many
things being said today which ought to be corrected. It's
always easy to know afterwards how one ought to have
behaved at the time, quite apart from the fact that as far

as I am personally concerned I really don't know why I should have behaved differently. What did I do? Nothing whatever. I was the local medical officer, as I still am. I can't remember what I am supposed to have said at the time, but anyhow that's my way, an Andorran always says what he thinks – but I must be brief . . . I admit that we were all mistaken at the time, which naturally I can only regret. How often do I have to say that? I'm not in favour of atrocities, I never have been. Anyway, I only saw the young man two or three times. I didn't see the beating-up that is supposed to have taken place later. Nevertheless, I naturally condemn it. I can only say that it's not my fault, quite apart from the fact that his behaviour (there's no point in concealing the fact) became (let us be quite frank) more and more Jewish, although the young man may really have been just as much of an Andorran as I am. I don't for one moment deny that we were somewhat influenced by the events of the period. It was, let us not forget, a turbulent period. As far as I am personally concerned I never took part in brutality or urged anyone to indulge in it. I can state that publicly. A tragic affair, undoubtedly. It wasn't my fault that things turned out as they did. I think I can speak in the name of everyone when, to conclude, I repeat that we can only regret the things that took place at that time.

12

The square of Andorra. The square is surrounded by soldiers in black uniforms, with ordered arms, motionless. The Andorrans, like a herd in the pen, wait mutely to see what is going to happen. For a long time nothing happens. There is only whispering.

DOCTOR Keep calm, everyone. When the Jew Inspection is over everything will remain as before. No Andorran has any-thing to fear, we've got that in black and white. I shall

remain the medical officer, the innkeeper will remain the
innkeeper, Andorra will remain Andorran . . .
A roll of drums.

JOURNEYMAN   Now they're distributing the black cloths.
Black cloths are handed out.

DOCTOR   No resistance now, whatever you do.
*Enter Barblin. She goes from group to group as though de-
mented, pulling people's sleeves; they turn their backs on
her; she whispers something that is unintelligible.*

INNKEEPER   Now all of a sudden they're saying he isn't one.

SOMEBODY   What do they say?

INNKEEPER   That he isn't one.

DOCTOR   But you can see that he is at a glance.

SOMEBODY   Who says that?

INNKEEPER   The teacher.

DOCTOR   Now we shall see.

INNKEEPER   Anyhow he threw the stone.

SOMEBODY   Has that been proved?

INNKEEPER   Proved?

DOCTOR   If he isn't one why is he hiding? Why is he afraid?
Why doesn't he come out into the square like the rest
of us?

INNKEEPER   Quite right.

DOCTOR   Why shouldn't he be one?

INNKEEPER   Quite right.

SOMEBODY   They say they've been looking for him all night.

DOCTOR   They found him.

SOMEBODY   I shouldn't like to be in his shoes.

INNKEEPER   Anyhow, he threw the stone –
*They stop talking as a Black soldier approaches; they have
to take the black cloths. The soldier passes on.*

DOCTOR   The way they distribute these black cloths without once
raising their voices. That's what I call organization. Just
look at it! That's efficiency!

SOMEBODY   They have a smell.
They sniff at their cloths.
The sweat of fear . . .
Barblin comes up to the group containing the Doctor and the

Innkeeper, tugs at their sleeves and whispers; they turn their backs on her; she wanders on.

DOCTOR That's nonsense.

SOMEBODY What did she say?

INNKEEPER She'll pay dearly for that.

DOCTOR No resistance now, whatever you do.

Barblin goes up to another group, tugs at their sleeves and whispers; they turn their backs on her; she wanders on.

INNKEEPER Has it been proved? You ask. When I saw it with my own eyes! Right here on this spot. Who else could have thrown the stone?

SOMEBODY I only asked.

INNKEEPER One of us perhaps?

SOMEBODY I wasn't there.

INNKEEPER But I was!

DOCTOR *puts his finger to his lips.*

INNKEEPER I suppose you think I threw the stone?

DOCTOR Quiet.

INNKEEPER Me?

DOCTOR We're not supposed to talk.

INNKEEPER Here, right here on this spot, the stone was lying here, I saw it myself, a cobble stone, a loose cobble stone, and he picked it up like this –

The Innkeeper picks up a cobble stone.

– just like this . . .

The Carpenter joins them.

CARPENTER What's going on?

DOCTOR Keep calm, keep calm.

CARPENTER What are these black cloths for?

DOCTOR The Jew Inspection.

CARPENTER What are we supposed to do with them?

The Black soldiers surrounding the square suddenly present arms: a Black, short, fat, pale, flabby, apparently harmless, crosses the square with brisk, short steps.

DOCTOR That's him.

CARPENTER Who?

DOCTOR The Jew Detector.

The Soldiers order arms with a crash.

INNKEEPER Suppose he makes a mistake?

DOCTOR He never makes a mistake.

INNKEEPER What would happen?

DOCTOR Why should he make a mistake?

INNKEEPER But just suppose. What would happen?

DOCTOR He has an eye for it. You can be sure of that! He can smell it. He can see it by the walk. If somebody walks across the square, he can see it by the feet.

SOMEBODY Is that why we have to take our shoes off?

DOCTOR He has been trained as a Jew Detector.

Barblin appears again, looking for groups to which she has not yet been. She finds the Journeyman, tugs his sleeve and whispers; the Journeyman pulls himself free.

JOURNEYMAN Leave me alone!

DOCTOR *lights a small cigar.*

JOURNEYMAN She's nuts: she says no one's to walk across the square, we're to let them take us all away. She wants to give us a sign. She's nuts.

A Black soldier sees that the Doctor is smoking and approaches him with fixed bayonet at the ready. The Doctor starts with fright, throws his cigar on the asphalt, stamps it out and turns pale.

They say they have found him . . .

A roll of drums.

This is it.

They put the cloths over their heads.

INNKEEPER I'm not going to put a black cloth over my head!

SOMEBODY Why not?

INNKEEPER I won't do it.

JOURNEYMAN Orders are orders.

INNKEEPER What's the use of it?

DOCTOR They do that wherever one of them has been hiding. That's what you get for it. If we had handed him over straight away –

The Idiot appears.

INNKEEPER Why hasn't he got a black cloth?

SOMEBODY They believe him when he says he isn't one.

The Idiot grins and nods and walks on, scrutinising the

*masked people and grinning. Only the Innkeeper is still
standing unmasked.*

INNKEEPER I won't put a black cloth over my head!

MASKED FIGURE Then he'll be flogged.

INNKEEPER Me?

MASKED FIGURE He hasn't read the yellow poster.

INNKEEPER What do you mean, flogged?
A roll of drums.

MASKED FIGURE This is it.

MASKED FIGURE Keep calm, everyone.
A roll of drums.

INNKEEPER I'm the innkeeper. Why don't you believe me? I'm the
innkeeper, everybody knows who I am, I'm the innkeeper, your innkeeper . . .

MASKED FIGURE He's scared!

INNKEEPER Don't you recognize me?

MASKED FIGURE He's scared, he's scared!
Some masked figures laugh.

INNKEEPER I won't put a black cloth over my head . . .

MASKED FIGURE He'll be flogged.

INNKEEPER I'm not a Jew!

MASKED FIGURE He'll be put in a camp.

INNKEEPER I'm not a Jew!

MASKED FIGURE He hasn't read the yellow poster.

INNKEEPER Don't you recognize me? You there! I'm the innkeeper.
Who are you? You can't do this to me. You there! I'm
the innkeeper, I'm the innkeeper. Surely you recognize
me? You can't leave me in the lurch like this. You,
Schoolmaster! Who am I?
*The Innkeeper has taken hold of the Teacher, who has just
appeared with the Mother, unmasked.*

TEACHER So it was you who threw the stone, was it?
The Innkeeper drops the cobble stone.
Why do you say my son did it?
*The Innkeeper masks himself and mingles with the other
masked figures. The Teacher and the Mother stand alone.*
That's right, hide under a cloth!
A whistle.

MASKED FIGURE What does that mean?

MASKED FIGURE Shoes off.

MASKED FIGURE Who?

MASKED FIGURE Everyone.

MASKED FIGURE Now?

MASKED FIGURE Shoes off, shoes off.

MASKED FIGURE Why?

MASKED FIGURE He hasn't read the yellow poster . . .

All the masked figures kneel down to take off their shoes. Silence. It takes quite a time.

TEACHER Look at them all on their knees!

A Black soldier comes. The Teacher and the Mother also have to take a black cloth each.

MASKED FIGURE One whistle means shoes off. According to the poster. And two whistles mean march.

MASKED FIGURE Barefoot?

MASKED FIGURE What did he say?

MASKED FIGURE Shoes off, shoes off.

MASKED FIGURE And three whistles means cloth off.

MASKED FIGURE Why cloth off?

MASKED FIGURE All according to the poster.

MASKED FIGURE What did he say?

MASKED FIGURE All according to the poster.

MASKED FIGURE What do two whistles mean?

MASKED FIGURE March?

MASKED FIGURE Why barefoot?

MASKED FIGURE And three whistles mean cloth off.

MASKED FIGURE Where are we to put our shoes?

MASKED FIGURE Why cloth off?

MASKED FIGURE Where are we to put our shoes?

MASKED FIGURE Cloth off means he's found the Jew.

MASKED FIGURE All according to the poster.

MASKED FIGURE No Andorran has anything to fear.

MASKED FIGURE What did he say?

MASKED FIGURE No Andorran has anything to fear.

MASKED FIGURE Where are we to put our shoes?

The Teacher, unmasked, walks in among the masked figures and is the only one standing up.

TEACHER Andri is my son.

MASKED FIGURE That's not our fault!

TEACHER Do you hear what I say?

MASKED FIGURE What did he say?

MASKED FIGURE He says Andri is his son.

MASKED FIGURE Then why is he hiding?

TEACHER I say Andri is my son.

MASKED FIGURE Anyhow, he threw the stone.

TEACHER Which of you says that?

MASKED FIGURE Where are we to put our shoes?

TEACHER Why do you lie? One of you did it. Why do you say my son did it –

A roll of drums.

You don't want to know the truth. Cover it up with a cloth! You don't want to know. Cover it up with a cloth! You'll still have your murderer serving you. What does it matter, so long as the innkeeper is still the innkeeper, the doctor still the medical officer. Just look at them! See the way they put out their shoes in a line. All according to the poster! And one of them is a murderer. Cover it up with a cloth! They only hate the one who reminds them of it –

A roll of drums.

What a people you are! God in heaven, who fortunately for you doesn't exist, what a people you are!

Enter the Soldier with the drum.

SOLDIER Ready? On your feet! Everybody over there! Take your shoes.

All the masked figures stand up with their shoes in their hands.

Put your shoes on the ground. But tidily. Like in the Army. Understand? Shoe next to shoe. Got it? The Army is responsible for law and order. And no answering back.

The Soldier examines the row of shoes.

I said shoe next to shoe. What sort of impression is that going to make?

MASKED FIGURE I'm the innkeeper.

SOLDIER Too far back!
The masked figure straightens out his shoes.
Right, everybody over there at the double. I shall read
out the order again.
Quiet.
'Citizens of Andorra! The Jew Inspection is a measure for
the protection of the population in liberated areas, and for
the restoration of law and order. No Andorran has any-
thing to fear. For instructions see yellow poster.' Quiet!
'Andorra, 15th September, Commander-in-Chief.' –
Why haven't you got a cloth over your head?

TEACHER Where is Andri? Where is my son?

SOLDIER He's here, don't worry, he didn't slip through our fingers.
He'll march. Barefoot like everyone else.

TEACHER Andri is my son.

SOLDIER We shall soon see about that –
A roll of drums.
Get back! Dress by the right! Close up!
The masked figures form up.
All right then, citizens of Andorra, do you understand?
Not a word is to be spoken when the Jew Detector is
here. Is that clear? Everything must be done right, that's
important. When the Jew Detector whistles, stop immediately. Understand? You're not expected to come to
attention. Is that clear? Only the Army comes to attention, because they have practised it. Anyone who is not
a Jew will be free to go. That is to say, you will go straight
back to work. I shall beat the drum.
The Soldier does so.
Then you will walk forward one after the other. Anyone
who doesn't stop when the Jew Detector whistles will be
shot out of hand. Is that clear?
The ringing of a bell.

TEACHER Why isn't the priest here?

SOLDIER He'll be praying for the Jew!

TEACHER The priest knows the truth –
Enter the Jew Detector.

SOLDIER Silence!

*The Black soldiers present arms and stand rigidly in this
position until the Jew Detector, who behaves like a simple
official, has sat down in the armchair in the centre of the
square. The soldiers then order arms. The Jew Detector
takes off his pince-nez, polishes them, puts them on again.
The Teacher and the Mother are now also masked. The
Jew Detector waits until the bell has stopped ringing, then he
gives a sign and two blasts are blown on a whistle.*

SOLDIER First one!

Nobody moves.

Come on, come on!

The Idiot is the first to move.

Not you!

Nervous laughter among the masked figures.

Silence!

A drumbeat.

What's the matter, damn you? All you've got to do is
walk across the square.

No one moves.

No Andorran has anything to fear . . .

Barblin, masked, steps forward.

Come on!

*Barblin goes up to the Jew Detector and throws the black
cloth down at his boots.*

Hey, what's the idea?

BARBLIN This is the sign.

Movement among the masked figures.

Tell him, no Andorran will cross the square! Not one of
us! Then let them flog us! Tell him! Then let them shoot
us all!

*Two Black soldiers seize Barblin, who struggles in vain.
No one moves. The Black soldiers all round have brought
their guns into the firing position. All without a sound.
Barblin is dragged away.*

SOLDIER . . . All right, now get moving. One after the other. Have
we got to flog you? Come on, next one. One after the
other.

Now they start walking.

Slowly, slowly! Next one!

Those who have gone past remove the cloths from their heads.

The cloths are to be folded up. But tidily, I said. Is this country a pigsty? The national emblem must be in the top right-hand corner. What will our foreign friends think of us?

Others walk too slowly.

Get a move on, can't you.

The Jew Detector studies their walk carefully, but with the casualness of habit and bored by his own self-confidence. One figure trips over the cobble stone.

Just look at that!

MASKED FIGURE My name is Prader.

SOLDIER Come on.

MASKED FIGURE Who tripped me up?

SOLDIER Nobody tripped you up.

The Carpenter takes off his cloth.

SOLDIER Come on, I said, come on. The next. And those who have gone past are to take their shoes at once. Do I have to tell you everything, God damn it? Is this a kindergarten?

CARPENTER Somebody tripped me up.

SOLDIER Silence!

One figure goes in the wrong direction.

You're like a bunch of chickens!

A few who have already gone past giggle.

MASKED FIGURE I'm the medical officer.

SOLDIER All right, all right.

DOCTOR *takes off his cloth.*

SOLDIER Take your shoes.

DOCTOR I can't see when I have a cloth over my head. I'm not used to it. How can I walk when I can't see the ground?

SOLDIER Come on, I said, come on.

DOCTOR It's an impertinence!

SOLDIER The next.

Drumbeat.

Can't you put your damn shoes on at home? I told you, those who have been passed are to take their shoes and go. What are you standing around gawping for?

Drumbeat.

Next.

DOCTOR Where are my shoes? Somebody has taken my shoes. Those aren't my shoes.

SOLDIER Why pick on that pair?

DOCTOR They are standing in my place.

SOLDIER You really are like a lot of kids!

DOCTOR Well, are those my shoes?

Drumbeat.

I'm not going without my shoes.

SOLDIER Don't start kicking up a fuss!

DOCTOR I'm not going barefoot. I'm not used to it. And speak properly to me, I won't be spoken to in that tone.

SOLDIER Well, what's the matter with you?

DOCTOR I'm not kicking up a fuss.

SOLDIER What the hell do you want?

DOCTOR My shoes.

The Jew Detector gives a sign. A blast is blown on the whistle.

SOLDIER I'm on duty!

Drumbeat.

Next.

No one moves.

DOCTOR Those aren't my shoes!

SOLDIER *takes the shoes from his hand.*

DOCTOR I shall lodge a complaint, yes, I shall lodge a complaint, someone has moved my shoes, I shan't budge a step, and certainly not if I'm shouted at.

SOLDIER Who do these shoes belong to?

DOCTOR They're not mine –

SOLDIER Who do these shoes belong to?

He puts them down at the front by the footlights.

We shall see!

DOCTOR I know very well who they belong to.

SOLDIER Get a move on!

Drumbeat.

Next.

No one moves.

DOCTOR Here they are!

No one moves.

SOLDIER Scared again, are we? Come on!

Once more they go one after the other. The procedure has become automatic so that it is now tedious. One of those who has walked past the Jew Detector and now takes the cloth from his head is the Journeyman.

JOURNEYMAN What was that about the national emblem?

SOMEONE Top right-hand corner.

JOURNEYMAN Has he been through yet?

The Jew Detector gives a sign. Three blasts are blown on the whistle.

SOLDIER Stop!

The masked figure stands still.

Off with your cloth!

The masked figure doesn't move.

Off with your cloth, Jew, do you hear!

The Soldier goes up to the masked figure and takes off his cloth. It is the Somebody, rigid with terror.

That's not him. He only looks like that because he's scared. It's not him. There's nothing to be scared about, man! He looks quite different when he's happy . . .

The Jew Detector has risen, walks round the Somebody and scrutinizes him for a long time like an indifferent but conscientious official. The Somebody's appearance visibly changes. The Jew Detector holds his ballpoint pen under the Somebody's chin.

SOLDIER Head up, man. Don't stare down at the ground like one of them!

The Jew Detector also studies his feet, sits down again and gives a negligent sign.

Clear off!

Tension relaxes in the crowd.

DOCTOR He doesn't make mistakes. What did I say? He doesn't make mistakes, he has an eye for it . . .

Drumbeat.

SOLDIER Next.

They start walking again in single file.

What sort of filthy behaviour is that? Can't you use your own handkerchief when you sweat? Whatever next!
A masked figure picks up the cobble-stone.
What do you think you're doing?

MASKED FIGURE I'm the innkeeper –

SOLDIER What are you messing about with that stone for?

MASKED FIGURE I'm the innkeeper – I – I –
The Innkeeper remains masked.

SOLDIER That's no reason to wet yourself!
There are giggles here and there, as people giggle over a well-liked but ridiculous figure; in the midst of this nervous hilarity come three blasts on the whistle, following a sign from the Jew Detector.

SOLDIER Stop. –
The Teacher takes off his cloth.
Not you, that one there, the other one!
The masked figure does not move.
Off with your cloth!
The Jew Detector stands up.

DOCTOR He has an eye for it. What did I say? He can see by the walk . . .

SOLDIER Three paces forward!

DOCTOR He's got him . . .

SOLDIER Three paces back!
The masked figure obeys.
Laugh!

DOCTOR He can tell by the laugh . . .

SOLDIER Laugh, or they'll fire.
The masked figure tries to laugh.
Louder!
The masked figure tries to laugh.

DOCTOR That's a Jew's laugh . . .
The Soldier pushes the masked figure.

SOLDIER Off with your cloth, Jew, there's no help for you. Off with your cloth. Show your face. Or they'll fire.

TEACHER Andri!

SOLDIER I shall count three.
The masked figure does not move.

One –

TEACHER No!

SOLDIER Two –

The Teacher pulls off the figure's cloth.

Three . . .

TEACHER My son!

The Jew Detector walks round Andri, examining him.

He is my son!

The Jew Detector examines Andri's feet, then gives a sign, just as negligently as before but a different sign, and two Black soldiers take charge of Andri.

CARPENTER Let's go.

MOTHER *steps forward and takes off her cloth.* No!

SOLDIER What the hell do you want?

MOTHER I shall tell the truth.

SOLDIER Is Andri your son?

MOTHER No.

SOLDIER Did you hear that! Did you hear that!

MOTHER But Andri is my husband's son –

INNKEEPER Let her prove it.

MOTHER It's true. And Andri didn't throw the stone, I know that too, because he was at home when it happened. I swear to that. I was at home myself. I know that and I swear it by Almighty God who is our judge in eternity.

INNKEEPER She's lying.

MOTHER It's true! Let him go!

The Jew Detector stands up again.

SOLDIER Silence!

The Jew Detector goes up to Andri and repeats the examination, then he empties out Andri's trouser pockets; coins fall out; the Andorrans recoil from the rolling money as though it were lava; the Soldier laughs.

Jew money.

DOCTOR He doesn't make mistakes . . .

TEACHER What do you mean, Jew money? It's your money, our money. What else have you got in your own pockets?

The Jew Detector feels Andri's hair.

Andri, why don't you speak?

ANDRI *smiles.*

TEACHER He is my son, he mustn't die, my son, my son!

The Jew Detector leaves; the Blacks present arms; the Soldier takes charge.

SOLDIER Where did you get that ring?

CARPENTER He has got valuables too . . .

SOLDIER Give it here!

ANDRI No.

SOLDIER Come on, hand it over!

ANDRI No – please . . .

SOLDIER Or they'll hack your finger off.

ANDRI No! No!

Andri struggles.

CARPENTER Look how he fights for his valuables . . .

DOCTOR Let's go . . .

Andri is surrounded by Black soldiers and out of sight when he gives vent to a scream; then silence. Andri is led away.

TEACHER That's it. Slink away to your homes – You didn't see it, you know nothing – go home and look at yourselves in your mirrors and be sick, be sick.

The Andorrans disappear in all directions, everyone taking his shoes.

SOLDIER He won't be needing shoes any more.

The Soldier goes.

SOMEBODY The poor Jew –

INNKEEPER What can we do about it.

CARPENTER I could do with a brandy. That business with the finger was going too far . . .

DOCTOR I could do with a brandy myself.

CARPENTER His shoes are still there.

DOCTOR Let's go inside.

CARPENTER That business with the finger was going too far . . .

The Carpenter, the Doctor and the Innkeeper disappear into the inn. The stage grows dark; the juke-box begins to play of its own accord, the same record. When the stage lights up again, Barblin is on her knees whitewashing the asphalt of the square; her head has been shaved. Enter the Priest. The music stops.

BARBLIN I'm whitewashing, I'm whitewashing.

PRIEST Barblin!

BARBLIN Why shouldn't I whitewash my father's house, Reverend Father?

PRIEST You're talking wildly.

BARBLIN I'm whitewashing.

PRIEST That isn't your father's house, Barblin.

BARBLIN I'm whitewashing, I'm whitewashing.

PRIEST There's no sense in it.

BARBLIN There's no sense in it.

Enter the Innkeeper.

INNKEEPER What is she doing?

BARBLIN There are his shoes.

INNKEEPER *is about to fetch the shoes.*

BARBLIN Don't touch them!

PRIEST She has lost her reason.

BARBLIN I'm whitewashing, I'm whitewashing. What are you doing? If you can't see what I see, then you can see what I'm doing – I'm whitewashing.

INNKEEPER Stop that!

BARBLIN Blood, blood, blood everywhere.

INNKEEPER Those are my tables!

BARBLIN My tables, your tables, our tables.

INNKEEPER Make her stop it!

BARBLIN Who are you?

PRIEST I've tried everything.

BARBLIN I'm whitewashing, I'm whitewashing, so that we shall have a white Andorra, you murderers, a snow-white Andorra; I shall whitewash all of you, all of you.

Enter the former Soldier.

Tell him to leave me alone, Father, he has his eye on me, Father, I'm engaged.

SOLDIER I'm thirsty.

BARBLIN He doesn't know me.

SOLDIER Who is she?

BARBLIN The Jew's whore, Barblin.

SOLDIER Go away!

BARBLIN Who are you?

Barblin laughs.

Where has your drum got to?

SOLDIER Stop laughing!

BARBLIN Where have you taken my brother?

Enter the Carpenter.

Where have you come from, all of you? Where are you going to, all of you? Why don't you go home, all of you, all of you, and hang yourselves?

CARPENTER What did she say?

BARBLIN Him too!

INNKEEPER She's off her rocker.

SOLDIER Get rid of her.

BARBLIN I'm whitewashing.

CARPENTER What's the idea of that?

BARBLIN I'm whitewashing, I'm whitewashing.

Enter the Doctor.

Have you seen a finger?

DOCTOR *speechless.*

BARBLIN Haven't you seen a finger?

SOLDIER That's enough of that!

PRIEST Leave her alone.

INNKEEPER She's a public nuisance.

CARPENTER Tell her to leave us alone.

INNKEEPER What can we do about it?

JOURNEYMAN I warned her.

DOCTOR The proper place for her is a lunatic asylum.

BARBLIN *stares.*

PRIEST Her father has hanged himself in the schoolroom. She is looking for her father, she is looking for her hair, she is looking for her brother.

All, apart from the Priest and Barblin, go into the inn.

Barblin, do you hear who is speaking to you?

BARBLIN *whitewashes the asphalt.*

PRIEST I've come to take you home.

BARBLIN I'm whitewashing.

PRIEST I'm Father Benedict.

BARBLIN *whitewashes the asphalt.*

PRIEST I'm Father Benedict.

BARBLIN Where were you, Father Benedict, when they took away
our brother like a beast to the slaughter, like a beast to
the slaughter, where were you? You have turned black,
Father Benedict . . .

PRIEST *says nothing.*

BARBLIN Father is dead.

PRIEST I know, Barblin.

BARBLIN And my brother?

PRIEST I pray for Andri every day.

BARBLIN And my hair?

PRIEST Your hair, Barblin, will grow again –

BARBLIN Like the grass out of the graves.

*The Priest starts to lead Barblin away, but she suddenly
stops and turns back to the shoes.*

PRIEST Barblin – Barblin . . .

BARBLIN Those are his shoes. Don't touch them. When he comes
back, those are his shoes.

Curtain.

Triptych

Three Scenic Panels

translated by

Geoffrey Skelton

The First Panel

Characters

The widow
Her daughter
Roger
Francine
A young clergyman
Funeral guests
An invalid
A child (non-speaking)
The deceased husband (non-speaking)

The sound of a bell tolling in a cemetery chapel; then silence and light: an empty white rocking chair, otherwise nothing. The stage is blacked out, except for a bright area the size of a living room. The widow, aged about sixty, comes in, and the first funeral guest.

GUEST: Dear old Proll!

WIDOW: Yes—

GUEST: The last time I saw him was at Easter a year ago. He was in splendid shape.

WIDOW: Yes—

GUEST: How we laughed!

WIDOW: Yes—

The widow struggles against tears.

GUEST: Sophie?!

The widow pulls herself together.

GUEST: He had a good death. Not many people nowadays have the good fortune to die at home, and seventy is a good age, after all.

The widow sobs, as the funeral guest stands helplessly beside her; it takes her some time to get a grip on herself again.

WIDOW: I can't really take it in. I still see him. Sitting there in his chair. I can see him. All the time I can hear what Matthis is thinking.

The funeral guest takes a pipe from his pocket.

GUEST: I can understand that.

A young clergyman appears to one side of the scene; he turns to the audience as if to a congregation of mourners.

CLERGYMAN: "But some of them said, 'Could not this man, who opened the blind man's eyes, have done something to keep Lazarus from dying?' Jesus again sighed deeply, then he went over to the tomb. It was a cave, with a stone placed against it. Jesus said, 'Take away the stone.' Martha, the dead man's sister, said to him, 'Sir, by now there will be a stench; he has been there four days.' Jesus said, 'Did I not tell you that IF YOU HAVE FAITH YOU WILL SEE THE GLORY OF GOD?' So they removed the stone. Then Jesus looked upwards and said, 'Father, I thank thee; thou hast heard me. I knew already that thou always hearest me, but I spoke for the sake of the people standing around, that they might believe that thou didst send me.' Then he raised his voice in a great cry: 'Lazarus, come forth.' The dead man came out, his hands and feet swathed in linen bands, his face wrapped in a cloth. Jesus said, 'Loose him; let him go.' " Amen.

The playing of an organ is heard, short and not too loud, during which the deceased man comes in, wearing everyday clothes; he sits down in the white rocking chair, unnoticed by the widow and the funeral guest, and remains motionless, his eyes open.

CLERGYMAN: "Although the doors were locked, Jesus came and stood among them, saying, 'Peace be with you!' Then he said to Thomas, 'Reach your finger here; see my hands. Reach your hand here and put it into my side. Be unbelieving no longer, but believe.' Thomas said, 'My Lord and my God!' Jesus said, 'Because you have seen me you have found faith. HAPPY ARE THEY WHO NEVER SAW ME AND YET HAVE FOUND FAITH.' "

The other funeral guests come in and group themselves inside the living room. There is a certain dignity in their silence, which is maintained as they greet one another. Not all are dressed for a funeral: there is a young woman in trousers, her only token of mourning a black head scarf; a youngish man is wearing a black turtleneck sweater. They stand there, waiting. The pause continues so long that dignity begins to turn into embarrassment. At last the daughter arrives, bearing a tray with sandwiches, and the first to help himself is the man in the sweater.

ROGER: Am I hungry! Starving—though I only had breakfast two hours ago.

He takes another sandwich.

ROGER: Thanks.

The daughter moves on.

WIDOW: Haven't you got a napkin?

ROGER: I've never spoken at a funeral before.

WIDOW: I'll fetch you a napkin.

The widow goes out.

DAUGHTER: Drinks are in the garden.

The funeral guests help themselves without haste.

GUEST: Have you got a match?

Continuing to speak in a low tone:

> That young man who spoke at the cemetery—in his sweater—I
> must admit I found it a bit embarrassing. . . .

The young clergyman approaches Roger, who is eating.

CLERGYMAN: Where is Mrs. Proll?

ROGER: No idea.

CLERGYMAN: I want to say good-bye.

Roger wipes his fingers on his handkerchief.

ROGER: Don't we all?

*For a while all the guests occupy themselves with eating, except
the young clergyman, who is trying to find the widow; Roger, who
has already eaten; the young woman in trousers, who is standing
to one side, smoking; and the funeral guest with his pipe. The
daughter returns and distributes paper napkins.*

DAUGHTER: The drinks are in the garden.

*The funeral guests go out slowly, each standing back to allow
precedence to another. There remain: Roger and the young
clergyman, and in the background the young woman in trousers,
smoking, now with an ashtray in her hand. The deceased man sits
in the white rocking chair, the others unaware of him.*

ROGER: Did you know him personally?

CLERGYMAN: No.

Roger lights a cigarette.

ROGER: He didn't believe in a life after death. I knew him, you
know. I spoke as I'm sure he would have liked.

The young clergyman remains silent.

ROGER: I thought a great deal of old Proll—

The young woman comes forward.

FRANCINE: Here is an ashtray.

ROGER: Oh, thanks very much.

FRANCINE: It's the only one here.

Roger taps his cigarette on it.

ROGER: Do you believe in a life after death?

She stubs out her cigarette in the ashtray.

FRANCINE: I really don't know. . . .

Roger looks at her.

FRANCINE: I say I don't know.

A late funeral guest arrives, an old man using two walking sticks; he looks around the room in some embarrassment.

ROGER: I don't doubt the existence of eternity. But what does it mean? For me it is the eternity of what once existed.

The invalid approaches.

INVALID: Where is Mrs. Proll?

ROGER: She went to get a napkin.

The invalid limps off.

ROGER: All I know is that human consciousness must have a biological basis. Even a bang on the head can make me unconscious. So how can my consciousness continue to exist once my brain has been destroyed—for example, by putting a bullet through my head?. . . What I'm really saying is that death, as a biological fact, is of no great significance: all it does is confirm the laws of Nature. But there is another side of death: its mysteriousness. I'm not saying there's nothing in that—just that it remains a mystery. And even if you reject the idea of an eternal life for every individual, something mysterious still remains, the feeling that death gives us the true picture of our lives: we live at last definitively.

FRANCINE: And what does that mean?

ROGER: It is *what* we have lived that counts. The various events of our lives, each one in its own place and time—there they stand, unalterable. And in that sense eternal.

The young clergyman is silent.

FRANCINE: Have you ever lost someone who was dearer to you than any other?

ROGER: Why do you ask that?

FRANCINE: Because you think so logically.

The widow comes in with a napkin.

CLERGYMAN: Mrs. Proll, I have to leave now.

The clergyman gives her his hand.

CLERGYMAN: The truth is the truth, whether your dear departed husband cared to see it or not. And he will see it, Mrs. Proll, I'm sure of that.

WIDOW: Thank you, Parson.

CLERGYMAN: A light will come, a light such as we have never seen before, and a birth without flesh; and we shall be different from what we were after our first birth, since we shall have lived. We shall feel no pain and shall no longer fear death, for we are born into eternity.

The widow accompanies the young clergyman out.

ROGER: I didn't mean to hurt anybody.

Voices in the garden.

FRANCINE: We can get drinks in the garden.

Roger and Francine go off into the garden. Only old Proll remains, in his white rocking chair. The voices in the garden are not loud but have become less inhibited. The widow returns:

WIDOW: Matthis, I know you didn't want a clergyman. How often have I heard you say that! But it couldn't be helped.

Laughter from a group in the garden.

WIDOW: They're all out in the garden now.

Silence in the garden.

WIDOW: You had a good death, Matthis. They all say that. Not many people nowadays have the good fortune to die at home. Remember your poor sister. And seventy is the Biblical age. . . . Matthis, is that what you want—that I should be afraid of you? I never treated you like an imbecile. How could you say such a thing? And in front of the doctor, too. And then you said it again to him: My wife treats me like a complete idiot. . . . Oh, Matthis!. . . What are you staring at?. . . I tell you it couldn't be helped, but you don't believe me. I told the young parson you never went to church—of course I told him that. . . . Why don't you look at me? Matthis, how cruel you can be!

Pause.

WIDOW: Oh, Matthis, my Matthis!

Pause.

WIDOW: It's a week now since you went out fishing for the last time. Exactly a week. And your shoes still everywhere, so that I find myself thinking, when it starts to rain: He'll be coming home soon.... You don't know what it means to be a widow. When the bells began to ring, I don't mind telling you, I felt relieved. And so did all the others.

Pause.

WIDOW: Not one of your Spanish War comrades has turned up. Perhaps they're all dead. And what can I say to these people? It was always you who did the talking....

Voices in the garden.

WIDOW: It was quite right what that young parson said: death should be a warning to us, and make us look at each other daily in a spirit of love. And there I was sitting beside you the whole night long, Matthis, and suddenly you tell me you want to be alone. That's what you said. And next morning, when I brought you up a cup of tea, you were dead. It was always the way *you* wanted it.

Pause.

WIDOW: You weren't afraid of death. How often you said that! You never thought of anyone but yourself—

From the garden the sound of a glass breaking.

WIDOW: We thought there would be at least a hundred people, and it would be too cramped in here. Lucky it's not raining... Matthis, I'm speaking to you.... Matthis! What have I done?... Don't you recognize your own Sophie?... I sent for the doctor, I nursed you, Matthis, day and night.... I lived with you for twenty-six years, didn't I?... Your shoes are everywhere, and what am I to do with all your rock crystals? It's not as if they're worth much, and a whole cabinet full of them .... I always believed in you, Matthis, you could never bear for me to show any doubt—you would just go off again with your fishing rod.... I firmly believed you had put everything in order—but nothing is in order.

Another short burst of laughter from the garden.

WIDOW: They're all remembering your jokes, and you leave me here alone.... Oh, Matthis, when I think of everything I put up with just to make sure you would always come home, and now—you want me to be afraid of you, Matthis, you don't love me.... Is it my fault you had to die?... Matthis, you

look younger now, but I can still recognize you, I knew you
when you were younger, didn't I? And now you just stare in
front of you, as if you didn't know me. . . . What have I
done? . . . I shall die, too, some day.

The doorbell rings.

WIDOW: All of us must die.

The doorbell rings again.

WIDOW: Still, someone spoke the way you would have liked. He
meant well, I think, that young man, but most of them found
it embarrassing.

The daughter passes through.

WIDOW: In your will not a single affectionate word. You know
that? Not one word of love . . . What did you marry me for? . . .
You wanted to be left alone. That was your last word—you
never bothered about what it means to be left a widow, you
always talked about your mother, how she blossomed. That's
what you said: blossomed. But your mother, when she
became a widow, was twenty years younger than I am. . . .
Matthis, I'm not complaining. You always think I'm complaining,
and then you just sit there in your rocking chair, not saying a
word. . . . God knows, my life has not been an easy one.

The daughter returns.

DAUGHTER: Someone has ordered a taxi.

The daughter goes into the garden.

WIDOW: Why do you stare at me like that?

The daughter's voice in the garden:

DAUGHTER: Who ordered a taxi?

WIDOW: Oh, I know your silence, Matthis, and the way you pick
up your fishing rod. Without saying a word. I know, all right.
And when I go to look for you because it's already dark,
because I'm anxious—you're not there beside the stream. . . .
Oh, the things I put up with, Matthis, just to keep us together!

Silence.

WIDOW: What have I said now—to make you grin like that?
Matthis, you're grinning! . . . I didn't treat you like an imbecile,
though maybe that model of yours did. Stare away! I forbade
her to come to the house after the funeral. What am I supposed
to do: express my sympathies to her? But of course I couldn't

keep her from coming to the cemetery and standing there with just a single rose in her hand.

She weeps silently.

WIDOW: They all show compassion toward me—all except you.

She pulls herself together.

WIDOW: You want to punish me for still being alive!

She starts to sob.

WIDOW: And how could you say to me—after twenty-six years, Matthis—that you found me unattractive? That's what you said: intellectually unattractive.

The first funeral guest comes in from the garden.

GUEST: Sophie.

WIDOW: You're going already?

GUEST: My taxi's here.

He gives her his hand.

GUEST: My dear Sophie—

Withdrawing his hand:

GUEST: Look after yourself.

The funeral guest goes off.

WIDOW: Yes, that's what you said, Matthis, as I was holding your hand. Three times you said it: that you wanted to be alone. . . . I made some more tea and brought it to your bed, and you said: Thank you for the tea.

Speaking as if to a disobedient child:

Matthis, why have you got dressed again?

Voices in the garden.

WIDOW: Matthis, I must go and join the guests—it was on my account they came, after all. . . . I haven't even thanked them yet for their flowers.

She straightens her hair.

WIDOW: And there is one thing you must understand, Matthis: one doesn't start going through someone's drawers the minute he is dead. You did tell me once, I know, but with all the things one has to think of, and then the undertakers having to know immediately whether cremation or burial . . . Ilse took a great deal off my shoulders, but that was something she couldn't have known. Why did you never speak to your daughter? It was only last night I found your note, Matthis, and by then it was too late. Please try to understand. They have to make their arrangements, too. . . . What are you staring at? . . . You always made the decisions, Matthis, but there's one thing I refuse to be deprived of: my belief that we shall meet again.

The funeral guests enter in groups.

WIDOW: You are going already?

Taking leave of the widow:

WOMAN: Sophie—

MAN: Mrs. Proll—

As they go off:

MAN: Just what I was thinking. Why do we meet so seldom? There are other occasions than funerals.

A mother with a small child approaches the widow:

MOTHER: You shake hands, too, dear.

The child is unwilling.

MOTHER: What manners!

Two men come in:

FIRST: Well, just look at me! Five pounds gone within a week. You can eat as much as you want, but no carbohydrates. As much meat as you like, even bacon. But no potatoes, no bread, no starch. And swimming is no help at all.

SECOND: Bacon has the most calories.

FIRST: It's not a question of calories—

They approach the widow:

FIRST: You'll call us?

As they go off:

FIRST: I must say, your sister is very composed.

While the other funeral guests are silently taking leave of the widow, Roger and Francine come in, the last to leave the garden.

FRANCINE: Oh, no, I don't mean Swedenborg and other people like that who rely on their hallucinations. I mean, it's not as

simple as you think. No human consciousness without a
biological basis. How do you know? A disembodied soul, not
even Plato could find a proof for that—quite right—but all the
same, Plato thought it not improbable. As Bloch does, too,
incidentally. There's a logic larger than the ordinary one.

The invalid approaches the widow.

INVALID: My dear Mrs. Proll.

Introducing himself:

INVALID: My name is Luchsinger. We were friends, Matthis and
I, we used to row in the same boat crew, though, goodness, it
was long enough ago, and then one goes on living in the same
town without ever seeing each other again—

He gives her his hand.

INVALID: Mrs. Proll.

WIDOW: Thank you for your huge wreath.

INVALID: I still feel so upset.

She releases his hand.

WIDOW: I'll see you out.

*The widow goes out with the invalid; only Roger and Francine
still have to take leave of her.*

FRANCINE: Will you hold my bag?

*She gives him her handbag, unties her black head scarf, shakes out
her hair, and combs it with her fingers before fastening the black
scarf on her head again.*

ROGER: I'll have to ask you for your name again.

FRANCINE: Francine.

ROGER: You're going into town, aren't you? I'd be glad to give
you a lift. I'm going there, too.

As they go off:

ROGER: What is your thesis about?

*The deceased man alone in his white rocking chair. Silence. The
deceased man gets up and goes out in the other direction. The
widow returns, sees the empty chair, and stops, as if frozen.*

WIDOW: Matthis!

The daughter comes in with the empty glasses.

DAUGHTER: I have to be back at work at two o'clock. But I'll wash up the glasses first. . . .

The daughter goes off.

WIDOW: Matthis, where are you?

The Second Panel

Characters

The old man
The garage mechanic
Katrin
The young clergyman
The neighbour with the flute
The tramp
Xavier
Klas
The old woman
An airline pilot (non-speaking)
The convict
A young Spaniard (non-speaking)
Ilse
A man with roses
A young bank clerk
Jonas
The invalid
A child (non-speaking)

In the foreground the white rocking chair, which is empty.
The stage is wide and empty and white. Somewhere on it old
Proll is standing, with a fishing rod in his hand, as if beside a
stream; not far from him, a garage mechanic in overalls is sitting.
For a short while one hears birds twittering. Then silence again.
In the background the young clergyman appears; he looks around
as if searching for someone, then comes to a stop. The sound of
birds again, followed shortly by renewed silence. The white light
remains unchanged.

OLD MAN: I'm fishing.

MECHANIC: I can see that.

OLD MAN: Then why ask?

The old man pulls in his line, which is empty, and casts it again.

MECHANIC: There used to be birch trees here—

Katrin comes in and sits down on the white rocking chair.

KATRIN: Yes, it was here I once sat. . . . Nothing is happening
   that hasn't happened before, and I'm now in my early thirties.
   There's nothing more to come. I sat rocking myself in this
   chair. Nothing more to come that I haven't already been
   through. And I shall remain in my early thirties. What I think,
   I have thought before. What I hear, I have already heard.

The sound of birds twittering.

KATRIN: It's April again.

The old man, fishing, and the garage mechanic:

MECHANIC: There used to be birch trees here, nothing but
   birches. And that was a real stream. Not a canal. In my time,
   that is. A stream with stones in it.

OLD MAN: That was a long time ago.

MECHANIC: You could catch trout here then.

OLD MAN: I know.

Pause.

OLD MAN: A stream with stones in it, that's right, and weeds covering the stones, so that you slipped when you tried to walk barefoot over them. And afterwards a green stain on your trousers—

He pulls in his line, which is empty.

MECHANIC: You're not catching anything.

The old man rebaits his hook, keeping silent as he does so; his manner shows him to be shortsighted.

OLD MAN: But you couldn't possibly remember the birches. When were the coachworks built? That's when the birch trees came down.

MECHANIC: I know that.

OLD MAN: How old are you, then?

MECHANIC: Forty-one.

The old man casts his line again.

OLD MAN: In those days I was still a schoolboy, and we used to catch the trout with our hands. Without a permit. That was forbidden. Only my father was allowed to catch them, with a rod. It was still a real stream then—

Pause.

MECHANIC: You should have struck then.

Pause.

OLD MAN: They all said: No new trousers for you, no new shoes, there's no meat, there's a slump going on. Only Father got sausages to eat.

The mechanic is silent.

OLD MAN: But it was long before the war that the birches were felled, and you say you're forty-one. So how can you possibly remember the birch trees and the stream?

Katrin in the white rocking chair; the young clergyman is now quite close to her; again one hears the birds twittering.

CLERGYMAN: Just listen to the birds!

Katrin, rocking herself:

KATRIN: Like in a cemetery . . . When I was a child, I used to walk through a cemetery every day, it was the shortest way to school, and in it there was a bronze bust, surrounded by

privet hedges: a man with a pointed beard. Not Lenin, but
some botanist. Later on I stopped being frightened of that
bust: he wasn't really looking at me. I touched his eyes once
with my finger: he wasn't really looking. I realized he wasn't at
all interested in the way people live now.

CLERGYMAN: May I ask you something?

KATRIN: Once someone cut back the privet, to keep the black
bust from being overgrown and to show the dates on the
pedestal: 1875 to 1917. A man in the best years of his life.
But I had the feeling he didn't want to return, even though the
birds were singing.

CLERGYMAN: Why did you take your own life?

KATRIN: That no longer interests me.

*A man comes in; he is in his shirt sleeves and is wearing slippers;
he is carrying a flute. He comes to a standstill and gazes around
him, as if looking for something.*

The old man, fishing, and the garage mechanic:

OLD MAN: Did you say something?

MECHANIC: No.

OLD MAN: Nor did I.

The old man pulls in his line, which is empty.

MECHANIC: Why choose here to fish?

OLD MAN: This is where I grew up. And went to school. There
used to be trout here, you said so yourself. This is where we
played cowboys and Indians. Where I once landed myself in
prison—but that was later on. . . .

The old man casts his line again.

*A young man comes in, dressed in military uniform; he has no
cap and no weapon, his uniform is torn in places and stained with
mud. He sees Katrin in the white rocking chair and comes to a
halt some distance away.*

The old man with the fishing rod and the garage mechanic:

OLD MAN: Jews! That's what my father always used to say:
they buy up all the land—for who else has money when there's
a slump? And they have ruined our countryside, the Jews.

MECHANIC: Well, it's true.

The man with the flute, standing to one side, begins practising.

KATRIN: Listen, Xavier, listen! Our neighbour's here, too. How awful! The dead never learn.

The man practises a difficult passage, then plays the whole melody through from the beginning, until he makes the same mistake again and breaks off.

KATRIN: Mr. Proll—!

OLD MAN: I'm fishing.

KATRIN: I'm sitting in your white chair. It's April. I've come to ask your advice—

The sound of birds twittering.

KATRIN: You'd rather not see me again, is that it, Mr. Proll?

A tramp appears and sits down on the ground, unnoticed by the others.

The old man, fishing, and the garage mechanic:

MECHANIC: Your name's Proll?

OLD MAN: Yes.

MECHANIC: Mine, too.

OLD MAN: You're also called Proll—?

He looks at the mechanic for the first time:

OLD MAN: I understand: you don't recognize me, for you never saw me as an old man. I lived longer than you did, Father.

MECHANIC: You're Matthis?

OLD MAN: People get shortsighted.

Both turn their attention back to the fishing rod.

MECHANIC: Why were you sent to prison?

OLD MAN: For evading conscription.

MECHANIC: What does that mean?

OLD MAN: Six months. Military detention, to be exact. Because I went off to Spain.

MECHANIC: Why Spain?

OLD MAN: To fight against Fascism. As it was then. You didn't live to see all that, Father.

Pause.

MECHANIC: You should have struck then!

OLD MAN: You think so?

MECHANIC: Well, of course.

The old man winds in his line, which is empty.

MECHANIC: You strike too late. That's what I was always telling you. Or too soon. You've always got your mind on other things. Or you don't fix the bait properly, though you've been shown often enough.

The garage mechanic rises:

MECHANIC: Here, give it to me!

He examines the fishing rod, the old man standing beside him like a son.

MECHANIC: How old was Mother when she died?

OLD MAN: You left her in debt, as you know. She had to go to work in a department store. Night work. Cleaning. She was a harder worker than you gave her credit for. Later she had a newsstand of her own, and went for a trip every year. A package tour to the Tirol or Venice, things like that. After your death she really blossomed. She used to say so herself: I've had more out of life since I've been a widow, she used to say.

MECHANIC: What are you using for bait?

The old man stoops down and picks up a can, which he holds out.

MECHANIC: Worms.

The garage mechanic takes out a worm and shows his son how to hold the rod while attaching the bait.

MECHANIC: Watch, now.

OLD MAN: Yes, Father.

MECHANIC: That's the way to do it.

OLD MAN: Yes, Father.

MECHANIC: And one more twist.

The garage mechanic casts the line.

MECHANIC: Isn't this my fishing rod?

OLD MAN: Yes, Father.

The tramp, crouched down alone:

TRAMP: Farther down the canal there are eleven foreign workers, but all they understand is Turkish. The boss, who skimped on the scaffolding, which was the reason it collapsed, is farther up the canal. And he doesn't understand Turkish.

CLERGYMAN: What is that supposed to mean?

TRAMP: There's no justice, Parson.

The garage mechanic, fishing, and the old man beside him:

MECHANIC: And you just up and went, leaving Mother at home—off to Spain!

OLD MAN: Yes, Father.

The garage mechanic is silent, watching the rod.

OLD MAN: Across the border on foot, then by rail as far as Lyons, where I'd been given an address. But it was a false one. I showed people my piece of paper, but there was no street of that name. Still, the taxi driver seemed to know what to do. He took me all through the town, charging nothing, and we were given something to eat and thirty French francs, a ticket to Marseilles—where I saw the sea for the first time in my life. The police in Marseilles had instructions to arrest people of our sort. We had to hang around in the harbour till we got the signal—from a policeman, in fact. It was a freighter, a French one, and next morning we landed in Valencia—

The garage mechanic pulls in the line, which is empty.

OLD MAN: Two weeks later we were at the front.

Katrin in the white rocking chair; the young man in military uniform watches her as she rocks.

XAVIER: Do you hear what I'm saying, Katrin?

KATRIN: I heard.

XAVIER: I'm talking to you, Katrin.

KATRIN: I know your lectures.

XAVIER: I don't think what I'm saying is nonsense. I mean about language. I'm not a linguist, but both of us know that the language you use is a man's language. Why do you keep quoting Sigmund Freud? Because your language doesn't

exist yet—the woman's language. How can a woman express
what she feels in this male syntax? When I read what women
are writing these days, I can understand it word for word, which
means that, when a woman wishes to express herself, she must
think like a man, she's at the mercy of this syntax that men
created for themselves. No sentence without a verb . . . Are
you listening? . . . How I should like for once to hear what
you are thinking, Katrin—you yourself, you as a woman!
That's what I mean—it won't be until women discover their
own language and until you see yourself as you are and express
what you feel, you, Katrin, you yourself as a woman, not
what Sigmund Freud or some other lord of creation has
invented for you—

Katrin has stopped rocking and is looking at him:

KATRIN: Xavier, we're dead.

He does not appear to hear her.

XAVIER: Ten whole days I waited for you.

KATRIN: I have listened to what you have to say. We can say it
all again, but it changes nothing, Xavier. Gradually one comes
to see that. You said my intelligence was one size too small,
and maybe you're right. We shouted at each other. We made
up and decided to begin again, from the start: we kissed, we
cooked a meal together and went to the seaside together, we
lived together—

XAVIER: We made up, didn't we?

KATRIN: Yes, Xavier, we kept making up.

XAVIER: Yet all the same you ran away.

Katrin starts rocking again.

XAVIER: Why are you silent?

KATRIN: I understand now.

XAVIER: Understand what?

KATRIN: That we just keep repeating ourselves.

Katrin is no longer rocking.

KATRIN: —we are dead, Xavier.

*The garage mechanic, fishing; the old man has gone, and the
young clergyman is standing beside the garage mechanic.*

CLERGYMAN: What's the name of this stream?

MECHANIC: Call this a stream? It was a stream once. Before the coachworks were built. Just take a look at the water. In my day you could see by looking in it whether the sky was overcast or not, what time of day it was. Is this water flowing, even? Can you tell? I can't.

Pause.

CLERGYMAN: I should like to ask you something.

MECHANIC: I was showing my son how to fish, but then off he goes, as always. I've shown him a hundred times. But he'll never learn.

CLERGYMAN: Was that your son?

MECHANIC: I'm a qualified mechanic. What can a man do when he's out of work? I got into debt renting a small filling station—

CLERGYMAN: SHELL.

MECHANIC: How did you know that?

CLERGYMAN: It's written on your back.

Pause.

CLERGYMAN: There's no time of day here.

The garage mechanic pulls in the line, which is empty.

CLERGYMAN: How did you die?

The garage mechanic casts the line again.

MECHANIC: Better ask my son.

The tramp, seated by himself:

TRAMP: Why doesn't he ask me? I died during a booze-up. Froze to death, I suppose. I was out for the count. Because I knew what lay ahead. I knew, all right. . . .

The old man, having left the garage mechanic fishing, is now standing before Katrin in the white rocking chair.

OLD MAN: Yes, Miss Schimanski, that was how you used to sit— just like that. In my chair. And sometimes you would rock it.

The sound of birds twittering.

KATRIN: It's nice here, Mr. Proll.

She rocks.

OLD MAN: You came to seek advice from an old man, and we

didn't even know each other. We were meeting for the first time.

KATRIN: The second.

OLD MAN: You said you'd been in my bookshop once before, but I hadn't noticed you. A lot of young people come to look at old books.

They regard each other.

KATRIN: You brought out some wine and two glasses.

OLD MAN: Yes.

KATRIN: You asked me what I did, how I earned my living, and I made you guess.

OLD MAN: Why didn't you want to tell me?

KATRIN: You didn't guess it.

OLD MAN: No.

KATRIN: I was glad of that.

Katrin removes her shoes.

OLD MAN: I didn't give you any advice, Katrin. I never even saw this young man. All I did was listen: Some dentist who wanted to marry you. A man of learning. That's what you said. And that you didn't love him. But a good fellow, and he knew your only reason for marrying would be so as not to have to go on working as a model. That's how I understood it: a good fellow who didn't want to turn you into an ordinary housewife. That's what you said. He knew you wanted to study.

KATRIN: Why are you looking at my feet?

OLD MAN: Because you have taken off your shoes.

KATRIN: Maybe I stayed too long.

OLD MAN: I was considering what advice to give a young lady in our society who had no wish to be a model, and you told me what you wanted to study—sociology, psychology.

Again the sound of birds twittering.

OLD MAN: Yes, Katrin Schimanski, that is just how you looked.

The tramp, sitting alone:

TRAMP: I don't hold out my hat now—the dead don't beg. They don't even curse. They don't piss, the dead don't, they don't stuff themselves with food and drink, they don't beat people,

the dead don't, they don't fuck. All they do is wander through
the eternity of the past and lick their stupid life stories till
they're licked right away.

He titters.

TRAMP: "La mort est successive."

Seeing that nobody reacts:

TRAMP: Diderot.

To the man with the flute:

TRAMP: Hey, feller, remember how we knocked heads once?
Though the knocking, to be frank, was all on your side. Once
on my arse, once on my head. But you were wearing a uniform
then. Am I right? A blue uniform with a white belt, and that
flute you're holding in your hand was a rubber truncheon.

Katrin in the white rocking chair and the old man:

KATRIN: You didn't give me any advice.

OLD MAN: No.

KATRIN: Why not?

OLD MAN: I knew you wouldn't take it, and that is also why
I never wrote to you.

Katrin laughs.

KATRIN: But, Mr. Proll, you did write to me!

OLD MAN: What do you mean?

Klas in pyjamas, gathering newspapers from the floor.

KATRIN: Klas—?

He continues gathering, as if he were alone.

KATRIN: What are you doing?

KLAS: Nothing, nothing at all.

KATRIN: I thought you had already read them.

KLAS: It's nothing, I say.

KATRIN: You and your tidying!

Klas carefully bundles the newspapers together.

KATRIN: Have you nothing better to do when you're at home than
go around checking whether all my bottles and tubes in the bathroom have their caps on, and shutting all the cabinet doors?

KLAS: Katrin—

KATRIN: I would have tidied up some time.

Katrin has leapt to her feet.

KLAS: What's the matter?

Katrin puts her hands over her ears.

KLAS: I'm not shouting, Katrin—

KATRIN: I get on your nerves!

KLAS: Not you, Katrin, just the hair in the toilet bowl—

KATRIN: Yes, I know!

KLAS: Then why don't you pull the chain?

KATRIN: I did pull it.

KLAS: Are you sure?

KATRIN: This is simply not true—

Klas stoops down.

KLAS: Here are your car keys.

KATRIN: Anything else?

KLAS: I'm not reproaching you, Katrin—we are living together, Katrin, and we are happy, it's only these trivial things that upset me so.

Silence.

OLD MAN: He's happy, he says.

KATRIN: I can't go on!

OLD MAN: She can't go on, she says.

Klas goes away, stooping again as he goes and picking up a brassiere as inconspicuously as possible.

KATRIN: That's how we spent our time. . . .

The sound of a toilet flushing.

OLD MAN: It's not meant as a reproach.

The man with the flute again practises the passage that always defeats him, starts from the beginning and comes once more to the difficult part, breaks off.

Katrin in the white rocking chair and the old man:

OLD MAN: I really can't remember writing to you after you were married. What did I say?

KATRIN: You gave me courage.

She rocks herself again:

KATRIN: Courage—just that . . . I can't remember the words, either. At first I thought it sad, that letter, but then it gave me courage: I ought not to sell myself. That, at any rate, was how I understood it. I should live with a man I loved, and altogether— It was a long letter, Mr. Proll, a fatherly one.

The sound of birds twittering.

OLD MAN: Now's it's April again.

A nurse comes in with a wheelchair in which an old woman is sitting.

OLD WOMAN: Here. Yes, it's nice here.

The nurse goes away, leaving the old woman in the wheelchair.

Katrin in the rocking chair and the old man:

OLD MAN: And what did we talk about then?

KATRIN: Have you forgotten that, too?

OLD MAN: Did I tell you about Spain again?

The sound of birds twittering.

OLD MAN: You got a divorce; it's April once more, and you have a boy friend, I hear, a student, and you're living together— yes . . . . And why did you come to me again?

Katrin rocks herself:

KATRIN: You told me about Spain.

The old man is silent.

KATRIN: What is it like to be old, Mr. Proll? Does one want to live through it all again, again and again?

Xavier and the young clergyman:

CLERGYMAN: How did you die?

XAVIER: Tragically!

CLERGYMAN: Why do you laugh?

XAVIER: Snow falling all night, fresh snow on a frozen surface,

then a thaw. Are you familiar with the mountains, Padre?
We'd already heard avalanches during the morning, and we
were pretty sure this steep slope wouldn't hold. I laughed when
I heard a sudden noise: Boom! Not loud, just a muffled
"Boom!"—as if the whole mountain were splitting. The first
thing to go was the snow barrier, as we feared; snow up to
our hips, you stand there as if you're stuck in cement and
can't move. Like in a dream. And then the real avalanche.

CLERGYMAN: You died for your country.

XAVIER: Suffocated for it. The nine others, too, probably the
whole patrol. Did you conduct the burial service?

CLERGYMAN: No.

XAVIER: The local people, who of course knew this slope well,
warned us about it, and I told our captain. But all he did was
roar at us: You shits, you shits! He insisted on our crossing
the slope—without him—as an exercise in obedience.

Xavier gazes around.

XAVIER: Why are none of these people alive?

*The tramp, all by himself, begins to recite, as if holding up
something at which he is looking:*

TRAMP: "Alas, poor Yorick! . . . he hath borne me on his back
a thousand times; and now, how abhorred in my imagination
it is! my gorge rises at it. Here hung those lips that I have
kiss'd I know not how oft. Where be your gibes now? your
gambols? your songs?"

He sees that nobody is listening.

TRAMP: I was listened to! I had the role of my life and twenty-
seven curtain calls every evening— One morning, when I woke
up, I was lying on a public bench, and the people were not
clapping, just passing by. I didn't need to bow any more. Or
go to rehearsals. All I needed was a piss, and that was just as
well, or I'd have gone on lying there forever—then instead of
later. . . . Are you listening, Parson? I'm telling how I came
to die. It took thirty years. You don't die all of a sudden.

*Xavier goes over to a man who is sitting and studying a map: a
pilot, as if in a cockpit, wearing a blue shirt with a tie, and badges
of rank on his shoulders; no cap, but earphones.*

XAVIER: Were you once alive?

The pilot does not hear him.

XAVIER: I remember reading the Air Ministry report—your last conversation with the control tower, recorded on a tape: WE HAVE TROUBLE WITH THE CABIN COMPRESSION —that was eleven minutes after takeoff, then: WE HAVE FIRE ON BOARD REQUEST AN IMMEDIATE LANDING OUR NAVIGATION IS NOT OK, and so on. You were told what to do: TURN RIGHT UNTIL I SAY STOP YOU ARE AT A VERY LOW SPEED COULD YOU INCREASE SPEED AND HEAD EAST. PLEASE INCREASE SPEED IF POSSIBLE. You heard all that: ALL UNDERSTOOD, and shortly afterwards GOOD-BYE EVERYBODY. That's what you said sixteen seconds before the crash: GOOD-BYE EVERYBODY,
The control tower repeated its instructions—

The pilot removes his earphones; a whistling tone is heard until he puts them on again.

XAVIER: Maybe I can show you on the map where you were at the end. . . . Incidentally, what you suspected was later confirmed. The experts, who spent months examining the wreckage, also believe there was a bomb in the rear luggage compartment, hence the loss of compression, the fire in the luggage compartment, the smoke in the cabin and later in the cockpit. I CAN'T SEE ANYTHING. Presumably you didn't obey the repeated instruction: OPEN YOUR WINDOW PLEASE. It wouldn't have helped much anyway, the experts think. The engines kept working right up to the end, but what happened to the steering they don't know—only you know that. . . . I made use of the report for my diploma. . . . Parts of a cheap altimeter were found in the wreckage, an instrument not belonging to the plane's equipment, and probably it was this that set the bomb off, when you reached three thousand meters. The plane couldn't be seen from the ground, but witnesses talked of hearing an explosion.

The pilot continues to study his map.

XAVIER: But why am I telling you all this?

The garage mechanic with the fishing rod; a convict comes in.

MECHANIC: There used to be birches standing here, and this was a real stream. The coachworks destroyed it all. They bought up the whole area. I was born here, but the Jews weren't—

He draws in his line, which is empty.

MECHANIC: You used to catch trout here.

He casts the line out again.

CONVICT: I didn't hang myself in my cell—often thought about it, but never did it. You get time off for good behaviour. After ten years. That's the usual way. And I had good behaviour, it's written in my file. Three years on the moors, six in the saw mills, till I had my accident. They said I was malingering, because it was Saturday and the doctor wanted to go sailing. They gave me an injection. This time next year I'd have got my release.

He turns to the man with the flute, who is just engaged in shaking saliva from his instrument.

CONVICT: They said I'd improved myself in those nine years, and that's the truth. I'd never have done it again. I'm sure of that, quite sure. In a year I'd have got my release—

Katrin laughs.

CONVICT: What's she got to laugh at?

Katrin in the white rocking chair and the old man, standing:

KATRIN: Yes, Mr. Proll, yes!

OLD MAN: You agree?

KATRIN: Yes, yes, call them up!

The old man makes gestures as if dialing a number.

KATRIN: That would solve it all.

The old man speaks as if into a telephone:

OLD MAN: Hello, this is Proll.

KATRIN: I've got a passport.

OLD MAN: I'll spell it: P R O L L. Right.

Katrin shows him her passport.

OLD MAN: No, young lady, not a charter flight.

KATRIN: For heaven's sake!

OLD MAN: We want a hot-air balloon.

Katrin rocks herself and laughs.

OLD MAN: She's putting me through.

KATRIN: How big should it be?

OLD MAN: I'll ask them what they've got.

KATRIN: And what colour.

The old man speaks as if into a telephone:

OLD MAN: Yes, we want a balloon. / Pardon? / Basket for two
people. / Yes, I know, young lady, a hot-air balloon is
unpredictable. / Pardon? / But of course, equipped with
sandbags, so we can ascend again if there's a bog or a high-
tension cable in the way. / Yes, I know about that: one pulls
a cord when one wants to land—when the lady in the basket
has had enough, for instance. *To Katrin:* She has to check how
many sandbags are included. *Into the telephone:* That'll do,
yes, I think it'll do. *To Katrin:* One dozen per person. *Into
the telephone:* Beg pardon? / Send the bill to the shop as
usual: Proll's Bookshop, 21 High Street. / That's immaterial,
the main thing is a hot-air balloon. Silver-gray.

KATRIN: White!

OLD MAN: Do you have a white one?

KATRIN: White as snow.

OLD MAN: White as snow, and filled with helium or whatever
you use nowadays. *To Katrin:* She has to check.

KATRIN: And where shall we fly to?

OLD MAN: That's unpredictable, she says. Depends on the wind
direction. Anyway, we won't have to bother about the Easter
traffic. Of course we may spend days over the Ruhr District,
getting suffocated, or hovering over the Vatican gardens,
which will upset the Swiss guards—

KATRIN: And who'll pull the cord?

OLD MAN: Equality of the sexes, strict equality.

KATRIN: That's agreed?

OLD MAN: There's no getting around it. You have twelve
sandbags, I have twelve sandbags, one slash of the knife and
we go hovering again. We each have a cord, that's quite clear,
and when I have got out, let's say on account of my age, then
the white balloon will soar off again into the sky: Katrin
Schimanski will hover on. . . .

Katrin rocks herself.

KATRIN: Proll, I love you!

Pause.

OLD MAN: How did it continue?

Katrin puts her shoes on again.

KATRIN: I wanted to walk to the station, you didn't believe me, I really did want to vanish, balloon or no.

The sound of birds twittering.

OLD MAN: There was something else you said.

Katrin rises and kisses the old man.

KATRIN: Proll, I love you.

She stands combing her hair.

KATRIN: And what else did I say?

She stops combing and laughs.

KATRIN: I know.

She continues combing her hair.

KATRIN: I gave you my arm and said: Daddykins. And we went for a walk.

Xavier and the pilot, who sits studying his map.

XAVIER: A lot of things remained unexplained. Despite the scientific investigation of all the wreckage. For example, no one could explain why you suddenly turned to the left—twenty kilometres from the runway, which was empty, the fire brigade at the ready, as you asked. According to the radar you were still nine hundred metres up at that time. The black box wasn't recovered, since there was another explosion when you crashed. The four engines were scattered over a two-hundred-metre radius. The woods—I only saw photographs—looked as if a typhoon had struck them. According to the Air Ministry report, two thousand fragments of human flesh were recovered, none weighing more than a kilogram. Unidentifiable, of course.

The pilot removes his earphones.

XAVIER: But why am I telling you all this?

The pilot rises and looks around him.

XAVIER: Whom are you looking for?

Katrin and the old man come to a halt.

OLD MAN: There used to be birches here, and the stream was a real one. In my young days. A stream with stones in it, and weeds growing on the stones, so one slipped, walking over them in bare feet—

KATRIN: You've told me that.

OLD MAN: The coachworks stood there.

KATRIN: What stood there?

OLD MAN: The coachworks, in which all my father's hopes rested. He was incorrigible; when he was given a tip after filling up a car, he held the door for the driver and felt all was right with the world, except for the Jews.

Looking around:

OLD MAN: That man there was my father.

KATRIN: The SHELL man?

OLD MAN: And she is my mother.

The garage mechanic, having stuck his rod in the ground, is standing in front of the old woman in the wheelchair.

MECHANIC: So you're Anna.

OLD WOMAN: Yes, Stefan.

MECHANIC: You lived a long time.

OLD WOMAN: To eighty-seven.

MECHANIC: I always used to think you were delicate, Anna, that you wouldn't make it.

OLD WOMAN: Those were hard times.

MECHANIC: I left you in debt.

OLD WOMAN: Yes, Stefan.

MECHANIC: How much?

OLD WOMAN: Forget it.

MECHANIC: Our boy hasn't forgotten it.

OLD WOMAN: Because he doesn't like you: the longer he survived you, the less he liked you. Because you had always been saying: This is how it's done, watch, like this.

MECHANIC: That's the thanks one gets.

OLD WOMAN: People's attitudes have changed a lot, you know. They suddenly begin to think they were brought up wrong.

She laughs.

OLD WOMAN: Yes, Stefan, that's what happens.

MECHANIC: I used to think: Wait till the coachworks are built.
And then they were built, but they had no job for me, though
I was born here and am a qualified mechanic, as you know. So
I thought: A filling station—

OLD WOMAN: I know.

MECHANIC: And I would have made it pay.

OLD WOMAN: Yes, Stefan.

MECHANIC: In spite of the rent money.

OLD WOMAN: You died too soon, Stefan. Before the bypass
was built. And it wasn't until after the war that trade improved.
I don't really understand it. It suddenly looked as if the war
had been worthwhile—

The garage mechanic looks at her.

MECHANIC: So you are my widow.

OLD WOMAN: Yes, Stefan.

MECHANIC: You're better-looking than you were, Anna.

Katrin and the old man come to a halt.

OLD MAN: There's Carlos!

*A young Spaniard, wearing the Basque cap of the Republican
militia and an ammunition belt, is kneeling on the ground, cleaning
an outmoded rifle.*

OLD MAN: He's nineteen.

KATRIN: What is he doing?

OLD MAN: I survived him by thirty years. . . . During the first
weeks all we had were those British rifles from the First World
War, and sometimes the ammunition didn't fit. He'd been an
unskilled labourer; I taught him to read and do figures.

KATRIN: You've told me that.

The young Spaniard removes the barrel.

OLD MAN: Afterwards it became my rifle.

Katrin and the old man continue their walk.

KATRIN: There's somebody who seems to know you.

In the background appears another old man, using two walking sticks. The invalid nods several times.

KATRIN: He wants to speak to you.

OLD MAN: Let's go.

KATRIN: What a lot of people!

OLD MAN: It's Easter.

The sound of bells ringing, then a Gregorian chant. It is the
Te Deum, *sung by the monks of the Benedictine Abbey of St.*
Maurice & St. Maur, Clervaux (Philips record A 02082 L, end of
side two). During the chanting and the ringing of the bells that
brings it to an end, all remain motionless.

Klas, in a light-coloured overcoat:

KLAS: We're in London, Katrin, in the British Museum. You are
stroking a basalt sphinx. And then we look at the mummies.
We are alive, Katrin, and it's Easter. It's not true, Katrin, that
I'm never satisfied.

Katrin and the old man continue their walk.

KLAS: Katrin—!

The sound of a toilet flushing.

KLAS: Is that all you remember, Katrin?

The young clergyman approaches Klas.

KLAS: I know, Parson, either one loves people as they are, or
one doesn't love them at all. Those bottles and tubes she
always leaves with their caps off, the newspapers on the floor
and the hairs in the toilet bowl, I know they're trivialities.
And I did stop mentioning them, too. It's not Katrin's fault
that untidiness upsets me. Katrin is different. I did try, Parson,
but all the same she insisted on a divorce.

CLERGYMAN: May I ask you something?

KLAS: We were so happy in London. A good hotel, comfortable,
she sang in her bath, and we saw a lot as well, Scott's ship, the
explorer who froze to death near the South Pole.

CLERGYMAN: How did you die?

The tramp, sitting alone:

TRAMP: You don't die all of a sudden. . . . I ate too much, that's why I got so heavy, the body part of me, and when I stopped eating it got thin, but I knew I should never be rid of it, the body part of me. I took it along to parties, where people talked and expressed opinions. And people listened to me, though my body was bored with my opinions. It hadn't yet begun to stink, I still had my hair and all the other things a man is supposed to have, and women were in love with my air of melancholy. Evening after evening I took my bow, went in front of the curtain, bowing the body part of me. Then one morning I woke up on a public bench; the Salvation Army talked to me, and I sang Hallelujah for a bowl of soup. I had some scissors in my pocket, and continued cutting my fingernails for another thirty years.

The old woman in the wheelchair and the mechanic:

OLD WOMAN: Yes, yes, Stefan, of course.

MECHANIC: He can't even fish properly.

OLD WOMAN: That's what you always said: He'll never amount to anything. You were always so impatient with our son.

MECHANIC: And you were always shielding him.

OLD WOMAN: He got a diploma, all the same.

MECHANIC: A typographer!

OLD WOMAN: All right, Stefan, you always feel as if no one but you ever worked, the father of the family, that only you were ever unemployed—

MECHANIC: I didn't go to demonstrations.

OLD WOMAN: All the same, you were unemployed.

MECHANIC: Did I ever sing the Internationale?

OLD WOMAN: No.

MECHANIC: How did he earn his living, then?

OLD WOMAN: Later on he ran a little printing press with his comrades, and it did quite well. It was what he knew, after all. But then the press was closed down, because they'd been printing pamphlets of some kind. At that time Matt despised me, and it made me weep, but he brought me his laundry, and I cooked for him. A man must eat, after all, and how he used to eat! Without saying a word, because he despised me. But if you depend on a newsstand for your living, you have to stock what people want.

Pause.

MECHANIC: And he can't even fish properly.

Pause.

OLD WOMAN: Then after the war he had an antiquarian book-shop, and suddenly he began to do quite well. He had books there you wouldn't find in an ordinary bookshop. Do you know what an antiquarian bookshop is?

An elegant-looking man in his middle thirties is holding a bunch of long-stemmed roses; he gives the impression of being embarrassed, and he turns to the nurse, who is carrying a tray of surgical instruments.

MAN: Oh, Sister—

ILSE: Are you looking for someone?

MAN: For a vase.

ILSE: Would you mind waiting a moment?

MAN: A large one.

The old woman in the wheelchair and the mechanic:

OLD WOMAN: Ilse!

The nurse stops.

OLD WOMAN: Why don't you speak to your father?

ILSE: He doesn't need me.

OLD WOMAN: So you say.

ILSE: He never even listens to me.

OLD WOMAN: But he often went for long walks with you; I've seen photographs in his album. You still had pigtails then, Ilse, and he put his jacket around your shoulders.

ILSE: Oh, yes.

OLD WOMAN: Because it was cold; and he made a fire among the rocks, so you wouldn't freeze.

ILSE: Oh, yes.

OLD WOMAN: And you say he never listened to you?

ILSE: Oh, yes, when I was a child.

OLD WOMAN: And you have forgotten all that?

ILSE: No, Granny.

OLD WOMAN: And the bicycle? I know about that because he had run out of money again, your father, and he borrowed it from me, because you wanted a bicycle, Ilse, and you got one.

ILSE: Oh, yes.

OLD WOMAN: Aren't you being unfair?

ILSE: I wrote to him when I got engaged, and in reply he sent me a picture postcard.

OLD WOMAN: So you said.

ILSE: A picture postcard, nothing else.

OLD WOMAN: Sometimes he was like that.

ILSE: I visited his grave once, and it was exactly as it always was when I wanted to tell him something—

She looks at the old man, then turns away.

MECHANIC: She's his daughter?

OLD WOMAN: A nice child. She used to help me sometimes at the newsstand, after school; she cut the titles off the unsold newspapers, so we wouldn't be charged for them.

A young man dressed in a neat and conventional suit stands examining his fingernails and arranging his tie and his cuffs.

YOUNG MAN: Ilse.

The nurse, holding the tray of surgical instruments, stops and looks at the young man.

YOUNG MAN: Don't laugh! It's what they expect, you know: neat, but not gaudy. The white shirt's obligatory. And no long hair, obviously. In the summer, when it's hot, we're allowed to take our jackets off, but not our ties, and clean shirts every day. The sleeves mustn't be rolled up. It doesn't look good when you're dealing with customers. Customers like to see you looking like one of themselves, as if you come from a good family. A bank is based on trust.

He arranges his cuffs again.

YOUNG MAN: Ilse, as of next Monday I'll be working at the cash desk!

Katrin and the old man come to a halt.

OLD MAN: He'll never marry her. I told her that. Once the bank finds out his father-in-law's a Bolshie—they don't like that.

They move on.

The young man in the neat and conventional suit stands alone after the nurse has gone; the young clergyman approaches him.

CLERGYMAN: How did you die?

YOUNG MAN: No idea.

CLERGYMAN: And so young?

The convict in the background:

CONVICT: I shot him.

The convict comes closer.

CONVICT: You don't know me—

YOUNG MAN: No.

CONVICT: We didn't reckon on anybody being at the counter after closing time. I confessed it all. You made no resistance, I admitted that too; you were counting banknotes and had no idea what was going on. I would have been released, for being of good behaviour this time next year. I'd never do such a thing again, and that's the truth, I'm sure of it.

Silence.

CONVICT: Why won't people believe me?

Silence.

CONVICT: Your name's Hubacher . Erich. Aged twenty-seven. You were a Boy Scout and you went to a trade school. I know all that, because it was read out in court. And the chief clerk said you were always very conscientious and punctual. I heard all that. You were engaged to a nurse.

Pause.

CONVICT: I shot you. Yes. From behind. Yes. Now you can see me. Nine years I sat brooding about it. Nine years! And he doesn't even ask me my name.

The convict moves on.

CONVICT: Nobody knows me here. . . .

The nurse brings a vase.

MAN: Thank you, Sister, very kind of you.

The nurse moves on, the man places the vase on the floor and arranges the roses in it.

Katrin and the old man come to a halt.

KATRIN: Daddykins—

OLD MAN: What is it?

KATRIN: We're going around in circles.

The old man sees the man who is arranging the roses.

OLD MAN: So that's what he looked like, your Rosenkavalier! What else can I call him? You never mentioned his name; all I ever saw were the roses in your room: thirty-five of them, all with long stems.

The man straightens up and examines the roses.

OLD MAN: Why don't you greet each other?

The man moves away.

OLD MAN: I understand.

KATRIN: I needed a man.

OLD MAN: And a new coat.

KATRIN: You understand nothing at all, Proll, because you are a bourgeois, like all the rest who wanted to possess me—

The man and the young clergyman:

CLERGYMAN: May I ask you a question? Such lovely roses! So you know this young lady?

MAN: What do you wish to ask?

CLERGYMAN: Why don't you speak to her?

MAN: We played records together. She sat down on the carpet, then I sat down on the carpet. I don't know what we talked about—we were playing records. . . .

Katrin has again sat down in the white rocking chair. The old man stands beside her.

KATRIN: I want to sleep, I want never to have lived at all, and to know nothing—just to sleep.

She closes her eyes.

OLD MAN: But you did live, Katrin.

She is silent.

OLD MAN: Why do you close your eyes?

Xavier crosses to a young man who has a suitcase in one hand and a woman's coat over the other arm; he puts the suitcase down.

JONAS: Katrin never came to fetch her things.

He places the woman's coat on top of the suitcase.

XAVIER: Bourgeois! She got that word from you. Whenever anything didn't suit her, out she came with her "Bourgeois!" You're the only one who isn't a bourgeois, because you sit at a typewriter writing about revolution.

JONAS: What are you trying to say?

XAVIER: When she walked out of our home, I waited ten whole days. And ten nights. Then I brought all her things to your place, thinking she was with you. She admired you. The way you talked about Bakunin. You explained Sigmund Freud to her, and Marcuse, and everything you wrote she took to be the truth. I thought you were having an affair. For a long time I thought that. And I didn't mind Katrin's living with you. Not in the least. But it was you who persuaded her.

JONAS: Persuaded her of what?

XAVIER: That I wanted to possess her.

JONAS: Do you think Katrin didn't know that herself?

Pause.

XAVIER: I saw her in her coffin.

JONAS: You loved her as a fashion model whose job it was to represent your idea of emancipation. If somebody other than yourself convinced her of anything, you began to doubt her intelligence; you can never believe that Katrin is able to think for herself.

XAVIER: That's what you said.

JONAS: Xavier, you're a bourgeois.

XAVIER: I saw her in her coffin—

The man with the flute is practising again.

TRAMP: "Has this fellow no feeling?"

NEIGHBOUR: What do you say?

TRAMP: I said what Hamlet, the Prince of Denmark, said when the gravedigger sang over the grave of his Ophelia.

He sings:

"In youth, when I did love, did love,
   Methought it was very sweet,
To contract, O, the time, for, ah, my behove,
   O, methought there was nothing meet."

NEIGHBOUR: You're interrupting me.

The tramp recites:

TRAMP: "Whether 'tis nobler in the mind to suffer
         The slings and arrows of outrageous fortune,
         Or to take arms against a sea of troubles,
         And by opposing end them?"

He hesitates.

"To die: to sleep; perchance to dream—"

He has forgotten how it continues.

The old woman in the wheelchair, alone:

OLD WOMAN: Matt—

OLD MAN: Yes, Mother?

OLD WOMAN: Matt, something else has come back to me.

The old man goes to the old woman in the wheelchair.

OLD MAN: What has come back to you?

OLD WOMAN: You once said you wanted to eat something that didn't exist on earth. You kept on saying it. I asked you if it were something sweet. You couldn't tell me what it was you wanted so badly, and I took you to the sweetshop—not the one on our corner, but a sweetshop in town. But you just kept shaking your head, though there were so many things there that were strange even to your mother. Yes, and then you flew into a rage, because the shop assistant and I laughed at you for wanting to eat something that doesn't exist. And you were still howling and stamping your feet when we got home.

OLD MAN: I don't remember that.

OLD WOMAN: You were five years old.

The old man looks around at the garage mechanic.

OLD MAN: He goes out whenever I come in.

OLD WOMAN: Ah, well, we're a family.

The old man looks at the old woman.

OLD MAN: Yes, Mother—

OLD WOMAN: What are you trying to say?

OLD MAN: You are content with your life.

OLD WOMAN: Yes.

OLD MAN: Would you like to live again?

OLD WOMAN: Oh, no.

The old man takes hold of the wheelchair.

OLD MAN: Where do you want to go now?

OLD WOMAN: To the stream.

OLD MAN: But it isn't a stream any more—

The young clergyman and a child with a satchel and a ball:

CLERGYMAN: You're waiting for your mother and father. Maybe you ran across the street to fetch your ball. They'll be along soon to take your hand, your mother and father. I know it. What was your name? What a nice ball you've got! . . .

Xavier approaches Katrin.

XAVIER: Has that clergyman been questioning you, too?

KATRIN: He's questioning everybody. That was his job, to comfort people with the promise of a life after death, and he can't understand there's no job for him here.

She rocks herself.

XAVIER: Katrin—!

He waits until she stops rocking.

KATRIN: We just keep on telling each other what we have already said. One comes to realize it gradually, Xavier: there's nothing more to come.

She rocks herself again.

XAVIER: Ten whole days I waited. Then I took your things to Jonas's place, thinking you would be with him. Why didn't you let me know? Then I heard you were working at Proll's bookshop—

Katrin is silent.

XAVIER: I'm sorry for old Proll. The only man who sees you as an individual, and in the end you lead him astray, too. At heart you think him disgusting—but you make an effort, because you need someone who considers you intelligent, and Mr. Proll, I can well believe it, makes an effort, too; he's old, and he's kind to you because he's old and is afraid of being left alone.

Katrin stops rocking.

XAVIER: Oh, Katrin!

KATRIN: That's what you said to me on the station platform, as I stood there crying, and I thought about what you said, Xavier, all night long—

The man with the flute starts to practise again.

KATRIN: He won't close his window. I shouted to him during the night: Can't you please shut your window?

The man with the flute continues practising, until he comes to the difficult passage, and breaks off.

XAVIER: Since when have you been collecting sleeping pills?

The tramp, sitting alone:

TRAMP: Now I remember.

He recites:

TRAMP: "No more; and by a sleep to say we end
      The heart-ache, and the thousand natural shocks
      That flesh is heir to, 'tis a consummation
      Devoutly to be wished. To die, — to sleep; —
      To sleep! perchance to dream: ay, there's the rub;
      For in that sleep of death what dreams may come?"

Katrin in the rocking chair and Xavier:

XAVIER: I looked at you in your coffin.

KATRIN: Did you?

XAVIER: A whole hour.

KATRIN: Did you remember how I used to laugh at your lectures in the kitchen, while you were washing up, and how you once slapped my face because I had slapped yours, and how childishly I behaved on the platform?

XAVIER: I spoke to you.

KATRIN: I didn't hear.

She rocks herself again.

XAVIER: Oh, Katrin!

She is not rocking now.

KATRIN: So you looked at me—for a full hour—with my sharp alabaster nose and white lips that seemed almost to be smiling, and these hands which had suddenly become virginal again.

XAVIER: I didn't kiss you.

KATRIN: Thanks.

XAVIER: What do you mean?

She is rocking again.

KATRIN: We don't hurt each other any more, Xavier, we're dead, Xavier, and what remains is that we didn't understand one another.

The old man with the fishing rod; the invalid, who previously greeted him with nods, is standing beside him.

INVALID: I know, I know, I should have come along earlier. I always meant to. We were friends once. Then suddenly it's too late. Yet I often thought about you. Whether you believe it or not. It was a great shock when I read one day that you were dead. I even used to dream about you—

The old man looks at him.

INVALID: Why didn't we ever have it out together?

The young clergyman returns.

CLERGYMAN: The pilot has found his child!

He stands there alone.

The old man with the fishing rod and the invalid:

INVALID: Matthis Proll—

OLD MAN: Yes?

INVALID: You haven't changed at all: you stand there fishing, while I wait around, hoping for a reconciliation. . . . We were in the same boat crew. You helped me with my diploma. When you returned from your beloved Spain, I let you live for six months in my house.

OLD MAN: I was grateful for that.

INVALID: Well, then.

The old man looks at his line.

INVALID: I had a talk with Sophie, that was after your funeral, and I spoke quite frankly. It's true I did now and again say Proll was a Stalinist and would always be a Stalinist.

OLD MAN: I never knew that.

INVALID: But it did damage your business.

The old man pulls in his line, which is empty.

INVALID: Are you listening to me?

The old man baits his hook.

OLD MAN: When was that uprising in Hungary?

INVALID: 1956.

OLD MAN: A long time ago.

INVALID: Matthis, that's what I mean—

OLD MAN: You became a company director?

INVALID: What has that got to do with it?

OLD MAN: Otherwise I know little about you. Somebody did mention later that you were using two walking sticks.

INVALID: Why didn't you ever phone me?

OLD MAN: Arthritis, is it?

INVALID: After all, you did know I was still alive, and we were living in the same town.

The old man is tinkering with his line.

INVALID: Sophie understood me, I think. Those were difficult times. Then. I didn't call you when your telephone was being tapped, that's true. But you didn't call me, either. Not once. You could have called me from a public phone. Please try to understand, I had the feeling that you despised me. And, incidentally, I did once write you a letter, though I didn't send it. I was also in your little bookshop once—

OLD MAN: When?

INVALID: You weren't there at the time.

OLD MAN: Did you find what you were looking for?

He throws out his line again.

INVALID: I wanted to ask your pardon, Matthis. I thought two intelligent men like ourselves, two grownup men—we can at least talk to each other, we were friends once—

The old man is looking at his line.

INVALID: I don't mean anything to you at all!

Katrin in the white rocking chair, and Jonas, who comes in with her coat and her suitcase, which he puts down beside her.

JONAS: Xavier has brought your things.

He lays the coat on top of the suitcase.

KATRIN: Did your revolution ever take place?

JONAS: I don't believe so.

KATRIN: You were out on the barricades.

JONAS: No.

KATRIN: But you're bleeding.

JONAS: They were shooting into the crowd.

The man with the flute starts practising again, but breaks off when he sees the clergyman beside him.

NEIGHBOUR: Does my practising disturb you?

CLERGYMAN: Nothing succeeds without practice.

NEIGHBOUR: Not all my neighbours are as understanding as you, Parson. Why don't I close the window? It's just that one sometimes forgets.

He starts to play again.

NEIGHBOUR: This is a difficult passage.

CLERGYMAN: May I ask you something?

NEIGHBOUR: I haven't much talent, Parson, I know that, but a man needs a hobby. Working all day long, sometimes nights, too. I wasn't allowed to practise in the hospital.

CLERGYMAN: I understand.

NEIGHBOUR: I'm convalescing.

CLERGYMAN: I understand

NEIGHBOUR: But it's not cancer, otherwise they wouldn't have allowed me home. Now I can practise again.

CLERGYMAN: Do you believe in God?

NEIGHBOUR: A colleague of yours was also asking me that. A Catholic. It was a Catholic hospital.

CLERGYMAN: There is only One God.

NEIGHBOUR: That's what your colleague said, too. . . . You know, Parson: when I became a policeman—first I took a course in architectural drawing, but there were no jobs to be had, so then I took up handball, I was a good handball player, and then I saw this poster: a safe, manly occupation for healthy young men. My fiancée thought I was disgusting to be thinking of my pension at the age of twenty-six. Today we're glad of it, I can tell you, really glad of it.

He shakes saliva from his flute.

NEIGHBOUR: God. I used to say: There must be something like that. And I believe it, too. Some order, that's what's needed. I'm an auxiliary, I don't give orders to shoot, Parson. That's all in the rule book. And when things suddenly start happening, one appreciates being given orders. . . . Whether it's the right ones who get killed at such times, no one can tell. Only God knows that. That's as far as I'd go.

The tramp, sitting alone:

TRAMP: IT'S A PITY ABOUT MANKIND. Strindberg. IT'S A PITY ABOUT MANKIND.

The old man with the fishing rod; Xavier is watching.

OLD MAN: Katrin has told me about you.

He pulls in his line, which is empty.

XAVIER: When was the last time you caught anything?

The old man baits his hook.

XAVIER: At school I was once sent out of the room and made to stand in the corridor for the rest of the lesson, because I asked whether there were any fish in the river Styx. I meant it purely as a factual question, but the whole class laughed, and the teacher felt insulted, for he didn't know, either.

OLD MAN: There are none.

He casts his line again.

OLD MAN: That time you came to the bookshop to see whether Katrin was really working there, whether she knew her way through the catalogue, could look up ANARCHISM, for instance—

XAVIER: So you remember that?

OLD MAN: You wanted to ask me something.

XAVIER: Yes.

OLD MAN: What was it?

XAVIER: And suddenly you were gone.

OLD MAN: Suddenly, for the first time, I had the feeling that Katrin found me disgusting. That's the sort of thing one doesn't forget.

Pause.

XAVIER: Did you consider Katrin intelligent?

OLD MAN: Was that what you wanted to ask?

The old man regards his line.

XAVIER: Mr. Proll, were you ever alive?

OLD MAN: Oh, yes—now and again . . . But here there is nothing to look forward to. That's the difference. For instance, when you came into my shop—I don't know what you hoped to achieve. Maybe you didn't know yourself. You were curious to see how Katrin would behave, how you yourself would behave. You were looking for something to happen that morning you came to the shop. A miracle, or no miracle, but something at least. All one's life one spends in constant expectation of something, from one hour to the next. . . . Here there is no longer expectation; there's no fear, either, no future, and that's why it all seems so trivial, when it has come to an end for all time.

The old man looks at Xavier.

OLD MAN: Katrin loved you.

The young clergyman approaches the tramp.

CLERGYMAN: The pilot has found his child!

TRAMP: Hallelujah.

CLERGYMAN: Why don't you look?

TRAMP: I can imagine it.

CLERGYMAN: Take a look!

The tramp turns and looks.

TRAMP: Just as Mummy filmed them.

CLERGYMAN: Aren't they happy?

TRAMP: Now the child throws, now Daddy catches, now Daddy throws, now the child catches—no, he misses, but Daddy fetches the ball and throws again, now the child catches. And Daddy claps his hands. Now the child throws again. But too low, and Daddy has to stoop. Exactly as it used to be! And now the child catches, now it throws, now Daddy catches again.

He is no longer looking:

TRAMP: Kodachrome.

CLERGYMAN: What did you say?

TRAMP: They're not playing ball, Parson, once they were playing ball, and what has been can't be altered, and that is eternity.

Katrin in the white rocking chair, and Jonas, who is standing, looking around him:

KATRIN: Where do you want to go, Jonas? Here you'll meet nobody you don't know already. Bakunin and all the rest of them, you'll never meet them—

Jonas looks at Katrin.

JONAS: I dreamed this once: a place I didn't know—just like this—and whom did I meet? Katrin Schimanski, and you seemed very odd. You knew everything. I wasn't at all afraid of you. For the first time. And there was really nothing to say. I told you I loved you. Not in so many words, but you understood. Why I didn't want you to come and live with me, no mention of that. We were simply here in this place, and I could see how pleased you were. You said: We can't touch each other. But you were tender in a way I'd never seen. . . . It was a long and rather complicated dream, but I know I never felt frightened. All so easy. It was only when I woke up that I remembered Katrin Schimanski was dead. A year ago. That's why you said: We can't touch each other.

The man with the flute, in shirt sleeves and slippers, practises his melody again, until he makes his usual mistake. The tramp, sitting on the ground far away from him, whistles the melody correctly. The man looks at the tramp.

TRAMP: What a patient fellow you are!

The man with the flute tries again.

*The old man alone with his fishing rod; he watches his line, while
the young Spaniard from the militia loads his clean rifle.*

OLD MAN: So you've loaded the rifle, Carlos, our British rifle.
I was there when you died, November '37. Some time later
I visited your village again, our billet there, but there's
nothing left to see. They still have a photograph of you, a
little one, now very faded: sitting just as you are now.

The old man looks at the young Spaniard.

OLD MAN: You believe in Stalin.

He looks again at his line.

OLD MAN: I survived you by thirty-two years, but your sisters
still recognized me, and so did your younger brother, who
buried you. A lot of your comrades were shot dead after
losing their rifles. Others died in prison, some of them under
torture.

Jonas is standing alone.

JONAS: The revolution will come. The minority know that, the
majority confirm it with their fear. The coming revolution
will make us immortal, even if we don't live to see it—

The tramp, sitting alone:

TRAMP: My memory is dried up, the role of my life is now
being played by others, and the dead are slowly growing
weary of themselves.

The young clergyman, standing alone:

CLERGYMAN: A light will come, a light such as we have never
seen before, and a birth without flesh; and we shall be different
from what we were after our first birth, since we shall have
lived. We shall feel no pain and shall no longer fear death, for
we are born into eternity.

*Katrin alone in the white rocking chair; beside her the suitcase
with her coat on it, on the other side the vase with the roses.*

KATRIN: Daddykins!

OLD MAN: I'm fishing.

KATRIN: How ordinary eternity is!

The sound of birds twittering.

KATRIN: And now it's April again.

The Third Panel

Characters

Roger
Francine
A news vendor
A gendarme (non-speaking)

A marble bench in a public place, nothing else visible. Night. Francine and Roger are sitting on the bench in the radius of light of an overhanging street lamp.

ROGER: Say something, Francine!

She is silent.

ROGER: There, right in front of us, the park railings, black Renaissance. I haven't forgotten those, with their gilded, pointed spikes. Yet I would have sworn the bench was cast iron and wood. And those traffic lights in the distance: silence on red, a sudden roar on green—

He takes a cigarette and lights it.

ROGER: Yes, Francine, it was here.

The sound of traffic in the distance, then silence. The traffic lights, which cannot be seen, change every fifty seconds. It is obviously a crossing where a big street meets a smaller one; in one direction the volume of traffic is large, and the sound of a great many cars can be heard when the light turns green, occasionally the harsh roar of a bus; in the other direction the cars are isolated, and the noise is not always the same every fifty seconds; the first phase lasts some time (up to seven seconds), the second phase, following after fifty seconds, lasts only a short while.

FRANCINE: You don't have to accompany me, Roger.

ROGER: That's what you said.

FRANCINE: There are times, Roger, when I hate you, but I shall never forget, Roger, that I once loved you very much.

ROGER: That's what you said.

FRANCINE: We should never have lived together.

Pause.

FRANCINE: At this time of night there are no trains. What is the point of going to the station so early? I can't see why you shouldn't come back to the hotel and rest until it's time for your train.

ROGER: That's what you said—

He smokes:

ROGER: — and I decided it would be better to go, not to the hotel with you, but to the station. And after that we never saw each other again.

He stamps out his cigarette.

ROGER: Your family looks on me more or less as your murderer. At any rate, that's what I hear indirectly. Others don't go quite that far. But they felt, our friends did, the need to take sides. The ones who adored Francine had to condemn me. When I mentioned your name, their silence was sometimes quite comical. I never found out how much they really knew about our relationship. They're tactful people, most of them. But at the time I lost several friends. I was told you wouldn't allow my name to be mentioned in your presence—

She takes a cigarette.

ROGER: This morning, just after I arrived, I met Madame Tailleur, or whatever she calls herself, that friend of yours. I wouldn't have recognized her, a ghost from the past. She wanted to know what I was doing in Paris. And the look she gave me! As if Paris were banned to me for all eternity.

He gives her a light; she smokes.

ROGER: My father—in all his eighty years I never found out what he really believed—he was no mystic, heaven knows, but he always knew what my dead mother was thinking. When he sold the house, never a doubt that his late wife approved. No need for her to know that he had messed things up with an inept bit of speculation, she was an understanding woman, and she always took his side. A convenient ghost. When we, his sons, didn't agree with him, it was always she who thought him right. He was an alcoholic. And he never doubted that she read the newspaper, too—his newspaper, of course. The long-haired youngsters: she hadn't lived to see those, but she found them as dreadful as he did. When he changed his political views, because they were proving too costly, and when he left the party, his dead wife left it, too. No doubt about it. I despised him, found all his communing with the dead repulsive. . . .

She sits silent, smoking.

ROGER: It was this bench, I'm certain of it. The only one under

a street lamp. We didn't feel like sitting in the dark. . . . A
year later I got married. You've never seen Ann. I got to know
her in Texas, and we have a son, as perhaps you've heard. He's
a schoolboy now.

She sits silent, smoking.

ROGER: Say something, Francine, tell me about yourself.

She smokes, her eyes straight ahead. He looks at her.

ROGER: We probably reacted exactly the same way after we
parted: you decided you were right, I decided I was right, and
all we had left was bitterness. Which is easier on the memory
than remorse. Your affair with Roger, mine with Francine,
maybe they differ in the degree of their significance, but the
dates are the same. . . .

*Silence, the heavy traffic is heard, then stillness, then the lighter
traffic.*

ROGER: If Ann were to walk down this avenue now, she wouldn't
be surprised to see me talking to you. She was jealous in the
beginning, because I was always justifying myself to Francine,
sometimes for hours on end. And she felt it was not her I
was contradicting, but you. Poor Ann, it wasn't easy for her.
I realized that later. But though I never mentioned your name
again, she could still feel your presence, inevitably. . . . Ann's
a photographer. . . . She's four years younger than you—that
is to say, she was. Now Ann is already somewhat older than
you. It's all very strange.

Pause.

ROGER: Incidentally, I did see you again—just once. Almost as
close as we are now. I don't think I was mistaken. You were
standing on the opposite escalator—it was in Berlin, at the
Zoo underground station, in the morning. Can that be right?
I was going down, you up, your hand on the railing, alone, and
you were looking straight ahead, not exactly radiating cheer-
fulness, but not unhappy, either. You were deep in thought.
Afterwards I felt I'd been quite right not to call out: Francine.

She extinguishes her cigarette against the marble.

ROGER: Or did you recognize me, too?

Pause.

ROGER: I never visited your grave.

A news vendor appears.

NEWS VENDOR: LE MONDE!—

Francine buys a newspaper; it takes some time, since she has to search for change, and obviously has difficulty with the unfamiliar coins without her glasses. At last she finds the right coin, and the news vendor goes off.

ROGER: You bought a newspaper—yes—to have something to read after we'd parted, when you were alone in the hotel bedroom.

She puts on her spectacles.

ROGER: Why did we part?

She glances at the title page.

ROGER: Vietnam . . . You knew how it would end before I did, though you didn't live to see it. But history proved you right. When I read about Chile today, I know exactly what Francine thinks about it.

She turns a page.

ROGER: Ernst Bloch is dead now, too—

She puts the newspaper down on the bench.

ROGER: The future holds nothing but fear.

Pause.

FRANCINE: Shall we go?

He does not move.

ROGER: Later I heard, from other people — and they couldn't have made it up, it can only have come out of your head—I heard I'd been blackmailing Francine for three whole years with threats of suicide.

He puts another cigarette between his lips.

ROGER: Did I do that, Francine?

He flips his lighter and takes the cigarette from his lips before he has lit it.

ROGER: Maybe you went through my drawers, I don't know, but you didn't find a revolver there. I didn't have one. I could always have jumped from the balcony. But I never threatened you with such nonsense. I did go to the Dolomites, that's true, but it wasn't meant as a threat—surely? What else, then? After a party where we'd all been drinking I did once try my hand at being a cat burglar—

He tries to laugh.

ROGER: Was that blackmail?

He throws his cigarette away.

ROGER: I think it's wretched of you, Francine, if that's the way you told our story: saying I blackmailed you for three years with threats of suicide.

She takes a cigarette and at the same time brings out her lighter, so that he can only look on as she lights her cigarette.

ROGER: That's how you smoked. And soon we shall start to feel cold. Later the gendarme will pass by and wonder why we are not in bed. I've never forgotten how you said: NOUS ATTENDONS LE MATIN, MONSIEUR! and how he gave a salute. Later still, when the traffic has stopped, we shall hear an ambulance siren in the distance. . . .

The traffic noises are still audible every fifty seconds: though becoming, not weaker, but shorter, so that the stillness gradually increases; sometimes only a single bus can be heard.

ROGER: Say something, Francine!

She smokes, looking straight ahead.

ROGER: For a time—after your death—I toyed with feelings of guilt. I set you up as my judge, in order to make you speak. But you didn't listen when I made my confession, and you looked at me as if it were impossible that I should ever understand. You said nothing—or you just repeated what you said then, here on this bench. . . . Francine, next year I shall be fifty, but you are always thirty-three.

He rises to his feet, without really knowing why he has done so; she continues to sit, unchanged; he stands with his hands in the pockets of his coat.

ROGER: WE SHOULD NEVER HAVE LIVED TOGETHER.

He looks at her:

ROGER: Do you know what I have often thought? That Francine is in love with her love. And that has nothing whatever to do with the man she may have met. Francine belongs in the ranks of the Great Lovers. She loves her bliss, she loves her fear and her longing and her bitterness, the exaltation of her yielding, and if the man thinks it has anything to do with him, he has only himself to blame. Francine is not in love with herself, I don't mean that. She just loves—like the Portuguese nun. She loves her love.

He sees that she is not listening to him.

FRANCINE: I shall work.

ROGER: So you said.

FRANCINE: Immerse myself in work.

She extinguishes her cigarette against the marble.

ROGER: That's what you said, and I understood that our parting was decreed, whatever else we would say that night.

She takes her lipstick from her handbag.

ROGER: Why didn't you want to have our child?

She makes up her lips without looking in her pocket mirror; he sits down again on the bench.

ROGER: And you never did have a child. So far as I know. Later I began to suspect that the people in Geneva might have made a mess of things that time.

He looks at her:

ROGER: Francine, was that it?

She puts her lipstick back into her handbag.

FRANCINE: It's two o'clock, Roger, and last night we hardly slept at all. Let's be sensible.

ROGER: That's what you said.

FRANCINE: What is the point of going to the station so early? I can't see why you shouldn't come back to the hotel and rest until it's time for your train.

He is silent.

FRANCINE: What's to happen now with the flat?

He is silent.

FRANCINE: It was you who decided we should part, Roger, last night. For once you showed more courage than I, and for that I am grateful.

ROGER: That's what you said.

FRANCINE: When you've been drinking you can never remember what you said.

ROGER: We had both been drinking.

Pause.

ROGER: What did I say, Francine?

Pause.

FRANCINE: Roger, I'm making no demands.

ROGER: That's what you said.

Pause.

FRANCINE: I can go to live with Marieluise. Anytime. But how do you imagine I can work in her attic?

He is silent.

FRANCINE: Roger, you have never helped me.

He is silent.

FRANCINE: You talk like a landlord. A mere transaction. You say: I'll make you a present of the flat, all it needs is fifteen minutes with a lawyer and the flat is yours, furniture included.

ROGER: That's what I said.

FRANCINE: That's your first thought: lawyers.

He is silent.

FRANCINE: Roger, I have only one request—

ROGER: And I stuck to that: I made no attempt to find out your new address, I didn't appear one day on your doorstep, I didn't ring your bell.

Pause.

FRANCINE: What can I do with six rooms by myself?

He is silent.

FRANCINE: How can you ask what work I shall do? When for a whole year I've been talking about qualifying as a lecturer. You don't take my work seriously.

He is silent.

FRANCINE: Don't worry about me. That's not what I need, your concern. I can read timetables for myself.

He is silent.

FRANCINE: All I need from our flat is my books. Nothing else. The dictionaries in particular. And my clothes.

ROGER: You sent for those.

FRANCINE: If any letters come for me—

ROGER: I always sent them on to Marieluise. As arranged. Some bills as well, perhaps—I don't know. And in the first weeks there were also some telephone calls. I didn't have any number to pass on.

Pause.

FRANCINE: Stop looking at me like a sheepdog.

He is silent.

FRANCINE: You'll go off to Austin, and we'll be relieved, both of us, not to have to prove anything to each other any more.

ROGER: I did go to Austin.

Pause.

FRANCINE: It would be better not to write to each other, Roger, ever. Let's promise that, Roger. Never.

He is silent.

FRANCINE: Roger, you don't need me.

He is silent.

FRANCINE: Who was it who whitewashed the whole flat when you were away in Trieste, all six rooms, standing by myself on the ladder?

He is silent.

FRANCINE: What could I find to do in Austin?

He is silent.

FRANCINE: When we went househunting together, you wanted a large old building with high ceilings, and I agreed with you. Yes, I felt positive that we were not just any old couple.

ROGER: We were Francine and Roger.

FRANCINE: Yes.

ROGER: And so we are.

Pause.

FRANCINE: Roger, I'm getting cold.

He is silent.

FRANCINE: You want me to need you, that's what love means to you. When you're feeling sure of yourself I'm a burden on you. It's when you're feeling unsure that you cling to me, and that's not what I'm here for, Roger.

He is silent.

FRANCINE: There are times when I hate you—

ROGER: That's what you said.

A gendarme comes in and stops before them.

FRANCINE: Nous attendons le matin, monsieur.

The gendarme salutes and goes off.

ROGER: Today, out in Orly—yesterday I didn't even know I'd be flying to Paris, and this morning, when I had the ticket in my hand and heard them announce the flight, I was still unable to tell myself why—it was only in Orly, after arriving there with no luggage, and when I was sitting in the taxi, that I felt this mad hope that it might all never have happened, and that we should meet you and I, in this avenue. . . . Incidentally, nobody knows I am in Paris. Except Madame Tailleur. WHAT ARE YOU DOING IN PARIS. This is what I'm doing: talking to the dead.

The traffic noise has subsided; now nothing is heard except an occasional bus, then silence again.

FRANCINE: Have you another cigarette?

He offers a pack of cigarettes, but no lighter.

ROGER: There are times when I forget you. I'm still wearing the watch Francine gave me. But it doesn't remind me of you. And there are places we visited together, Strasbourg, for instance—the cathedral there reminds me of other cathedrals, not of Francine. That's how it is sometimes. I wouldn't confuse your handwriting with anybody else's, were I to see it, no, but I can't recall what it was like. And your body, your naked body . . . Oh, that can be agony—in the street, among the crowds at the traffic lights, I see hair that is your hair exactly. I know it's not possible, but I don't start walking when all the others do, I wait until I have forgotten you again.

FRANCINE: Have you a light?

He gives her a light.

ROGER: Sometimes I dream of Francine. You are always different from the person I know, and usually in the company of strangers. I try to show you that by stretching out my arms, I can fly above the roofs. Which is not allowed, of course. Sometimes you are tender towards me, Francine, in my dreams. I know that tells me nothing about you, Francine, none of it is news of you.

Pause.

Perhaps we parted to show ourselves we could live without each other, and so we could, as long as you were alive.

She looks straight ahead, smoking.

ROGER: Did you go to Hanoi?

She looks straight ahead, smoking.

ROGER: You're tired, Francine.

FRANCINE: Desperately.

ROGER: That's what you said.

She looks straight ahead, smoking.

ROGER: Do you recognize this piece of paper?

He takes a piece of paper from his wallet.

ROGER: How that got into my wallet I've no idea. Like something drawn by a child. Railings. But nothing behind them. Could it be yours? I never saw you drawing.

She extinguishes her cigarette against the marble and again takes her lipstick from her handbag to paint her lips, this time looking into the small pocket mirror; a single bus is heard, then silence.

ROGER: I suppose you heard that I met her once, your Marieluise. At a party. We were standing at a cold buffet, and I probably asked her how Francine was getting on— otherwise I shouldn't have heard the words I did: YOU HAVE NEVER LOVED ANYBODY, ROGER, AND YOU NEVER WILL LOVE ANYBODY. I assumed this judgment came from you, and I left.

She moves her lips to settle her makeup.

ROGER: Would you still say that today?

She puts her lipstick back in her handbag.

ROGER: I know next to nothing about your life after we parted that night. You stayed in Paris. I kept my promise, I never went in search of you, as long as you were alive—

A single car is heard.

FRANCINE: Perhaps that was a taxi.

She has risen to her feet.

FRANCINE: It's two o'clock. Roger, and last night we hardly slept at all. Let's be sensible.

She looks at her watch:

FRANCINE: Half past two.

He remains seated and looks at her.

ROGER: Is that the suit you were wearing?

Again a single bus, then silence.

ROGER: When I heard about your operation, the first one— the people didn't know I knew Francine Coray, so they spared no details—I wrote you a letter, but I didn't send it. I didn't dare to, Francine. Then, six months later, there was talk of X-ray treatment. . . . That time I did fly to Paris, but out there in Orly I knew some white nun would come and tell me my presence was not desired.

He puts a cigarette between his lips.

ROGER: I knew Francine was going to die.

He takes the cigarette from his lips.

ROGER: Say something, Francine.

Silence.

ROGER: Incidentally, I'm now alone again. My boy is allowed to visit me once a month, and for a fortnight each year. Ann is living with another man. It may even have been from me that she learned what was once said of me over a cold buffet: YOU HAVE NEVER LOVED ANYBODY. . . . A statement like that sticks like the mark of Cain.

He lights his lighter, then extinguishes it.

ROGER: I imagine you burned all my letters. I hope so—that they're not lying around in that woman's house, Madame Tailleur. . . . I haven't burned yours, Francine, though I haven't reread them, either. I should be afraid to. Phrases like in the Song of Solomon, but now they no longer apply. I've put them in a cardboard box, your letters, and sealed them in the approved way: with a candle and sealing wax, a drop of wax on the string, then a thumb on the hot wax, my finger-print as seal.

He lights a cigarette.

ROGER: You were no longer a student when you decided

against having our child, and I'd just passed my fortieth
birthday. I didn't insist on it, no, I certainly didn't. On the
journey to Geneva I asked you again, two or three times. You
never realized how shocked I was by your determination. No,
I didn't let you see that—on the contrary, in fact. I professed
to understand you completely. Maybe my masculine understanding hurt you, I don't know. We were alone in the
compartment, you pulled your coat over your face. But we
were still in love for some time after that—

*The siren of an ambulance is heard in the distance; it comes
closer, though not very close, then fades again.*

ROGER: What had really come between us, long before that,
we didn't talk about at all that night. Not a word. At any
time. Just like any other couple.

*She sits down again on the bench, her handbag under her arm,
ready to leave.*

ROGER: What did we talk about until three in the morning?

Again a single bus, then silence.

ROGER: Once, in one of my dreams, I saw you drawing or
painting. One sheet of paper after another. What you were
drawing so intently I couldn't see. All I saw was one piece of
paper after another, and you, a grown woman, looking
happy, as absorbed as a child, earnest but happy. My presence
didn't upset you. Then I asked you to give me one of your
drawings, you didn't say I could, but you left it to me to
take one or not—and then I woke up. When I turned on the
light, I felt pleased, quite convinced I possessed a drawing
of yours. A sign. I looked for it on the floor, on the table,
in the pockets of my jacket—of course I didn't find anything.

He takes the piece of paper from his coat pocket.

ROGER: I suppose I must have scribbled this myself.

Slowly he crumples the piece of paper.

ROGER: Your silence, Francine—I understood your silence, as
long as you were still alive.

The gendarme comes in exactly as before.

FRANCINE: Nous attendons le matin, monsieur

The gendarme salutes and goes off.

ROGER: One shouldn't talk with the dead.

She puts the newspaper into her handbag.

FRANCINE: You don't have to accompany me, Roger. Straight on, turn right through the gate, then straight ahead and through the other gate and straight on across the bridge—I know, I can find the way.

He stamps out his cigarette.

ROGER: When I got the news, a printed card, incidentally, with a text chosen by your family—before then it had always seemed possible that we might meet again. Quite by chance. You never sought a meeting, I know that, Francine, and I didn't dare to, and then suddenly the thought that we might see each other again had vanished.

He rises to his feet.

ROGER: But I did accompany you.

She remains seated.

FRANCINE: We did once have a good time together, Roger, a great one. I thought the two of us, you and I, would rethink the whole world. Everything. And there must be something like that: a couple that sees itself as the first couple ever, as the inventor of the idea of couples. Us! The world may be shocked by our arrogance, but it can't hurt us. We have known grace. That's what I believed. And we knew the idea of possession didn't enter into it. Otherwise we should have got married. Once, at the very beginning, you said: There is nothing on this earth that cannot be rethought. And that was the bond between us, Roger. We mustn't let anyone know that we, Roger and Francine, were rethinking the world, including all its dead. The orgies of argument we enjoyed, Roger! And I felt certain we loved more than just each other. You me and I you—all that is interchangeable. So you said! But what brought us together was not interchangeable. Other couples were just man and woman, we decided, and we were that, too, but on top of everything else: as a sort of extra bonus. And you know, Roger, our desperation at that time was never petty—wrong-headed perhaps, but never petty, and we could say terrible things to each other—things we could no longer say now. . . . That's when we bought the big flat. We talked a lot of rubbish, Roger, sometimes I and sometimes you, and sometimes both of us together, but at that time I really did believe I could rethink things, you could rethink things. We weren't dead, Roger, never dead—as we are now.

He looks at her the way one looks at a person who cannot know what he has been saying, and keeps silent.

FRANCINE: And we were proud of each other, you know. We didn't treat each other with kindness or compassion, or expect it, either. We saw each other as two people who had been singled out—yes, I mean that: singled out—me by you and you by me. We moved no mountains, and you often laughed at my optimism. You know, Roger, even in our mistakes we became bolder. We didn't misuse our feelings of tenderness, using them to hide from each other, or to comfort ourselves. . . . Yes, Roger, that's how it was. For a time.

He sits down again.

ROGER: Go on!

FRANCINE: Roger, I'm getting cold.

ROGER: I'm listening.

She is silent.

ROGER: When memory suddenly finds itself alone in the world, it becomes another story, Francine, a very different one. My need to feel I was in the right—that has vanished since you died, and memory suddenly starts to release other things, now I see you in front of me.

He gazes at her tenderly:

ROGER: You with your narrow forehead and your big teeth, a blond horse with spectacles!

She removes her glasses and puts them into her handbag.

ROGER: And with your streaming eyes.

Pause.

ROGER: Incidentally, our flat no longer exists. The house has been torn down—

Pause.

ROGER: A short while ago I had a conversation with a girl. I hardly know her, an ambitious youngster in search of a scholarship—that's why she came to see me. She had been having an abortion, she said: she felt I ought to know, so I wouldn't think she was always late for appointments. Maybe her frankness embarrassed me, she said, but she was anxious that I should understand her. It was, as she told me: BECAUSE I DON'T KNOW WHO THE FATHER IS. . . . Up till then it had never occurred to me that our case might have been the same.

Pause.

FRANCINE: There are times, Roger, when you would like to slap my face. You don't do it because you know it would mean you would never see me again.

ROGER: That's what you said, Francine; then you took your handbag—I could have sworn it was a blue one—

She picks up her white handbag.

ROGER: —and got up.

She rises to her feet.

ROGER: And off we went with scarcely a word: straight on, turning right through the gate, then straight ahead and through the other gate, and straight on across the bridge to our white hotel.

She is standing, he remains seated, in the manner of a person sitting alone, hands in pockets, not knowing what to do next, staring straight ahead into the darkness.

ROGER: Suddenly—have you ever had this experience?—suddenly I realize it isn't true, something I had always maintained, which I had once believed. Suddenly it might all be quite different. It can seem like an awakening, in the middle of the day. A sentence I once heard, maybe years ago, comes into my mind, and suddenly it means something quite different. That is happening more and more frequently to me now. Without any reason I can see. I wake up, realizing that a joke I made yesterday isn't a joke at all. Or I remember some sentence which for years had aroused my indignation, and to which I reacted indignantly at the time. But now: I can't really see why that particular remark upset me so. I don't understand why I reacted as I did. . . . I don't know if you've ever had that experience, Francine.

Pause.

ROGER: Do you know, there isn't a single photograph of Francine that reminds me of you? Except a childhood photograph: young Francine, looking as I've never seen you look, together with a large sheepdog.

Pause.

ROGER: Say something!

Pause.

ROGER: Once, after you'd been to Moscow, you spoke about
Lenin—how the sight of him in that mausoleum made you
feel sick, his wise head empty of thought for the past fifty
years. . . . That's the trouble: we live with the dead, and they
don't change.

Pause.

ROGER: I'm looking forward to a holiday in Iceland with my
youngster. I've been telling him how volcanoes and glaciers
originate, and now I have to show him that there are such
things. He's too old for fairy tales. We're going to Iceland
this coming summer. For a fortnight. With a tent and
sleeping bags.

Pause.

ROGER: Francine, say something.

FRANCINE: You don't have to accompany me.

ROGER: No, Francine—say something you didn't say then.
Something you thought later. Something you would say
now—that would set us free of our history, Francine.

*Again the siren of an ambulance is heard in the distance; the
sound comes nearer, then fades in the opposite direction.*

FRANCINE: Roger, I really am cold.

ROGER: Once, months ago, I had the idea that I ought to shoot
myself through the head, so that I could hear Francine again.

FRANCINE: And you're cold, too.

He remains seated.

ROGER: Francine, say something.

He suddenly shouts:

ROGER: Say something!

Pause.

FRANCINE: Roger, we've said it all.

ROGER: Have we?

FRANCINE: I told you I would work. Or go to Hanoi, if that
were possible, to report on things from the other side.

Pause.

FRANCINE: It was you who decided we should part, Roger. For

once you showed more courage than I, and for that I am
grateful.

Pause.

We should never have lived together.

Pause.

How can you ask what work I shall do? When for a whole
year I've been talking about qualifying as a lecturer. You don't
take my work seriously.

Pause.

Stop looking at me like a sheepdog.

Pause.

You'll go off to Austin, Roger, and we'll be relieved, both of us,
not to have to prove anything to each other any more.

Pause.

Roger, you have never helped me.

Pause.

What can I do with six rooms by myself?

Pause.

Roger, you don't need me.

Pause.

Don't worry about me. That's not what I need, your concern.
I can read timetables for myself.

Pause.

It would be better not to write to each other, Roger, ever.
Let's promise that, Roger. Never.

Pause.

We did once have a good time together, Roger—

ROGER: Go on!

Pause.

FRANCINE: All I need from our flat is my books. Nothing else.
The dictionaries in particular. And my clothes.

Pause.

Roger, I'm making no demands.

Pause.

When we went househunting together, you wanted a large old
building with high ceilings, and I agreed with you. Yes, I felt
positive that we were not just any old couple.

Pause.

That's your first thought: lawyers.

Pause.

Roger, I have only one request: that you never try to find out
my new address. Do you promise that? I don't want you
appearing one day on my doorstep, ringing my bell.

Pause.

Roger, I'm cold.

Pause.

You want me to need you, that's what love means to you.
When you're feeling sure of yourself, I'm a burden on you. It's
when you're feeling unsure that you cling to me, and that's
not what I'm here for, Roger.

Pause.

What could I find to do in Austin?

Pause.

There are times when I hate you, Roger, but I shall never
forget that I once loved you very much.

ROGER: Go on!

FRANCINE: There are times when I hate you—

ROGER: Go on!

FRANCINE: There are times when I hate you—

*She stands and looks on as, without haste, he reaches into his
coat pocket, as if he were searching for his lighter, and, still
without haste, releases the safety catch of a revolver. He does it,
not in the manner of a man who is used to it, but as if it had been
explained to him.*

ROGER: Go on!

FRANCINE: You never loved anybody, Roger, you are not
capable of that, and you never will love anybody.

Pause.

ROGER: So that remains.

She looks on as, without haste, he puts the revolver to his temple, as if he were alone; no report, but sudden darkness, then daylight: the bench is empty, the traffic sounds, now loud, are heard again every fifty seconds, the silence between each change very short.

Methuen World Classics

Aeschylus (two volumes)
Jean Anouilh
John Arden (two volumes)
Arden & D'Arcy
Aristophanes (two volumes)
Aristophanes & Menander
Peter Barnes (two volumes)
Brendan Behan
Aphra Behn
Edward Bond (four volumes)
Bertolt Brecht (four volumes)
Howard Brenton (two volumes)
Büchner
Bulgakov
Calderón
Anton Chekhov
Caryl Churchill (two volumes)
Noël Coward (five volumes)
Sarah Daniels (two volumes)
Eduardo De Filippo
David Edgar (three volumes)
Euripides (three volumes)
Dario Fo (two volumes)
Michael Frayn (two volumes)
Max Frisch
Gorky
Harley Granville Barker
    (two volumes)
Henrik Ibsen (six volumes)

Lorca (three volumes)
David Mamet
Marivaux
Mustapha Matura
David Mercer (two volumes)
Arthur Miller (four volumes)
Anthony Minghella
Molière
Tom Murphy (three volumes)
Peter Nichols (two volumes)
Clifford Odets
Joe Orton
Louise Page
A. W. Pinero
Luigi Pirandello
Stephen Poliakoff
    (two volumes)
Terence Rattigan
Ntozake Shange
Sophocles (two volumes)
Wole Soyinka
David Storey (two volumes)
August Strindberg
    (three volumes)
J. M. Synge
Ramón del Valle-Inclán
Frank Wedekind
Oscar Wilde